READINGS FROM
TALCOTT PARSONS

KEY TEXTS
Series Editor: Peter Hamilton
The Open University

KEY TEXTS

Series Editor: PETER HAMILTON

The Open University, Milton Keynes

Designed, like *Key Ideas,* to complement *Key Sociologists,* this series provides concise and original selections from the works of sociologists featured in *Key Sociologists*. The selections, made by the authors of *Key Sociologists* volumes, will enable the books to be used as part of a teaching package connecting study of the essential texts to introductory analyses of the sociologists' works.

READINGS FROM TALCOTT PARSONS

PETER HAMILTON, The Open University, Milton Keynes

READINGS FROM EMILE DURKHEIM

KENNETH THOMPSON, Faculty of Social Science, The Open University, Milton Keynes

READINGS FROM THE FRANKFURT SCHOOL

TOM BOTTOMORE, Professor of Sociology, University of Sussex

READINGS FROM TALCOTT PARSONS

Editor:
PETER HAMILTON
The Open University

ELLIS HORWOOD LIMITED
Publishers · Chichester

TAVISTOCK PUBLICATIONS
London and New York

First published in 1985 by
ELLIS HORWOOD LIMITED
Market Cross House, Cooper Street
Chichester, Sussex, PO19 1EB, England
and

TAVISTOCK PUBLICATIONS LIMITED
11 New Fetter Lane, London EC4P 4EE

Published in the USA by
TAVISTOCK PUBLICATIONS
and ELLIS HORWOOD LIMITED
in association with METHUEN INC.
733 Third Avenue, New York, NY 10017

© 1985 P. Hamilton/Ellis Horwood Limited

British Library Cataloguing in Publication Data
Parsons, Talcott
Readings from Talcott Parsons. – (Key texts)
1. Sociology
I. Title   II. Hamilton, Peter, *1947*–   III. Series
301'.01   HM24

ISBN 0–85312–854–5 (Ellis Horwood Limited)

Typeset by Ellis Horwood Limited
Printed in Great Britain by R. J. Acford, Chichester

Contents

For Susan, Toby, Oliver and Max

PETER HAMILTON has been Lecturer in Sociology at the Open University, Milton Keynes, since 1973. He was Visiting Research Fellow at the Station d'Economie et Sociologie Rurales in Paris between 1981 and 1982.

He is the author of a number of well-known books and many articles on the sociology of knowledge, introductory sociology, rural sociology and French society. He is the Editor of three Ellis Horwood/Tavistock series, *Key Sociologists*, *Key Ideas* and *Key Texts*. These include a text, *Talcott Parsons*, published in 1983 by Ellis Horwood/Tavistock.

Introduction

Talcott Parson's work straddles the gulf between the social theories of the founding fathers and the professionalized sociology of the present day. Parsons was — to use C. Wright Mills's pejorative but half-admiring term — a 'Grand Theorist' in the Durkheim, Weber or Simmel mould. But he was also a *professional* sociologist, in the sense that he played an important part in the development of sociology as an organized discipline, in the period after 1945. His work during this period has often been taken as typifying a major sociological school — usually called *functionalism* — which held sway as a virtual orthodoxy in Anglo-Saxon sociology from the 1940s to the 1960s. Whilst I would argue with the assumption that Parsons's work was in fact typical of the wider functionalist tradition, there can be little doubt that his theories played a central part in the rise of that paradigm within sociology. The decline and replacement of the functionalist paradigm was similarly associated with critical attacks on Parsonian theory, which was conceived — at least by the critics — as the keystone of functionalism.

This is not the place to enter into a lengthy analysis of why Parsons's work presents a very distinctive form of functionalism: indeed he always repudiated such a labelling, preferring to describe his work in the 1950s and 1960s as 'functional analysis', and throughout most of his career professed himself to be more interested in *human action*, conceived as a group of interacting systems in which the biological concept of function was useful, but not the goal of explanation. A confirmed anti-positivist and anti-behaviourist, this aspect of Parsons's theories tends to be underplayed by the critical view of his later work as a sort of positivistic, behaviourist functionalism.

The readings from Parsons's considerable work (over 160 published items, from major books to short review articles) which are contained in this collection cover the full range of his published writings. The selection is intended to provide students and other readers with an introduction to the *central* theoretical and conceptual issues which mark the development of his distinctive approach to sociology. For obvious reasons a reader such as this cannot possibly claim to be a comprehensive selection of Parsons's work: its aim is to present a representative cross-section. The principle selection has been based upon my *Key Sociologists* series volume *Talcott Parsons* (Ellis Horwood/Tavistock, 1983) and reflects the main phases of Parsons's intellectual development, from his first publications in 1928/9 up until those published after his death in 1979.

In this brief introduction to the pieces selected for inclusion in the reader, my aims are twofold: firstly, to provide a brief overview of Parson's life and career and, secondly, to discuss his intellectual development, with particular reference to the readings which follow.

LIFE AND CAREER

Talcott Parsons was born in 1902, in a small mid-western town called Colorado Springs. His father was a Congregational minister in the town, and the atmosphere of family life was permeated by an ascetic Protestantism which had strong social reform overtones. Edward Parsons was also a college teacher of English, and Talcott's early life was spent in the rather limited social world typical of small American colleges in the first quarter of this century.

Parsons aimed for a career in either biology or medicine when he went to Amherst College (Massachusetts) in 1920. However, his interests rapidly turned towards the social sciences, and especially what was then called 'institutional economics'. This was close to what we would nowadays call political economy: the study of the *social* consequences of economic processes. It was an interest which fitted well with the social reformist conscience of Parsons's family. But it also brought Parsons into contact with sociology through the courses taught by Walter Hamilton and Clarence Ayers, which were heavily influenced by the work of Thorstein Veblen (1857–1929) as well as some European sociologists such as Emile Durkheim.

After graduating from Amherst, Parsons was offered a year's foreign study by an indulgent uncle. Rather than opt for an American graduate school he chose to go to Europe, and attended the London School of Economics in 1924–25. Its attraction to the young Parsons was perhaps the somewhat radical stance of some of its chief figures – Harold Laski, R. H. Tawney, Morris Ginsberg, L. T. Hobhouse, etc. – although in fact he seems to have been most impressed by the lectures of Bronislaw Malinowski, the social anthropologist.

Malinowski and his colleague A. R. Radcliffe-Brown were in the forefront of a new *functionalist* social anthropology which concerned itself with explaining human institutions in terms of their functions for the survival of specific societies. It is clear that the way in which Malinowski and Radcliffe-Brown used the 'functional' analogy from biological science to describe social processes was attractive to Parsons, as it combined two of his main interests – biology and sociology – in a single theoretical model. It was a theme to which Parsons would return at many points during his intellectual career.

Although Parsons followed no specific course of study at LSE, it is evident that the experience was a formative one. By a happy chance, it was followed by a further year spent at the University of Heidelberg, on an exchange fellowship.

Parsons arrived in a Heidelberg still intellectually dominated by the influence of Max Weber, who had lived and worked in the city from 1896 to 1918. Weber's work – which seemed to deal authoritatively with the connections between the economy and society – captivated Parsons. He was soon engaged in a doctorate on *The Concept of Capitalism in Recent German Literature*, and read widely in the work of Weber, Marx, Sombart and a number of minor authors. He was also fortunate in following a course in neo-Kantian philosophy taught by an old friend of Weber's, Karl Jaspers, which helped him to grasp the methodological base of Weber's work.

On his return to the USA, Parsons worked initially as an instructor in economics, first at his old college, Amherst, and subsequently at Harvard University. At this time (1926–34), following his doctoral thesis and the subsequent publication of papers based on it (one of which is reproduced in edited form in this collection) Parsons was firmly esconced within the discipline of economics. However, his interest in sociological theory remained such that he felt that 'economic theory should be conceived as standing within some sort of theoretical matrix in which sociological theory also was included' [1].

This led Parsons to read widely in economics: his interest in the failure of most conventional economic theory to deal with the social consequences of economic policy led him to look in particular at the work of those economists who dealt with the social bases of economic action, such as Marshall, Pareto, and of course Weber. It was during this period that Parsons began to play an important part in making Weber more accessible to a non-German audience: his translation of *The Protestant Ethic and the Spirit of Capitalism* appeared in 1930, and remains the standard work.

In the early 1930s a Department of Sociology was established at Harvard, and Parsons moved into it as a lowly 'Instructor' under the somewhat autocratic emigré Russian, Ptirim Sorokin. The Department rapidly grew in stature, attracting many eminent scholars as staff or visiting lecturers. Parsons and Sorokin seem never to have hit it off as colleagues, and it was to take Parsons until the late 1930s before he could obtain promotion to a post worthy of his intellectual reputation. However, Harvard provided a relatively secure environment for his scholarship, and Parsons soon began to gather a group of graduate students around him, many of whom were later to become eminent figures in their own right within sociology — such as Robert Merton, Kingsley Davis and Wilbert Moore for example. Parsons was clearly an exciting and inspirational teacher, and many of those who were attracted to Harvard because of Sorokin, stayed as graduate students because of Parsons.

Parsons's move from economics to sociology reflected his developing perception of economics as a 'special case' of sociology. The aspects of human behaviour and action with which economics dealt could not, he believed, be properly conceptualized except in the context of an encompassing social theory.

Parsons read widely in the work of neo-classical economists, the grand theorists of sociology, and philosophy during this stage of his career. The outcome of this search for a wide-ranging social theory was initially *The Structure of Social Action* (published in 1937). At least partly because of his 'European' background, Parsons's work took a markedly anti-American stance insofar as contemporary social science was concerned. Parsons opposed the prevailing positivism and empiricism which characterized the main American schools. Perhaps his disdain for his native thinkers was excessive, and reflected his somewhat unorthodox training, but it did allow him to construct a quite remarkable *convergence* of intellectual strands from the most significant streams of European social thought. Although this major new work was a very considerable contribution to sociological theory, its reception in

America was unenthusiastic outside of Harvard, no doubt mainly because Parsons chose to ignore the dominant sociology of his day, exemplified by the Chicago School.

The Structure of Social Action has been represented by some commentators (notably Alvin Gouldner [2]) as typical of an intellectual retreat from the social ills of 1930s America which characterized the 'ivory tower' intellectuals of Parsons's circle. However, Parsons's sights were fixed on social issues of considerable significance, and the book represented for him 'a clarification and development of my own thought about the problems of the state of Western society' [3] – problems which were focused moreover in the rise of Fascism in Germany and Italy on the one hand, and in the Communist revolution in Russia on the other. Parsons saw in both major threats to the continuation of capitalist democracies such as America, which for all its faults represented a system which allowed greater liberty and freedom to the individual than either of its putative competitors.

In developing this convergence of social theory – embodied in what Parsons termed *the voluntaristic theory of action* – he had been influenced by a Harvard physiologist with sociological leanings (L. J. Henderson) to consider Pareto's work. There was indeed a so-called 'Pareto circle' at Harvard, in which Parsons was for a time a participant, and which was influential in propagating the social and economic theories of the Italian thinker. But although Parsons clearly thought Pareto's ideas important, and analysed them at some length in *The Structure of Social Action,* he did not thereafter devote much attention to the Italian's work.

After the publication of *The Structure of Social Action* Parsons's position within Harvard, and in the sociological profession generally, improved considerably. He was securely established at Harvard, and he began to develop his work into areas which he called 'the socio-psychological complex', where the overlapping concerns of sociology, psychology and anthropology came to the fore. In particular, he became increasingly attracted to the work of Sigmund Freud, via his contacts with Elton Mayo at the Harvard Business School, the author of a number of influential studies in the sociology of organisations. He also collaborated increasingly with the psychologists Gordon Allport and Henry Murray, and the anthropologist Clyde Kluckhohn, all of whom contributed to the development of a Freud-influenced 'culture and personality' movement of some significance in American social science during the 1940s and 1950s.

During the Second World War Parsons worked as a consultant to the US Government on questions relating to the post-war reconstruction of Germany. In addition he of course continued his work at Harvard, and wrote a number of interesting papers on German society and culture. In 1942 he took over from Sorokin as head of the Department of Sociology, and developed a new, interdisciplinary Department of Social Relations which opened its doors in 1946 under his chairmanship. The Department had a strong sociology, psychology and anthropology base, and attracted many of the very best graduate students. In its first 10 years over 80 Ph.D.s were awarded, of which many were taught by Parsons, names such as Harold Garfinkel, Clifford Geertz, David Aberle, Robert Bales, Bernard Barber, Edward Devereux, Marion Levy, Morris Zelditch among them. As a result, a dense 'communication network' of ex-Parsons students radiated out from Harvard into the expanding sociological profession, and were influential in the propagation of his ideas through the 1950s and 1960s.

Parsons was extremely active during the period from 1945 to 1956 – publishing over 27 items, of which a number were major works. Some were collaborative enterprises which reflected the increasingly interdisciplinary nature of his work, whilst others (such as *The Social System* of 1951) represented a step forward in the development of his sociological theories, as he moved towards the elaboration of a model of human action using systemic concepts within a framework of functional analysis. This phase of his work (I will return later to a discussion of the distinct *phases* of Parsons's theoretical development) is thus often termed his 'structural-functional' or 'functionalist' period, although both terms are ones which he rejected. By 1950 Parsons was at the pinnacle of his profession: elected President of the American Sociological Association in 1949, Parsons's work had become the basis of a dominant *paradigm* within sociology. Parsons's key works of this period – *The Social System* and *Toward a General Theory of Action* (both 1951), *Working Papers in the Theory of Action* (1953) and *Economy and Society* – represent his distinctive contribution to the 'structural-functionalism' which dominated American sociology until the late 1960s.

As with all paradigms in natural and social science, there comes a point where their original theoretical novelty is worked out, and they cease to provide the stimulus for fruitful research. When this occurs, critiques of the basic theory become more prominent, and may in some cases form the nucleus from which other paradigms develop. Thus from the late 1950s onwards a number of critiques of structural-functionalism in general, and of Parsonian systems theory in particular, began to appear and to gain support. Such critiques came from a number of positions, which perhaps emphasizes the heterogeneity implicit in sociological theory: C. Wright Mills attacked Parsons's 'Grand Theory' from a

Veblenesque concern with what he saw as its retreat from practical reality and concrete social problems into a conceptual ivory tower; Ralf Dahrendorf contested Parsons's emphasis on what he took to be an 'utopian' belief in value-consensus and proposed instead that greater attention should be paid to explanations of 'constraint, conflict and change'; George Homans questioned the need to go beyond the individual in explanations of social behaviour, asserting that it could be explained only be reference to psychological factors; and David Lockwood opposed what he saw as Parsons's attempt to construct general social theory on an incomplete model of social reality which took normative order as its sole base, rather than including *power* and *conflict* as in his preferred Marxian approach. Such critiques were the vanguard of a process of critical disengagement of American sociology from domination by a Parsons-centred structural-functionalism. During the 1960s this process gathered steam, materially assisted by the renaissance of Marxian approaches which were so closely associated with the Parisian revolution in 1968 and the 'student power' conflicts which occurred in all Western societies from about 1967 to about 1973. But the reaction was not exclusively dependent on the 'rediscovery' of Marx. Several other trends in social theory contested the intellectual terrain: *ethnomethodology*, in Harold Garfinkel's[†] influential formulations which began to attack the apparently 'positivistic' bias of functionalism; *exchange theory*, inspired by George Homans; various types of phenomenologically orientated 'reflexive' theories; Lewis Coser's elaboration of a so-called *conflict theory*; and updated versions of *symbolic interactionism* such as that developed by Erving Goffman.

As noted above, many of the critiques of Parsonian systems theory in particular or of structural-functionalism more generally, focused on the apparent inadequacies of such theoretical approaches in the matter of conflict, power and social change. This area seemed to be the major drawback of functionalism for in proposing that social institutions should be analysed in relation to how they maintained system equilibrium, it seemed that disequilibrating forces – oppositional values, class conflict, power relationships, etc. – were being swept under the carpet. Parsons was clearly aware of such criticisms, and whereas in the earlier stages in his career he had considered political issues on a more *ad hominem* basis – treating only those which in some way or another perplexed him such as Facism and McCarthyism – in the late 1950s and early 1960s he began to develop a more systematic

---

† Paradoxically, Harold Garfinkel had been a student of Parsons in the 1950s, and suggested in his *Studies of Ethnomethodology* (1967) that his work began from various insights contained in *The Social System*.

approach to politics and subsequently to issues of social change and development. In an article reviewing C. Wright Mills's famous study *The Power Elite*, Parsons began to draw out some of the implications of his discovery of the *generalized media of exchange*, initially worked out with Smelser. He saw not only that the economy was a social system, but also that the *polity* could be approached in similar ways. Notwithstanding the tendency of political theorists to treat power as a 'zero-sum phenomenon' — or in other words to assume that there is a *fixed* amount of power in any political system which is simply moved from one group to another in the political process — Parsons began to develop a theory which defined power as an exchange medium which operates like money in the economic system: it is subject to expansion or contraction according to the availability of 'credit' facilities. Although he never wrote anything on the 'polity' to compare with *Economy and Society* or *The Social System* in scope, a number of essays produced up to the mid-1960s and reprinted in *Politics and Social Structure* (1967) indicate his increasing concern to adapt systems theory so as to answer criticisms of its conceptual inadequacies.

Parsons himself appeared to believe that his interest in questions of *generalized media of exchange* between *action systems* had directed his work out of 'structural-functionalism' and towards a 'cybernetically' oriented action theory in which the emphasis was upon how a symbolic 'programme' of control operated in action systems. In this process of theoretical development, Parsons returned increasingly to biological analogies and to the major developments in genetics which occurred during the 1950s and 1960s. As was noted at the beginning of this chapter, he had begun his undergraduate studies in biology, a subject in which he continued to have a lay interest until the end of his life. During the 1930s he had followed the work of Claude Bernard, W. B. Cannon and of course his colleague L. J. Henderson with considerable interest. Indeed, the physiologist Henderson appears to have been the original source of Parsons's concern with conceptions of *system*, which the former had applied to his own exposition of Vilfredo Pareto's sociological theories on a base derived essentially from biological science.

Paradoxically, the wide-ranging development of Parsons's theories in the final phase of his work coincided which a demise of the paradigm he had done so much to create. This must be at least partly explained by the observation that Parsonian systems theory did not seem to offer fruitful lines of research in a period marked by a strong demand for *critical* social theories. It is ironic that Parsons's own work paved the way for such interests to develop, because its success as a model of social systems in dynamic equilibrium drew attention to the increasing number of challenges to equilibrium which marked the 1960s and early 1970s: the civil rights and student power movements, the 'hippie' counter-culture and, most important of all, the Viet-Nam war. Parsons himself applied his theories to some of these issues (notably that of racism) but seems to have avoided any commentary on the South East Asian tragedy.

Parsons retired from Harvard in the early 1970s, at a time when the great interdisciplinary enterprise of the 1940s was being dismantled, as sociology formed itself again into a separate department within the University.

Parsons's formal disengagement from Harvard in 1973 symbolized the trend away from structural-functionalism or 'systems theory' within sociology. But it did not result in any slackening of his tremendous output of work. During the 1970s he collaborated extensively with some of his ex-students, at the University of Pennsylvania (chiefly Renée Fox and Victor M. Lidz) in a faculty seminar which was to produce his final publications – the two essay collections *Social Systems and the Evolution of Action Theory* (1977) and *Action Theory and the Human Condition* (1978) of which the latter is by far the most interesting. At the end of his life it would seem that Parsons felt able to attempt one further extension of his action theory to take in both science *and* religion, for one previously unpublished essay in *Action Theory and the Human Condition*, 'A paradigm of the human condition', attempts to conceptualize the most comprehensive aspects of human existence. Finally, then, Parsons's own 'general system of action' becomes a subsystem of the 'human condition' in much the same way as earlier the 'social system' itself had been a subsystem of the general theory of action. The last decade or so of Parsons's life was a period in which he utilized the developing insights of his theoretical advances to treat an extensive range of issues. We find him writing on medical sociology, on death, on various aspects of religion, on law, on political power, on stratification, on education and socialization, on the family, on modern capitalism, on psychoanalysis, and on deviance as well as contributing commentaries and dicussions of the work of his intellectual mentors and on theory in general.

Talcott Parsons died in 1979, near the Univerisity in Munich where Weber spent his last years. It is ironic but perhaps fitting that Parsons should have met death in the same city and in the same season of the year as his intellectual mentor, Max Weber.

THE THREE PHASES OF PARSONIAN THEORY

This collection of readings from Parsons's work is designed to reflect the development of his theories over his very lengthy career. It thus complements my previous book on Talcott Parsons in the *Key Sociologists* series, in taking a three-phase model of Parsons's work as the principle of selection for the readings in this volume.

The three-phase model I have used presents Parsons's intellectual development in terms of three distinct, though interrelated phases. I call these Parsons[1], Parsons[2] and Parsons[3], and each is related to certain key ideas and concepts which trace the formation and extension of stages in the evolution of the 'general theory of action' with which Parsons was always concerned.

Parsons[1] comprises the initial phase of Parsons's work, and contains his gradual development of a voluntaristic theory of social action opposed to the positivistic, utilitarian and reductionist views of sociology. The central work of this phase is his book *The Structure of Social Action* of 1937.

The second phase, Parsons[2], is really the most important. It contains Parsons's movement away from the confines of social action theory in the direction of structural-functionalism, towards the elaboration of a more general 'theory of action' containing the crucial concepts of 'system' and 'system needs'. Three books comprise the key works of this phase: *The Social System*, 1951, and *Toward a General Theory of Action*, also 1951, and a book written collaboratively with Neil Smelser, *Economy and Society* (1956).

In the Parsons[3] phase it is possible to discern some important developments of the Parsons[2] theories, especially in terms of a cybernetic model of social systems and a concern with the empirical problems of defining and explaining social change. Several books are central to this final phase. There are two short books: *Societies* (1967) and *The System of Modern Societies* (1971), and two collections of essays, *Sociological Theory and Modern Society* (1967) and *Politics and Social Structure* (1971). Just before his death, two further collections of essays appeared, *Social Systems and the Evolution of Action Theory* (1977) and *Action Theory and the Human Condition* (1978), which contained significant theoretical development. This final phase has exhibited a considerable refinement of Parsonian theory, particularly in respect of elaboration of the concepts of generalized media of exchange first begun in *Economy and Society*. Also, in a number of empirical areas, Parsons has further extended his theories and their conceptual structures to deal (although not unproblematically) with substantive issues.

In addition to the three main phases of Parsons's work — Parsons[1], Parsons[2] and Parsons[3] — both this collection and my earlier study of his theories include an earlier formative stage as an integral element. This Parsons[0] phase essentially covers the period from Parsons's return from Germany in 1927 through to the writing of *The Structure of Social Action* in 1934–6.[1]

Although the Parsons[1] stage begins with his careful and thoroughly original formulation of a voluntaristic *theory of action* in his first major work, it would be wrong to ignore some interesting sociological and economic work produced before that time. So the Parsons[0] stage stretches from his doctoral dissertation (at Heidelberg 1926–27), through a short period teaching at Amherst College, to his early years at Harvard University. It is worth mentioning because during this time (c. 1925–34) Parsons was able to resolve three main problems.

Firstly, he was trying to achieve an adequate conceptualization of the relationships between economic and sociological theory (a theme which continued concerns first approached in his thesis, on the analysis of capitalism as a socio-economic system in the works of Karl Marx, Werner Sombart and Max Weber). Secondly, he was involved in an attempt to work out the implications, methodological and epistemological, of what was meant by the concept of a 'theoretical system' in social science. Thirdly, he was engaged in exploring the theoretical and methodological bases of the idea of *social action* within social thought.

This collection includes readings from a representative selection of the small number of papers written between 1927 and 1935 which reflect these concerns. It is worth stating here that these studies effectively 'cleared the intellectual ground' for Parsons, allowing him to concentrate on the central concerns with voluntarism, and the normative integration of social action, and to definitively cast off his ties to economics and steer more firmly towards sociology.

NOTES AND REFERENCES

[1] Talcot Parsons, personal communication to author, 13 May 1974.
[2] Alvin W. Gouldner (1970) *The Coming Crisis of Western Sociology*, London, Heineman, pp. 175–178.
[3] Talcott Parsons (1977) On building social system theory: a personal history, in *Social Systems and the Evolution of Action Theory*, New York, Free Press, p. 29.

Part One

The Parsons⁰ Phase

The three readings reprinted in this Part cover the period from Parsons's dissertation for his Heidelberg doctorate, up to the writing of *The Structure of Social Action* and his positing of a *voluntaristic* theory of action. They thus chart his movement from a primary concern with economic theory and its treatment of the socio-economic system of capitalism, to a position where the normative basis of social action had come to be his main concern.

'Capitalism' in Recent German Literature: Sombart and Weber (1928/9) was based on the Heidelberg dissertation, although it also reflects Parsons's readings of neo-classical economic theory during his initial period as graduate student and instructor in the Department of Economics at Harvard. The paper is of interest in the way it shows how Parsons was aware of the whole *Kapitalismus Streit* (debate about capitalism) which had so animated the German scholars of Weber's generation — a debate which centred around the definition of the characteristic features of capitalism as a socio-economic *system*, and which opposed the 'materialist' theories of Marx to the more 'idealist' theories of Weber and Sombart.

In *Economics and Sociology: Marshall in Relation to the Thought of his Time* (1931) we find Parsons deeply embroiled in the problems of utilitarian and neo-classical economic theory, and in particular their failure adequately to account for the normative basis of economic action. It is interesting to see Parsons examining Marshall's ideas from a sort of sociology of economics viewpoint — at one point he describes Marshall as a living example of the spirit of capitalism, in Weber's terms. The article clearly marks a turning point for Parsons in his consideration of the relationship of economics to sociology: he is quite clear that the way out of the problems of economic theory — in particular its failure to deal with the 'real world' of economic behaviour which always represents exceptions to its neat laws — is via sociology, because economic activity can only exist within a matrix of non-economic, and especially *sociological*, factors.

Finally, the essay on *The Place of Ultimate Values in Sociological Theory* (1935) represents a clear statement of Parsons's faith in a *voluntaristic* theory of action as the basis of social theory. By emphasizing the crucial importance of free will, Parsons is indicating his opposition to positivist or behaviourist methodologies which seek to reduce the *normative* character of social action to physiological or biological processes. The article represents a foretaste of what was to come in *The Structure of Social Action*.

"CAPITALISM" IN RECENT GERMAN LITERATURE: SOMBART AND WEBER

Anglo-American economic thought, at least in its predominant trend, is a child of the individualistic and rationalistic philosophy of the seventeenth and eighteenth centuries. One of the salient characteristics of this whole trend of thought has been its rather abstract generality; its formulation in terms implying, or at least not denying, universal applicability wherever human economic life is lived. With the general attitude thus assumed it has perforce tended to neglect the economic problems connected with the growth and development of types of economic society, and in particular with the working out of the differences between, and the specific characteristics of, the different cultural epochs.

There has been, however, another major strain in modern thought, which has laid its main emphasis on this aspect of the problems of society, and in particular of economic life. Its principal, though by no means exclusive, field of influence has been Germany, and its intellectual soil more than anything else the romantic movement in its many different phases. It has been pre-eminently occupied with the problems

Abridged and reprinted, with permission, from *The Journal of Political Economy*. Vol. 36, (December, 1928), No. 6, pp. 641–661; and Vol. 37 (January, 1929), No. 1, pp. 31–5.

of history, and among its most important accomplishments is the formulation of various philosophies of history, in Germany notably those of Hegel and Karl Marx. It forms the background of the theories which this paper is to discuss.

The more immediate background is formed by two main influences: first, the historical school in economics, with its attack on orthodox theory, and, much more important, its emphasis on the relativity of economic systems and epochs, and the necessity of analyzing each on its own merits with a view to working out its own particular character istics rather than getting at general economic laws. Secondly, Karl Marx and the discussion after Marx in Germany of the problems of socialism. And here two main aspects are of importance: First, the economic interpretation of history, the problems connected with which play a major part in the thought of Sombart and Weber. Secondly, Marx is the special forerunner of the particular theory with which I am here concerned: that of capitalism as a great epoch in social and economic development.

In both Sombart and Weber there are views of history which are largely to be understood as answers to the questions raised by the economic interpretation, and in each there is a further development of the idea of capitalism as an epoch of history, tinged with the views of Marx, but at the same time showing important divergences from him and from each other.

The purpose of this paper is not primarily to subject these theories to a critical examination, but to put them before American readers in a more condensed and systematic form than that in which they are available in German, and to project them onto the background of their relations to the general development of social thought. What there is of criticism will be largely incidental to these main tasks.

In the works of Werner Sombart is to be found the first of the two great theories of capitalism with which we have to deal [1]. The aim of his work as he lays it down in the introduction to the *Modern Capitalism,* is to present a systematic, genetic treatment of the development of European and American economic life as a whole. His view of economic science is, one may say, historical, but at the same time theoretical. It is historical in that he goes so far as to deny the existence of economic laws transcending history, at any rate beyond what might be considered physical and technical conditions of economic activity (for instance, physical diminishing returns). But aside from this negative attitude to orthodox economic theory, which I do not share, he sees the positive task of economic science in the historical presentation and analysis of concrete economic systems and modes of life.

In this sense he digs out and reduces to order an enormous mass of historical material, filling for *Modern Capitalism* alone, six large volumes. He is certainly not alone concerned or satisfied with working out an ideal type of capitalism which has for him only abstract interest, but his theory is a means of illuminating and understanding the concrete historical development. But he is not a "mere" historian. He is interested, not in working out the particular circumstances of the economic history of any single country for its own sake, but in presenting European economic life as a whole, in its great common trend, and in getting at the laws of its development. His aim is thus definitely theoretical, and his work should be judged as a whole from that point of view. The term "theory," however, is here used in a different and more general sense than that common in economic science, to mean, not merely a system of equilibrium, but any consistent and unified system of concepts to be used in the analysis of social phenomena [2].

In conformity with this general view of economics stands the leading concept of his work, that of the economic system. He defines it as follows: "Under this term I understand a peculiarly ordered form of economic activity, a particular organization of economic life within which a particular mental attitude predominates and a particular technique is applied." [3] This economic system is to be constructed in the purity of an "ideal type" to be used for the analysis of concrete reality, and will be found to correspond more or less closely to the historical facts. The empirical equivalent of the economic system is for Sombart the economic epoch, a period of time in history within which a particular economic system or form of economic life has predominated.

Every economic system has, he maintains, three aspects: a form of organization, a technique, and a mental attitude or spirit [4]. Of these three, the side which he most strongly emphasizes is that of the spirit. In Sombart's own words: "It is a fundamental contention of this work that at different times different attitudes toward economic life have prevailed, and that it is the spirit which has created a suitable form for itself and has thus created economic organization." [5] Each spirit is for him a thoroughly unique phenomenon, occurring only once in history. There is no line of development leading from spirit to spirit, and thus from system to system, and each is, therefore, to be considered by and for itself.

He uses the conception of the spirit as the means to bring order and unity into the historical material. It is one of the most striking features of Sombart's work that he is able to interpret a whole epoch of history in such an illuminating and convincing way in terms of one great leading idea. It gives a unity to his presentation which marks a great advance over the entirely disconnected studies of historical facts presented by the historical school proper. It does not give the impression that he is "philosophizing" independently of the facts. On the contrary, he is able to achieve an amazing degree of concreteness in his picture.

The emphasis on the spirit as the moving force of economic and social development is that part of the theories with which this paper deals, which is most distinctively German, and which brings out most clearly the relations they bear to the main currents of European thought. At bottom it goes back to German idealism and the conception there developed of the "life of the spirit." It may be said that Kant's great synthesis saved this whole line of thought from the inundation which threatened to submerge it by reconciling it with mechanistic science. The synthesis, however, was not without its difficulties; and since Kant there has been a pendulum-like movement in German thought, tending to exaggerate first one and then the other of the two great elements of the compromise. In Hegel the pendulum swung far over to the "spiritual" side; then with Feuerbach and some of the young Hegelians it swung just as far the other way. At this point began the application to the analysis of capitalism, starting at the left, so to speak, with the historical materialism of Marx [6]. It was in terms of the Marxian view that the problem was presented to Sombart, and in a sense he represents the extreme of the swing back again toward Hegel. There is, however, the important difference that while retaining in essentials the matter-spirit alternative, Sombart has discarded the peculiar evolutionary form, the dialectic, in which the doctrine appeared in both Hegel and Marx (though in different senses), and has substituted his own type of "cultural morphology." This he derived from conceptions long existing in various forms of historical thought, especially its more romantic aspects.

Sombart proceeds immediately to the application of his idea of the spirit of economic life when he begins to lay the scene for modern capitalism by sketching precapitalistic economy. He distinguishes two precapitalistic systems in Europe: self-sufficient economy (*Eigenwirtschaft*) and the handicraft system. But for his purposes they are much the same and are treated as such because in spirit they are almost identical. The principal characteristic common to them is that economic life was regarded purely as a means for the satisfaction of human needs. Moreover, these needs were neither unlimited nor fluctuating, but were traditionally fixed for each person according to the social station into which he was born. He was expected to receive the support necessary for a given status (what Sombart calls the *Bedarfsdeckung-sprinzip* and sharply distinguishes from the principle of unlimited acquisition or *Erwerbsprinzip*). With this traditional character of precapitalistic economic life he contrasts the rationality of capitalism.

Starting as he does from the postulate that economic systems are separate and unique, Sombart is bound to make the most of the differences between them and to minimize the elements of continuity. It is thus the logical necessity of his whole viewpoint which leads him to his well-known and highly controversial thesis that medieval commerce was essentially a handicraft and thus sharply distinguished from that of modern times [7]. Economic historians of liberal leanings would strongly disagree with him, and there is a prima facie case for the accusation of at least serious one-sidedness [8].

Sombart's most precise formulation of the essence of capitalism is as follows:

> It is an economic system, as above defined, which is distinguished by the following characteristics: (1) Form, organization. (a) It is a system based upon private initiative and exchange; (b) there is a regular co-operation of two groups of the population, the owners of the means of production and the propertyless workers, all of whom (c) are brought into relation through the market. (2) Spirit, mental attitude. It is dominated by the principles of acquisition, of competition, and of economic rationality. (3) The corresponding technique is the revolutionary technique of modern times, emancipated from the limitations of the organic world [9].

Each of these three aspects may now be dealt with in turn. The basic units of the system are the capitalistic enterprises. In function these are, in contrast to the medieval manor, almost indefinitely varied, but in structure and manner of working they show important similarities.

First of all there is division of labor within the enterprise, especially as between the functions of ownership and management on the one hand, and those carrying out orders on the other. This cleft forms the starting-point of the modern labor movement and of modern socialism, phenomena which are peculiar to the modern era and only to be understood in relation to their capitalistic origin. Only in modern times has there been, according to Sombart, an industrial proletariat as we know it, although there have often been relatively propertyless classes. Further in the course of development comes a more and more complex subdivision of functions, particularly in the first set, through progressive divorce of ownership from management.

Now the interconnection of all these independent units through the market and the price mechanism has most important consequences. All the qualitative differences of the most diverse economic goods are reduced to a single common denominator, money. This quantitative measure gives a means of comparison of diverse goods on the one hand. On the other hand it gives an objective purpose for all economic activity, which is primarily the making of profit in terms of money, and only indirectly the securing of goods for which money can be exchanged. Thus a wedge is driven between the "natural" end of economic action, the satisfaction of needs, and the means to that satisfaction. Every capitalistic enterprise is forced by its very nature to pursue a given end common to all enterprises, in the pursuit of which there is no stopping-place.

From this viewpoint Sombart defines capital as "the sum of exchange value which serves as the working basis of a capitalistic enterprise." [10] He thus gives it substantially the same meaning which it has in accounting practice, and defines it in terms of its function, and not as a category of goods. Secondly, he makes it a historical concept which has no meaning apart from the capitalistic system. It is Sombart's solution of the difficulty of bringing capital and capitalism into a satisfactory relation. Its great merit is that it avoids the confusion which Weber brings into his idea of capitalism as a historical epoch by basing his concept on a general and abstract definition of capital [11]. Thus it appears that Sombart sees capitalism as an objective system the end of which comes to be the acquisition of profit. It is the compulsion on the individual business man to seek this end which Sombart, following Marx, calls the "necessity of capital to reproduce itself" (*Verwertungsstreben des Kapitals*).

The existence of such an objective and acquisitive system is the dominant fact which Sombart wishes to explain in terms of his theory of the spirit of capitalism, in accordance with his general position regarding the relation of spirit and form of organization. This is not to be taken to mean that Sombart's theory is dependent upon any particular psychology. Both Sombart and Weber would strongly repudiate that suggestion. In the first place they are interested in the action of the individual *as a whole* and hold that any further analysis of him lies beyond the province of social science. The whole individual is the "atom" from which they start. Secondly, they are interested in the *differences* between mental attitudes at different times and places, not in the universal elements which form the subject matter of psychology. That is the essence of the historical nature of their work. In this respect there is an important difference between them and the American "institutional" economists. The results of psychology, say Sombart and Weber, may be used to supplement the economist's knowledge, but psychology is no part of the proper study of economics or sociology, and its relevance to their problems is on essentially the same plane as that of the other non-social sciences which supply data to economics.

The spirit of the entrepreneur of the capitalistic spirit is in Sombart's view made of two main components: the bourgeois [12] spirit and the spirit of enterprise. The spirit of enterprise is a general phenomenon, by no means peculiar to capitalism, but common to most phases of the social world which came into being with the Renaissance. It is the same spirit that created the modern state, the new religion, science and technique. It is a spirit of worldly character, restless, roving, and adventurous. It finds an especially favorable field of action in capitalistic acquisition. The endlessness of competitive activity in a race without a fixed goal is well suited to its striving toward infinite aims (*Unendlichkeitsstreben*). Capital is used as an instrument of conquest and domination.

The principles of the spirit of enterprise are two: that of acquisition and that of competition. In the pursuit of gain all the many motives of the many different types of men are objectified, are made to express themselves in one set of terms, the pecuniary success of the enterprise, quite oblivious whether the original motive might be desire for power, mere venality, the love of activity for its own sake, or what not. The making of profit becomes an end which dominates the whole system.

The acquisitive principle is strengthened in its effect by that of competition. This it is which makes gain a measure of success, and because of it acquisition comes to be without limit. It occurs in two ways: negatively, in that acquisition loses all relation to the personal needs of the entrepreneur; positively, in that not acquisition alone is the aim but acquisition in competition with others. Therein lies the dynamic force of capitalism in increasing the intensity of economic life. As a result acquisition finally becomes generalized so that the whole world is seen from the point of view of business interests; nature and other men are looked upon as means of production. Economic activity, which is originally purely a means to an end, becomes an absolute end in itself, the expression of a religion [13].

Organically bound up with the spirit of enterprise is the other main component of the capitalistic spirit, the *bourgeois* spirit. Its leading principle is that of rationality. Its task is to make life systematic, disciplined, secure; to subject the plans of the entrepreneur to careful scrutiny and meticulous calculations of profit and loss. It appears largely in the form of a business ethics whose typical virtues are reliability, temperance, frugality, industry, thrift.

It can easily be seen in what relation the two components of the capitalistic spirit stand to each other. The creative impulse is without question to be attributed to the spirit of enterprise. It is responsible for the destruction of the old order and for the creation of the new. On the other hand, the *bourgeois* spirit has created the framework within which the spirit of enterprise has been able to develop itself. Rationality is a necessary condition of the development of modern large-scale industry.

There is, however, for Sombart a process of development within the capitalistic spirit. The earlier period is one of the predominance of the spirit of enterprise, with on the whole a defective development of rationality. Later, on the other hand, the *bourgeois* spirit gains the upper hand, and the spirit of enterprise, while it does not disappear, is so to speak tamed and brought into the service of the rational pursuit of purely capitalistic aims. Thus the spirit of enterprise becomes objectified and harnessed to the capitalistic system; it becomes divorced from the pursuit of personal aims and comes to serve an entirely abstract one.

Finally, however, the same fate befalls the *bourgeois* spirit also. While capitalism takes on more and more bourgeois characteristics, the entrepreneurs as such need not do so. On the contrary, the *bourgeois* virtues are transferred from the person of the entrepreneur to the enterprise. It becomes industrious and thrifty; it possesses the necessary solidity to enjoy good credit, quite independently of the possession of such qualities by the individual entrepreneur. Even saving tends to become divorced from the will of the individual and to be carried on by the entreprise. This is what he calls the process of "objectification" of the capitalistic spirit.

Thus Sombart sees at the end of capitalistic development the creation of a "monster," the capitalistic enterprise, possessed of a purpose, an understanding, and a set of virtues all its own, going its own way independently of human will. Not that it is independent of human activity in itself. That is just where it is most objectionable to Sombart. It calls for more intensive intellectual activity and absorbs a greater proportion of human energy than any other form of economic organization. But this intellectual activity has come to be in the service of abstract non-human ends. It is no longer free, but is forced to follow paths marked out in advance by the "system". It forms a treadmill in which everyone is caught, unable to escape.

The spirit of capitalism is the leading concept of Sombart's work.

In terms of this everything else is to be understood. Its origins in the history of thought lie in the "conservative" [14] wing of the romantic movement. From that point of view capitalism appears chiefly as a destructive force tearing down the social ties of an older and more "organic" civilization. Here is the origin of Sombart's adverse ethical judgment of capitalism. It is interesting to note that, in common with almost all social thinkers who for so many centuries have been radically opposed to the existing order, he invokes a "state of nature," namely, the precapitalistic era, by which to measure the shortcomings of capitalism. But while the state of nature of the radical philosophies of the eighteenth century was a state of extreme individual freedom, i.e., freedom from social ties, Sombart takes to a large extent the very society which they were fighting against as his natural state. With it goes an interpretation of the institutions of those times as natural "growths," which is the opposite pole from that of a Voltaire or a Godwin.

[. . .]

Max Weber has none of Sombart's concentration of attention upon a single line of development. His researches extend over the whole of human history. He investigates the classic world, China, India, ancient Judea, and others. But it always remains his purpose to throw light upon the problems of modern society, and especially upon modern capitalism [15]. [. . .]

The "ideal type" (*Idealtypus*) is Weber's special instrument of sociological analysis. He asserts that the historical social sciences are faced with an infinite variety of facts from which a selection for purposes of analysis must be made. The objective of these sciences is the knowledge and understanding of specific individual culture phenomena in their uniqueness, as different from all others even of similar character. These "historical individuals" [16] he seeks to "understand" in terms of the human motives which have given rise to the social action summed up in them. The standard under which a group of actions is to be brought together as a historical individual is the "significance" (*Bedeutung*) of those actions for human ends and values. Hence the discovery of uniform relations and their formulation in terms of "laws" cannot be the objective of such a science.

That "understanding" Weber attempts to attain by means of the ideal type. It is a special *construction* in the mind of the investigator of what social action would be if it were directed with perfect rationality [17] toward a given end. It is not a reflection of actual behavior, since it is purposely a "fictitious" construction, which can never occur in reality. Nor is it an abstraction in the ordinary sense which operates under the assumption "other things being equal," for even with respect to the elements with which it specifically deals it makes assumptions contrary to fact. Nor can it be a hypothesis to be "verified," nor a general concept of a class (*Gattungsbegriff*) under which many "cases" may be included. It is a picture of what things would be under "ideal," not actual, conditions.

Given this instrument of analysis the investigator may compare with it the actual record of events in many different instances and thus attempt to "understand" them, each in its individual uniqueness, by seeing how far they conform to action rationally directed toward the given ends, and to distinguish such elements as are not "understandable" in these terms. Furthermore, the single ideal type is directed toward understanding, not the whole of the "historical individual," but only one side or aspect of it. A whole would thus be analyzed in terms of several ideal types. Finally, this ideal type is never the end of the scientific investigation, but always a *means* to understanding. It has no "reality" in itself; it does not "reproduce" reality, but is a fiction, always involving assumptions purposely contrary to fact. Its function is to form a standard for the systematic selection, arrangement, and analysis of the historical facts.

In this process Weber does not exclude "values" from his consideration in terms of them, and to include in his analysis only what can be understood in such terms. But none the less he claims objectivity for his method, since it takes the values as given and attempts no ultimate judgment or criticism of them. He does, however, deal with them in attempting to refine the values he finds in history into ideal types of themselves [18].

Investigation of Weber's work, [19] however, has shown that while all this is true of one class of ideal type, there is another group of concepts which Weber calls ideal types, but which are of a quite different nature. They are directed toward *one particular* historical individual and are applicable only to it, are thus *historical* and not general concepts like the others. Secondly, they attempt to work out the *whole* "essence" of the thing, not just one side of it. Such a concept cannot be purely a means, but its construction must be in some measure the end of the investigation in question. That Weber calls both ideal types without distinguishing them leads to serious confusion, a confusion which is especially marked in his analysis of capitalism, as I shall show at the end of the discussion.

The propositions of abstract economic theory were thought by Weber to be ideal types in the first sense, a view perhaps not very different from its conception as an "engine of analysis" which has become common in English theory in recent times. In the latter of the two senses the "theory" of Sombart may be said to consist of ideal types, of which that of capitalism was the most interesting for this paper. It is a picture of the rationalized and distilled "essence" of the epoch, free from all the irrationalities of the actual historical material. But it is definitely historical, not general.

Unlike Sombart, Weber never developed a unified theory of capitalism. In spite of the fact that a very large proportion of his sociological work was devoted to this problem, he left only a number of fragments which from our point of view are to be regarded as special investigations [20]. It is thus unavoidable that in piecing these together a certain element of construction should enter in.

At the outset there is the difficulty that Weber seems to have used the term "capitalism" in two different senses without clearly distinguishing them. It is necessary to analyze them both and to keep them distinct from one another. They may be called "capitalism in general" and "modern capitalism."

The first is, one may say, an ideal type in the former of the foregoing senses. It is a general concept in terms of which many different sorts of capitalism, such as, for example, colonial, finance, and political, may be analyzed. It is thus not a historical concept in the same sense as Sombart's capitalism, but stands above and beyond all historical periods, serving in the analysis and comparison of one aspect of many of them. It is built upon a general economic concept of capital which Weber defines as "goods which are devoted to securing a profit in exchange," [21] i.e., having about the same connotation as Boehm-Bawerk's "private capital." Thus capitalism is a system in which such goods are used, or play a prominent part, and may be defined most generally as a system of (rationally conducted) exchange for profit. It is a purely economic category, and Weber explicitly excludes all social components, such as a factory system using free labor, etc., from it.

It is unnecessary to point out that this is not a solution of the problem of modern capitalism which has absorbed Sombart's attention and which is the subject of this paper. And Weber is quite clear about that. In spite of his continual references to capitalism in antiquity and other times, he is very careful to point out the vital differences between all those and modern society.

There is, however, some relation to modern conditions in that all capitalism is classed as essentially acquisitive. "A capitalistic action is one which is oriented to the exploitation of opportunities for profit

in exchange, that is (formally) peaceful opportunities." [22] Thus it is
directed toward acquisition and not toward the satisfaction of need,
driving the same "wedge" between the immediate and the ultimate end
of economic action, as Sombart pointed out. But although capitalistic
activity is directed toward acquisition, Weber refuses to identify capitalism or the spirit of it with a psychological instinct or impulse of acquisition. He says: "Capitalism may even be identical with the suppression,
or at least the tempering, of this irrational impulse. But that does not
mean that capitalism has nothing to do with acquisition. On the contrary, it is identical with the struggle for gain in a *continuous, rationally
conducted capitalistic enterprise,* a struggle for ever renewed profit,
for rentability. And it must be. In a capitalistic order of society as a
whole an enterprise which did not strive for gain would be condemned
to destruction." [23]

Thus Weber emphasizes the same thing as Sombart: that capitalism
forces the individual business man into the race for profit, not because
he is venal by nature, not because it represents the highest values in
life for him, but because his enterprise must earn profit or go under. It
is the objective system to which the individual must conform if he
wants to do business at all. The remarkable thing is that this objectivity
appears at a point where Weber is obviously speaking of capitalism in
general, whereas Sombart makes it a characteristic of modern capitalism.
The key may perhaps be found in the words "in a capitalistic order of
society as a whole." Weber says there were capitalistic enterprises at
many times and places, and hence, in a broad sense, capitalism; but he
would maintain that only in the modern occident has there been a
sufficient number of them to dominate society as a whole. Hence the
difference between the different sorts of capitalism would be for him
one degree. But that is not the whole story, as will be shown presently.

In the foregoing quotation a further element has appeared which
was not contained in his original definition of capitalism, but evidently
applies to "capitalism in general." That is, the struggle for gain is in a
"continuous, rationally conducted capitalistic enterprise." This rationality, by which he means neither "reasonableness" nor a high degree of
theoretical scientific development, but a thoroughgoing systemization
and adaption of practical life to a particular set of ideals, indicates what
features of modern society are of importance for his theory of capitalism. That it appears in his discussion of general capitalism indicates
that he did not clearly distinguish in his own mind the two separate
concepts of capitalism to be found in his work.

But even with this hint it cannot be capitalism in this simple
form to which Weber refers as "the most fateful force in our modern

life." When one comes to inquire what he did mean by that statement one finds him analyzing a highly complex "constellation" of factors which together form a unique and unified whole, what he has called a historical individual.

His first contribution is a negative one, the definite exclusion of the "capitalistic adventurers" from any essential place in modern capitalism. Such people are, he says, found at all times, and are in no way peculiar to ours. The particular basis of their exclusion is the irrational character of their activity which is directly opposed to the systematic and rational spirit of modern capitalism. This indicates the most essential substantive difference between the theories of Weber and Sombart. Sombart's spirit of enterprise is not for Weber harnessed to the chariot of capitalism, but remains outside it, even though it may appear prominently in capitalistic times.

The common characteristic of all the principal features of modern society, non-economic as well as economic, Weber sees in their peculiar type of rationality. Its principal institutions belong to his general type of "rational organization," or what he calls in a special sense "bureaucracy." [24] Its main characteristics are: rationality, resting on a complex, hierarchically organized division of tasks, each with a sharply marked-off sphere of "competence"; specialization of functions, whereby a special premium is placed upon expert knowledge of whatever kind it may be; and impersonality, in the sense that the ends which the organization serves are impersonal (acquisition, political domination, etc.) and that commands are given and obeyed by virtue of a "legal" authority vested in the position of the individual who gives them, not his personal qualities.

The two most important non-economic institutions for Weber are the modern state and modern science, both of which are organized on definitely bureaucratic principles. He particularly emphasizes this aspect of science, which was originally based far more on the purely individual accomplishment of genius.

The specific characteristic of modern capitalism on the economic side is that Weber calls the rational organization of free labor. "Only the occident has known rational capitalistic enterprise with fixed capital, free labor, and rational division and integration of labor, with a division of functions through exchange on the basis of capitalistic acquisition." [25] This is in turn the key to some other economic features of modern society. Of course modern capitalistic acquisition is achieved by at least formally peaceful means, and Weber emphasizes the aspect of stability as a condition of accurate calculation. This is largely carried out by another typical feature of modern times, a rational system of bookkeeping [26].

The development of bookkeeping makes possible still another highly important phenomenon, the rigid separation of the private interests of the business man from those of the business unit; not necessarily a spatial separation, though this comes to be usual, but in thought and for purposes for calculation the individual is split into two. One is a producer who as such is part of a great mechanistic system with no individuality of his own. The other is a consumer who has still a part of his life left to devote to his family, recreation, cultural interests, etc. But the relations between the two tend to weaken, and the business side of life to run on its own tracks without regard to the private side.

It is Weber's peculiar view that this all-important bureaucracy is essentially the same phenomenon whether it appears in a great corporation, a government department, or a political party machine. Its spread rests primarily upon its purely technical superiority to all other forms of large-scale organization of human activity. Capitalism is, one may say, simply bureaucratic organization placed in the service of pecuniary profit.

Weber's view of the relation of bureaucracy to capitalism stands in close relation to the socialistic contention that in the transition from capitalism to socialism the state will tend to disappear. Weber would not put it quite that way, but would say that the sharp distinction between economic and political organization tended with the bureaucratization of economic life to fade out, and that the line of development was in the direction of a fusion of the two. The fusion is, moreover, characterized for Weber by the fact that the economic element comes to predominate over the political. The acquisitive nature of capitalism permeates all modern bureaucracy as distinguished from that of other times, and thus justifies the name "capitalism" as the most apt designation of modern society. The element of competition, which is of primary importance for Sombart, recedes quite into the background for Weber. In fact all the specific elements of capitalism which we think of as contrasting it with socialism — competition, private property, production for exchange, class antagonism between *bourgeois* and proletariat, although a part of Weber's theory — are of secondary importance as compared with the great central fact of bureaucracy. The final result of the development, a great unified organization in the service of economic production, would not be far from socialism as ordinarily conceived.

[...]

Finally, another cause of Weber's difficulties lies in his method.

He wishes to work in terms of comparative sociology by means of ideal types. He thus takes sections and aspects of all sorts of societies away from their context and tries to compare them, but in so doing he loses the very thing he is looking for, the very individuality which they can have only in that context. Thus he speaks of the various sorts of capitalism, of bureaucracy, and so forth. On the other hand, in his treatment of the spirit of capitalism he follows an entirely different procedure. Here he works out as an organic whole, as an "historical individual," a set of ethical ideals, and tries to understand contemporary civilization in terms of them. This sort of capitalism is unique, existing only in modern times in Western society. But on trying to develop this concept he comes into conflict with his other conception of "capitalism in general" and is unable to reconcile them. He does, however, try, and in the attempt he is forced to characterize modern capitalism in terms of one feature, the rational organization of labor, superimposed upon his capitalism in general. But this feature loses its original nature as a "fictitious" ideal type and becomes identified with historical reality. Because it originates as an ideal type it is impossible to establish an organic connection between it, on the one hand, and the spirit of enterprise and several other features of modern society on the other, because they belong for him in quite different and distinct sociological categories. And the tendencies of development which he works out for this isolated element of society he tends to hypostatize as true for society as a whole. In doing so he does violence to the facts and presents a picture different from what it would have been had he not been forced by his method to break up the the organically connected historical individuals with which he started.

The real trouble is that Weber treats as "ideal types" two fundamentally different sorts of concepts. The one deals with generalized "aspects" of phenomena for comparative purposes, the other with unique historical epochs, cultures, etc., as wholes and by and for themselves. Because he does not clearly distinguish these two types of concepts he constantly wavers between them. Because the second class of ideal type does have a historical significance he does not strictly adhere to his methodological principle that a *general* ideal type is purely a fiction, a means for further analysis, and has no reality in itself. In fact his "capitalism in general," and more especially his "bureaucracy," which start off as such ideal types, come in the end to have this definite historical reality from which he deduces very important consequences. In thus attempting to apply a method suitable only for comparative purposes to the analysis of a culture as a whole he seriously confuses the picture which he gives. I think there is no doubt that the logical basis of Weber's iron-bound process of rationalization lies in the isolation of one aspect of social development and the attribution of historical reality to an ideal type which was never meant to represent it. If this error is corrected the absolute domination of the process of rationalization over the whole social process falls to the ground.

In conclusion, the significance for social science in general of the work of Sombart and Weber is to be sought in four principal directions:

1. As far as general social theory is concerned, it bears most directly upon a set of problems which are not primarily economic, but are certainly, in a broad sense, sociological, namely, those growing out of the economic interpretation of history. I have attempted to show the great importance of the influence exercised by the Marxian thesis in shaping the views of these men. In fact, German sociology, in so far as it aims at an appraisal of the moving forces in social life, has its starting-point to a very large extent in Marx. Here is a set of problems which sociology cannot afford to neglect.

2. It bears upon some important methodological questions concerning this peculiar type of "historical theory." Its aim is to throw light on the individuality of "historical individuals," periods, epochs, cultures, institutions. Sombart attempts it by a "genetic," Weber ostensibly by a comparative, method, but really by a combination of both. Are the two methods supplementary to each other, or mutually contradictory? We have seen the confusing results of Weber's failure to distinguish them.

3. With regard to the positive problem of capitalism itself, Western analysis of modern economic society has been largely concerned with the application of general economic theory to it. This, no matter what its value for other purposes, has tended to blur over its distinctive features as compared with other historical or theoretically possible types of economic order. Even historical analysis has operated largely from the viewpoint of unilinear evolution. So it seems to me that the totally different approach of these investigators merits serious attention and should prove very fruitful. Furthermore, the positive results which are common to both authors, the objectivity of the capitalistic system, its connection with ethical values, and the peculiar predominance of economic influences under capitalism, have received a wide acceptance in Germany and merit much more discussion than they have had in this country.

4. However exaggerated Weber's view of the dominating importance of "bureaucracy" may be, it certainly calls attention in a most striking way to an aspect of our modern society which we have all felt to be

there, but which has received far less attention from the economists than it deserves. Orthodox economic theory does not furnish the technique or set of concepts necessary for its study. Weber, with his sociology of ideal types, has made an attempt to grapple with the problem which deserves recognition and which should lead to much further investigation.

READING 1:
NOTES AND REFERENCES

[1] The first edition of Sombart's great work, *Der moderne Kapitalismus,* appeared in 1902. It met much adverse criticism and in the years following he undertook practically to rewrite the whole. Several special studies were published from time to time (*Der Bourgeois,* 1913, *Die Juden und das Wirtschaftsleben, Krieg und Kapitalismus, Luxus und Kapitalismus*) and in 1916–17 the first two volumes of the new edition of the *Kapitalismus* appeared. They dealt with the precapitalistic systems and the early capitalistic period, from the breakdown of the Middle Ages to approximately the end of the eighteenth century. The third and last volume, dealing with "mature capitalism" (*Hochkapitalismus*) down to the World War, appeared in two instalments, 1926–27. Other works of Sombart bearing on the problems of capitalism are *Die deutsche Volkswirtschaft in roten Jahrhundert, Der proletarische Sozialismus* (1924; 2 vols.), the article "Die prinzipielle Eigenart des modernen Kapitalismus," *Grundriss der Sozialoekonomik,* Vol. IV; and various articles in periodicals, especially the *Archiv fuer Sozialwissenschalft und Sozialpolitik.*

[2] See E. Salin, *Weltwirtschaftliches Archiv,* 1927. It will be impossible to present here any large proportion of Sombart's particular historical interpretations. But they should be included in any complete view of his work.

[3] *Kapitalismus,* I, 21–22.

[4] The two German terms which Sombart uses are *Wirtschaftsgesinnung* and *Wirtschaftsgeist.* Both are difficult to translate. I shall in general use "spirit" and hope its exact meaning will become clear in the course of the discussion.

[5] *Kapitalismus,* I, 25.

[6] There has been considerable controversy in the literature on historical materialism as to just what Marx and Engels meant by it. Some interpreters (for instance B. Croce, *Historical Materialism and the Economics of Karl Marx*) maintain that it is to be

considered, not a theory of the forces in social evolution, but rather an heuristic principle. Whether that be the correct interpretation of Marx or not, the sense in which I am taking him has certainly had the greatest influence on Sombart (see *Der proletarische Sozialismus*) and also on that aspect of Weber in which I am primarily interested.

[7] *Kapitalismus*, I, 279 ff.

[8] On Sombart's own ground it seems somewhat incomprehensible that he is able to speak of *two* precapitalistic systems, since the most characteristic criterion of any system is the spirit, and in this case both are dominated by practically the same spirit.

[9] "Prinzipielle Eigenart des mod. Kapitalismus," *Grundriss der Sozialoekonomik*, Vol. IV.

[10] *Kapitalismus*, III, 129.

[11] See below, with reference to Weber. That Sombart's way of looking at capital is not necessarily to be considered as inconsistent with a general analytical system of economic theory as attested by the case of Schumpeter (*Theorie der wirtschaftlichen Entwicklung*, 2nd ed., Munich, 1926), whose view in this regard is very similar to that of Sombart. Yet Schumpeter is one of the staunchest supporters of those claims of economic theory which Sombart denies.

[12] Sombart himself uses the French word *bourgeois* to designate the whole capitalistic man, not one aspect of him. For the single rational aspect he uses the German *Bürger*. It seems best, however, since there is no proper English equivalent of the latter, to translate *Bürger* by *bourgeois*, ignoring Sombart's distinction.

[13] For this viewpoint see T. N. Carver, *The Religion Worth Having*. For Sombart's explanation, "Die prinzipielle Eigenart, etc.," *Grundriss der Sozialokonomik*.

[14] In the sense of identification with an "organic" view of society and more or less feudal ideals, not of defense of the status quo.

[15] See Karl Jaspers, *Max Weber: Gedächtnisrede* (Tübingen, 1921).

[16] The German term is *Historisches Individuum*. It refers to a cultural phenomenon in which many men may be involved.

[17] The "perfect rationality" meant by Weber may not always be a perfect, but rather a relative, rationality, the degree of which depends on the purpose for which the ideal type is constructed. It is always used to separate the relatively rational from the relatively irrational elements of the situation to be analyzed. However, the ideal type based upon the perfectly rational adaptation of means to given ends (what he calls *zweckrational*) is the

most important class for Weber. As he says (*Wirtschaft und Gesellschaft*, 2 and 3): "For scientific analysis working with ideal types, all irrational, emotionally determined complexes of behavior, which influence action, are most easily investigated and presented as 'deviations' from a construction of the purely rational (with regard to means) order of occurence of them." And again: "The construction of a strictly rational course of action serves the sociologist in these cases, on account of its evident understandability and lack of ambiguity, . . . as an ideal type for the purpose of understanding real action which is influenced by irrationalities of all kinds, in terms of their 'departure' from what the action would be if it were purely rational." Only in this sense is Weber's sociology to be considered rational. It makes no assumption as to the actual relative importance of the rational elements in social life.

[18] This question of the objectivity of his type of social science is one of the most difficult aspects of Weber's position. It unfortunately cannot be discussed here. For his viewpoint see "Die Objectivitaet Sozialwissenschaftlicher Erkenntnis, *Ges. Aufsaetze zur Wissenschaftslehre*, pp. 146 ff.

[19] For the best analysis of Weber's methodology see A. von Schelting, "Die logische Theorie der historischen Kulturwissenschaften von Max Weber usw.," *Archiv für Sozialwissenschaft und Sozialpolitik*, Bd. 49. Parts of Weber's own writings which deal with the problem of the ideal type are: several of the essays in the volume *Gesammelte Aufsätze zur Wissenschaftslehre* and the first part of "Wirtschaft und Gesellschaft," *Grundriss der Sozialoekonomik*, Vol. III.

[20] Those of Weber's works which bear upon this problem are above all the three volumes of the *Gesammelte Aufsaetze zur Religionssoziologie*, especially the first essay, "Die protestantische Ethik und der Geist des Kapitalismus"; various parts of his great general work on sociology, *Wirtschaft und Gesellschaft*, the essay "Agrarverhältnisse im Altertum" in the *Ges. Aufsätze sur Sozial- und Wirtschaftsgeschichte;* and the *General Economic History* (English translation of *Wirtschaftsgeschichte* by Professor F. H. Knight).

[21] *Agrarverhältnisse im Altertum*, p. 13.

[22] *Wirtschaft und Gesellschaft*, p. 48.

[23] *Religionssoziologie*, I, 4.

[24] "Bureaucracy" is here used in a more general sense than that of common speech. It refers to any large-scale organization of the sort indicated, and does not carry any of the implications of

cumbersomeness, red tape, etc., which are so often associated with it. See *Wirtschaft und Gesellschaft,* pp. 125–30, 650–78.

[25] *Wirtschaft und Gesellschaft,* p. 96.

[26] Sombart also makes a great deal of this point, going very thoroughly into the history of bookkeeping methods. *Kapitalismus,* II, p, 10 ff., 159–62.

ECONOMICS AND SOCIOLOGY: MARSHALL IN RELATION TO THE THOUGHT OF HIS TIME

In the last issue of this Journal I undertook to analyze Marshall's writings with a view to culling out certain vital elements to be found there which were logically separable from his "organon" of economic theory strictly defined. The outcome of that investigation was the thesis that running throughout Marshall's work is a line of thought which is almost everywhere coördinate in importance with what I have called his "utility theory," namely, his belief in the importance, both ethically and for explanatory purposes, of certain types of activities pursued largely as ends in themselves, and of certain types of character of which these activities are partly the expression, partly the formative agent. Marshall's attitude toward and interest in these activities and qualities of character play a decisive part in determining his position on a number of important problems, both of technical economic theory and of broader scope. Such considerations are among the things involved in his attitude toward Ricardo, his doctrines of the supplies of the agents of production, his views of real cost, his attitude toward laissez-faire, social evolution and human nature. [. . .]

The issues with which this discussion is to be concerned can

Abridged and reprinted, with permission, from *Quarterly Journal of Economics*, Vol. 46 (1932), pp. 316–347.

perhaps best be raised by pointing out a striking relationship which Marshall's idea of "free enterprise" bears to the doctrines of another recent writer on modern capitalism, Max Weber, who is the representative of a totally different school of thought [1].

Weber finds the dominant characteristic of modern capitalism in a certain peculiar rationality of the conduct of life, a rationality sharply opposed to the irrationalities both of "traditionalism" and of undisciplined instinct, whim, impulse or sentiment. It is characterized on the part of the individual by a careful systematic planning of his life as a whole and the elimination of all activities inconsistent with such a comprehensive plan. In actual economic life it results in the far-reaching application of science to industrial technique and business organization, the long-time planning of operations, the vivid realization of the future — all serving to make the whole economic organization predominantly into what Weber calls a "bureaucratic" type. This rational bureaucratic organization of modern society is most conspicuous in the economic sphere, in enterprises producing goods for a competitive market. The making of profit and the increase of capital being the common aim of all such enterprises, the system as a whole is most appropriately called capitalism.

But the very impersonality of profit as an aim raises the question of motivation. Is such activity carried on to satisfy individual desires by the expenditure of the profits? Is the rationality of capitalism peculiar only in the perfection with which it adapts means to *universal* human ends? Weber definitely rejects such views. There is nothing natural and universal about the capitalistic way of life such that, given favorable external conditions, it will become established of itself. On the contrary it is an entirely unique phenomenon, which has appeared only once in history in an equally unique constellation of circumstances. It is not explicable in terms of the wants which are expressed in consumers' demand, assumed to be given from the point of view of the productive process. Nor is it explicable in terms of wants in the sense of instincts, such as acquisition of workmanship.

Then what does account for it? In its fully developed form the competitive discipline is enough, the system is self-sustaining. Any individual who failed to conform to its rules and ways would be eliminated from the struggle. But selection alone cannot account for the *origin*. The standards of this particular selective process themselves are not universal; they had to originate somewhere. Their origin Weber finds above all [2] in the Protestant Ethic which created a state of mind favorable to such a way of life. Through the idea of a "calling," a task to which every man felt himself to be assigned by divine Providence, economic activities came to be pursued not as means to other worldly ends, but from the mundane point of view as ends in themselves — justified to the individual by their relation to his eternal salvation.

Weber's main emphasis throughout is on the importance of this "ascetic" element in modern economic life, as against the more ortho-dox view that it is merely the result of "natural" tendencies of behavior, instinctive or hedonistic. His explanation of modern capitalism is in a sense in terms of wants, but not in the same sense as that of utility theory. The "ascetic" aspect means on the whole an inhibition of wants in the latter sense, which, however, greatly favored capitalism because it promoted accumulation. On the other hand the "wants," or perhaps rather values behind the system are expressed directly in economic activities, not in demand; in the system and rationality of conduct, in industry and frugality, in short the "economic virtues."

This suggests some interesting points of correspondence between Weber and Marshall. In the first place, both are agreed that modern capitalism, or "free enterprise" is characterized by a peculiarly high degree of rationality; it is in fact the result of a long "process of ration-alization." They are also agreed that, in so far as rationality is a mark of "economic" conduct, the development of capitalism is characterized by an increasing importance of economic factors in social life. Moreover, both emphasize the importance of the economic in another way. Economic development leads to a greater spread of the competitive price system, so that an increasing proportion of men's lives is deter-mined by their relation to it. Weber greatly emphasizes the compulsive nature of competition, while Marshall does so only by implication; it is for him an important agent in keeping up the springs of energy and enterprise. This makes it possible to say that, in a sense, both hold an "economic interpretation of capitalism" tho not of history as a whole.

But in both cases, and this is the most significant agreement, these first two elements, rationality and dependence on the com-petitive price system, derive their meaning largely from a third factor, Weber's "callings," pursued first for the glory of God, later, with the dying out of the religious motives, as ends in themselves; and Marshall's "activities." For both, especially, the rationality in question is relative to these activities, centering around them as a nucleus. Weber makes the relativity highly explicit, contrasting this form of rationality with many others that are possible. Marshall's conception of rationality is much more absolute, but his ruling out the rational satisfaction of those wants which he calls "artificial" from a rôle in social progress clearly shows the relation of rationality to activities in his doctrine. With Marshall as with Weber this same element is the basis of the denial that civilization can be understood either in terms of biological instinct, the "wants" which rule the lower animals, or of "artificial wants" which would be either primarily hedonistic or random.

Moreover Marshall agrees with Weber, and on similar grounds, that the concept of selection is inadequate as a general explanatory principle. Weber's position, cited above, is that while selection [3] can sometimes explain the maintenance of a given social organization once established, it can never explain the origin of the standards of selection themselves. Marshall, in more directly ethical terms, says survival power is the power "to *thrive in* the environment, not necessarily to *benefit* the environment." [4] Given the fact that the development of free enterprise has in Marshall's view meant specifically moral advance, it is quite clear that a process of "benefitting the environment" must have gone on continuously, i.e. that the competitive process has been supplemented by another source of standards.

As will be shown later, Weber's general sociological position is fundamentally different from Marshall's. Hence Weber's scientific motives for studying modern capitalism in the terms in which he did are completely foreign to Marshall. [5] Then whence the remarkable correspondence? The explanation seems to be that Marshall was a living example of the "spirit of capitalism" of which Weber was talking. While he happened to be right about the rôle of certain ethical qualities in modern life, the reason for his ability to see them was not, as with Weber, an extraordinarily wide perspective, but his own deep-rooted belief in them. It was here that Marshall, the seer and reformer, [6] made his contact with Marshall, the scientist. This reforming zeal was at least as important an influence in his life as a whole as his purely "positive" scientific interest.

Marshall's own ethic was also certainly a derivative of the Protestant Ethic of which Weber speaks. As Keynes tells us "The Marshalls were a clerical family of the West of England" and his father tho not himself a clergyman was "cast in the mould of the strictest Evangelicals." [7] While Marshall himself was a free thinker in his adult life, he retained all the more tenaciously the ethical fruits of his strict religious bringing up. Moreover, he himself ascribed considerable importance to religious factors of the Reformation in "strengthening the English character." [8]

[...]

I now come to what is, from a scientific point of view, the most important stage of the argument. Marshall puts forward the views which have been under discussion in these two papers under the rubric of economics. They involve, however, implications for his conception of the whole social process so broad that it is justifiable, even tho Marshall himself would have repudiated the suggestion, to regard his body of "economic" thought taken as a whole as a sociology. While he thought he was avoiding anything beyond legitimate economic analysis, and even held that, at least in his day, a science of society as a whole was not attainable, [9] he did not succeed in avoiding the wider problems. The only trouble is that his treatment of them is unsatisfactory.

It has been shown, I think, that his position follows not unnaturally from that of his predecessors. They really left only the alternative that sociology was either applied biology or psychology, or that it was simply economics in the sense of utility theory. In so far as utilitarianism represented the "liberalism" sketched above, freed from hedonism, it was a sociology which consisted solely of a universal application of economic theory in the "utility" sense. As compared with any of these, Marshall's position, regarded as a sociology, is a distinct advance. He is able to account for a group of phenomena which are of great importance, but have no place in any of the above frameworks. So much must be said for him in spite of the difficulties of his position. But is his widening of the boundaries of economics to include the study of activities and character a service to economics? To be sure it places the phenomena studied by utility theory in a wider perspective and hence gives a more correct total view of them. But this may not be the best way of gaining such a perspective. Is not the perspective which Marshall gains on the process of want-satisfaction more than counter-balanced by his conspicuous lack of perspective on the activities themselves? From the above analysis it must be concluded that the main lines of Marshall's treatment of activities, in so far as it is more than a bare recognition of their importance, results from its assimilation to the tradition of English economics. Only a separation can avoid Marshall's difficulties.

But how can this separation be brought about without losing sight of the importance of the activities? Marshall is quite right in holding that they cannot adequately be dealt with in terms either of a biological struggle for survival or of a study of human nature. The character in which he is interested is not an inborn trait of man's biological or pyschological nature; it is socially conditioned. In part no doubt it is economically conditioned. But Marshall is committed from the start to the view that it is best studied as part of the system of economic equilibrium. The only remaining alternative seems to be to turn its explanation over to a still wider science: sociology. But there is a sense in which it can be said that the whole English intellectual tradition of which Marshall was a part had no place for sociology [10]. Within the scope of that tradition the only phenomena not specifically explicable in terms of the principles of non-social sciences, biology and psychology, are those ordinarily understood as economic — the rational pursuit of individual want-satisfaction. But by sociology I should mean a science which studies phenomena specifically social, those arising out of the *interaction* of human beings as such, which would hence not be reducible to the "nature" of those human beings. The biological and psychological factors would assume the position of limiting conditions, knowledge of what might be of great importance in understanding any *particular* concrete problem but which would not be a part of the specific logical subject matter of sociology. Economics, on the other hand, would be a part of sociology dealing with one aspect of social phenomena, which would need to be supplemented by other sociological factors before it could give adequate solutions of concrete problems. Does such a science exist at all? What would be the position of economics within it? Above all how would it deal with problems such as those Marshall tried to solve by his treatment of activities and character within the framework of economics? Is it capable of dealing with types of "activities" which cannot be so easily assimilated to the conceptions of a narrower economics as those of Marshall? The starting point of this final stage of the inquiry is the recognition that the universal importance which Marshall attaches to *his* activities cannot be founded in the facts alone; it is at least partly a matter of the perspective imposed by his sociological framework and can only be escaped by altering that framework.

It is fortunately not necessary to venture into entirely unexplored territory in order to show that a way out of Marshall's impasse is possible. Let us here consider two general conceptions of the scope and problems of social science and of the relation of economics to sociology which offer an escape from his difficulties. I choose these two, Pareto and Max Weber, not because I wish to hail them as the only possible alternatives to the "Anglo-American" tradition of which Marshall forms a part — whether they are cannot be decided within the scope of the present study — but because they both have a peculiar relevance to Marshall's problems.

The anti-intellectualist movement and its relation to Anglo-American social thought has already been touched upon. Pareto is the most eminent sociological representative of the movement in continental Europe; the revolt against exagerrating the rôle of reason may be considered his starting point. He, however, has escaped the predominant tendency of Anglo-American anti-intellectualism of psychologism and survivalism; hence for present purposes his doctrine is to be differentiated sharply from the latter.

Pareto, as the leading representative of the "mathematical school" of economics, made important contributions to economic theory [11]. It is interesting to note that, however much his theoretical system differs from that of Marshall in form, in substance it is very similar to what I have called the latter's utility theory. It was, on the other hand, a keen realization of the inadequacy of economics in this sense for the understanding of concrete social phenomena which led Pareto finally, in his old age, to formulate a whole system of sociology [12]. Its beginnings are to be found in his work on socialism [13]; and it is to be remarked that tho he did not devote a special work to the problem of protectionism this occupied a large place in the development of his thought [14].

Pareto defined economics as the science of "logical" action − what I have called "rational" − as opposed to "non-logical." He is insistent that "Non-logical" is not necessarily "illogical" from the point of view of the outside observer. His criterion of "logical" is the correspondence of the subjective with the objective end of a given act. By thus trying logical or economic action up with the existence of a subjective end, a "want," Pareto cuts himself off sharply from any economic "behaviorism"; for the behaviorist by categorically denying the relevance of the "subjective" to his scientific problems, has no possible means of distinguishing the logical from the non-logical when the latter is not illogical. Thus, for Pareto, economics is the study essentially of the logical − or rational − process of the satisfaction of "wants" (goûts) in so far that it is permitted by the "obstacles," the cost factors, whether they be scarcity of natural resources, disinclination to work, or to save, or anything else [15]. Pareto studies the economic process in terms of a general equilibrium theory. The "wants" are definitely taken for granted as ultimate for economic purposes. At the same time force and fraud are ruled out, partly because of the dominant part played by deliberate choice on the part of consumers. But since consumers, and sellers, choose between the alternatives actually open to them, the exercise of economic "power" is not excluded.

But, as Pareto insists throughout, this economic theory is abstract. It deals only with certain selected elements of social life, and before being applied to any concrete problem needs to be corrected by the reintroduction of the elements from which abstraction was made. A systematic study of the more important of those other elements forms the principal content of his sociology. In formulating it he takes his departure from a study of non-logical action. He distinguishes two fundamental elements which are involved; the professed motives of action (values, ideals, and the like) which he classifies as "derivations," and which he finds to vary enormously; and, more constant than they, certain more or less universal tendencies of action which he calls "residues." It is important to note the great caution with which Pareto defines the "residues." They are simply the relatively constant factors in non-logical action. He is particularly careful not to identify them with instincts. The residue is not a psychological but a sociological conception. They are not constant attributes of an abstract human nature but relatively constant tendencies of the behavior of human beings *in society*. It is change in the residues and their combinations which primarily accounts for social change, tho of course that change may be due to the changing composition of a population with respect to hereditary type, as well as to change within the same hereditary type [16] due to social influences. It is the position which marks Pareto off from " psychologism."

His anti-intellectualism appears in the general contention that the residues far outweigh the derivations in importance, tho he is careful not to exclude the latter from some rôle in the social equilibrium. Finally besides these two factors, and the economic, Pareto lays great stress on the fact of social stratification of the higher layers, the élite, and their relation to that of the lower are determined.

Had he discussed Marshall's activities and character Pareto would probably have ascribed them primarily to a particular combination of residues, partly perhaps influenced by past derivation of a religious nature. This would be a combination which gave a specially large importance to economic, or logical action. Its rise to predominance, Pareto would explain in terms of a particular process of circulation of the élite which favored this type. But these phenomena would be placed in a very different general framework from that of Marshall. Instead of being the one combination favored by the historical process as a whole, it would be only one of a large number of possible combinations. Pareto is not committed by his methodological position, as Marshall is, to one special type of unilinear evolutionary process leading to the progressive elimination of certain factors of social causation. On the contrary he brings about a very convincing reinstatement of some of those factors, notably force and fraud. Moreover, so far as he has any theory of the historical process as a whole, it is not Marshall's unilinear evolution but a succession of never-ending cycles of change. The doctrine, receiving, as it does a notable revival in Pareto's work, is a measure of the radicality of his departure from the tradition which has been under discussion here. Thus Pareto, while he would be able to find a place in his scientific scheme for Marshall's problems, commands an immensely widened perspective which enables him to escape the provincial narrow-mindedness of which Marshall is guilty.

The other alternative conception to that of Marshall which I wish to consider is Max Weber's. Weber is a true representative of the main currents of German social thought, which never has been very closely related to that of the Anglo-Saxon world. The central interest of Weber, as of Pareto, was in "economic" problems, the explanation of the phenomenon of modern capitalism, But as he soon realized that economics alone is incapable of solving his problems, he pushed further on to develop a science of sociology. The motivation of the two men in undertaking this task was strikingly similar.

Their conception of economics is also very similar. Weber makes it the science which studies human actions in so far as they are directed toward the acquisition of utilities (*Nutzleistungen*) [17]. So far, like the British and Pareto, by defining economic action in terms of its subjective aim, he radically repudiates economic "behaviorism." But, in accord with Pareto, he denies that this means basing economics on psychology. Utility here refers only to the actual end of action, the motive of concrete choices, not to the ultimate psychological "drives." Economic action is moreover in principle rational, tho it may in practice be tinged with traditionalism or other non-rational factors. But it is not the whole of the rational. It does not at all include one of the fundamental types of rational action, that concerned with putting ultimate values directly into practice (*wertrational*). It concerns only action in the service of limited finite ends, and not even all of that. The use of force, even tho it be rational, is excluded, as is 'technique" [18]. On the other hand the ends which are compared are taken as data. The explanation of their origin is not the task of economics. Non-rational action is understood largely in terms of its deviation from rational types.

For present purposes the most important non-economic category of Weber's sociology is that of action in direct pursuit of ultimate values (*wertrationales Handeln*). The conception is a leading one in the whole line of thought of which he is representative. It implies that not merely individuals as the sociological "liberal" might admit, but historical epochs and cultures are characterized by the predominance of sets of ultimate values which form an essential element in the understanding of the social phenomena connected with them. Besides this category he adduces others of a non-economic nature; emotional determination, force, tradition, which do not necessarily involve recourse to bio-psychological explanations. Nevertheless it is the specific rôle of "values" which is characteristic of German Sociology. They may be wholly independent and logically unconnected, as for Sombart and

Spengler, or connected on a dialectic process as for Hegel, or Marx, or they may form the main differentiating elements in a branching-tree conception of social development, as for Weber. In any case they introduce a highly important element of relativism into sociology. They encourage the conception of a society dominated by such a system of values as a closed, complete whole, sharply differentiated from others, rather than as a transistory stage in a continuous process.

It is in these terms that Weber approaches the problem of capitalism. He considers it as a system sharply differentiated form others which have existed in history. The "activities" involved in it are specific products of highly specific influences, among which the ethic of Protestantism occupies the central place. There is no reason to suppose that without the presence of such a specific constellation of factors any such way of life would ever have come into existence. It is emphatically not the sole result of the whole evolutionary process; Weber is immune from such surreptitious teleology. Similarly the civilization of India is to be understood to a large extent in terms of the peculiar values it embodies — again mainly religious — and not as merely a "retarded" stage of social development as a whole. Thus Weber, like Pareto, achieves a wide perspective on the characteristics of modern capitalism, which was closed to Marshall. In his case also it is the totally different sociological framework which enables him to do this. Nothing would be further from the truth than to suppose it was *more knowledge,* in any quantitative sense, that gave Weber and Pareto their advantage over Marshall. On the contrary, it is their strictly theoretical insight; in other words, clarity of thought on fundamental problems. That is the point of this whole analysis.

To conclude. These two papers have been concerned with supporting the following line of argument. Marshall in his economic writings does not confine himself to the narrow range of problems of value and distribution which are ordinarily thought to have constituted the field of orthodox economics. On the contrary, parallel with, and inextricably bound up with his "pure theory" runs a second line of doctrine concerning the relation of economic activities to human character. In his own estimation this second line is at least as important as the first. It must be considered as a theory and not as the "application" of his real theory.

The peculiar way in which Marshall deals with these problems and the way he fuses his thought concerning them with his pure economic theory implies a position on the broadest questions of social theory so definite that it must be held to constitute a system of sociology. The characteristic features of this sociology are not a matter of Marshall's more or less random observations on things lying outside his field, but grow out of the logical exigencies of fitting his own central doctrines into the framework of sociological theory dominant in the England of his time. This is the real reason why Marshall's doctrines are of more than historical interest. They throw a bright light on the whole structure of English social thought.

Considered as a sociology, his work represents in some respects an improvement on that of his predecessors. But both his own strong belief in the importance of the activities which form his central theme, and the narrowness of the tradition into which he had to fit them, combined to lend a certain lack of perspective to his treatment of the activities which closed his eyes to the importance of many other things. His views of their place in social evolution will not stand criticism in terms of the wide sweep of history with which sociology after all must concern itself.

It is possible to escape this lack of perspective, but only by undertaking a thoro reconstruction of the intellectual tradition of which Marshall formed a part. The first essential step in such a reconstruction is the limitation of the field of economics so as to deprive it of the tendency it shows in Marshall's hands to expand into a general sociology with a very particular bias. This demarcation has been the starting point of the two systems of sociology just sketched. Both make room for an important and legitimate science of economics within the framework of a sociological scheme so broad as to counteract any tendency to economic one-sidedness. But both are built on a logical basis radically opposed to that of most previous Anglo-American social thought. This is not a plea for unqualified acceptance of the doctrines either of Pareto or of Weber, indeed in some resects they are incompatible with each other. Other possibilities equally promising may exist, or are likely to be developed in the future. But I think any system of sociology satisfactory from the viewpoint of this paper will necessarily involve departures from the main lines of the Anglo-American tradition as radical as those of Pareto and Weber.

In any case, I make a very serious plea that the theoretical questions here raised be faced. They cannot be evaded either by complacent and unquestioning acceptance of tradition or by flight to the "facts." Marshall himself once said "the most reckless and treacherous of all theorists is he who professes to let facts and figures speak for themselves." [19] In the field of the ultimate questions regarding the basis of his science he stands convicted by his own indictment. Let us hope that others who have this experience to build upon will not turn even further away from such questions than he did. Science, if it failed to map out its course, would be as lost in the uncharted seas of "fact" as a ship without a navigator.

READING 2:
NOTES AND REFERENCES

[1] See Max Weber, "The Protestant Ethic and the Spirit of Capitalism," London and New York, 1930. This essay, while containing the core of Weber's theory of capitalism, is only a fragment of the whole, which he unfortunately never formulated in one place.

[2] Of course other conditions had to be favorable. Weber has often been unjustly accused of holding that capitalism was "created" by Protestantism, out of a vacuum as it were. Such is by no means his position.

[3] Combined of course with the formative effect of a social environment upon individuals.

[4] *Principles*, p. 596; also *Industry and Trade*, p. 175.

[5] Moreover, any important reciprocal influence is out of the question. It is practically certain that Marshall never read Weber's essay and even had he done so he could not have been greatly influenced by it — the point of view is too different. The main lines of Marshall's views were certainly fixed before Weber's essay was written (1904).

[6] See Keynes, *Memorials*, pp. 11,12.

[7] *Memorials*, p.1.

[8] "The isolation of each person's religious responsibility . . . is a necessary condition of the highest spiritual progress." "The natural gravity and intrepidity of the Acin races that settled on the shores of England inclined them to embrace the doctrines of the Reformation; and these reacted on their habits of life." *Principles*, p. 742.

[9] *Principles*, Appendix C, p. 770.

[10] Of course if sociology means simply the science of society as a whole, comprising a study of all the factors bearing on society in whatever manner in its specific subject matter, it is out of the question that there should be no place for it; but that does not make it an independent science. On the other hand, if the central subject-matter of sociology be limited to the *social* (or "cultural") factors, as I prefer to do, it is quite possible to dispute its independent existence on the ground that its alleged subject-matter does not exist except as a resultant of factors already adequately treated by other sciences. The quarrel here is analogous to that

over the question whether biological phenomenon are reducible to applications of the laws of physics and chemistry. I am quite aware that the similar denial that social phenomena are reducible to applications of biological and psychological principles involves a philosophical stand. It is ultimately the character of English philosophy which is the basis of the whole position which shuts out sociology in this sense.

[11] In his *Course d'économie politique,* 2 vols., 1896; and *Manuel d'économie politique,* 1906.

[12] *Traité de sociologie générale,* 2 vols. 1917–19.

[13] *Les systèmes socialistes,* 2 vols., 1902.

[14] In both cases his problem was to explain why men acted counter to the deductions of pure economic theory, which sees in harmonious coöperation of the factors of production the way to maximum satisfaction and in protection a necessary destruction of wealth.

[15] By thinking in terms of "obstacles" Pareto intentionally avoids the morass into which Marshall fell on the question of real cost. In effect he limits it to opportunity cost.

[16] Moreover the standards of the selective processes by which the biological composition of a population changes are partly social, not biological-environmental alone. Pareto, like Marshall and Weber, sharply repudiates what he calls "social Darwinism."

[17] See *Wirtschaft und Gesellschaft,* Ch. II, p. 31.

[18] Technique is concerned solely with choice of means of unmistakable ends, while economic action is concerned with comparison of and choice between immediate, tho not ultimate ends since the latter cannot be "weighed." Weber's conception of economies clearly includes the use of power, though not that of force. See *Wirtschaft und Gesellschaft,* Ch. II, p. 32.

[19] Present Position of Economics, *Memorial,* p. 168. Of course Marshall is perfectly correct, especially as against the Historical School at which the remark was aimed. I am merely construing his statement even more widely than he intended in order to turn it against him.

Reading 3

THE PLACE OF ULTIMATE VALUES
IN SOCIOLOGICAL THEORY

The positivistic reaction against philosophy has, in its effect on the social sciences, manifested a strong tendency to obscure the fact that man is essentially an active, creative, evaluating creature. Any attempt to explain his behavior in terms of ends, purposes, ideals, has been under suspicion as a form of "teleology" which was thought to be incompatible with the methodological requirements of positive science. One must, on the contrary, explain in terms of "causes" and "conditions," not of ends.

Of late years, however, there have been many signs of a break in this rigid positivistic view of things. The social sciences in general have been far from immune from these signs, and in sociology in particular they have combined to form a movement of thought of the first importance. One main aspect of this movement has been the tendency to reopen the whole question of the extent to which, and the senses in which, human behavior must or can be understood in terms of the values entertained by men. In the present essay I wish to attempt a

Abridged and reprinted, from *International Journal of Ethics*, Vol. 45 (1935), pp. 282–316.
† In keeping with Parsons's remarks on the original paper, his footnotes have been suppressed from this reading. The original did not contain detailed references.

formulation of the kind of conception of human action which I take to be implied in some of these recent developments of sociological theory. In particular, what is the status in that conception of the element which may provisionally be called "ultimate values"? I shall not attempt here to trace the process by which this conception of human action has been built up, but merely to outline the conception itself.

One of the most conspicuous features of the positivistic movement just referred to has been the tendency to what may be termed a kind of "objectivism." Positivism, that is, has continually thought in terms of the model of the physical sciences which deal with an "inanimate" subject matter. Hence the tendency has been to follow their example in thinking of a simple relation of observer to externally observed events. The fact that the entities observed, human beings, have also a "subjective" aspect has a tendency to be obscured, or at least kept out of the range of methodological self-consciousness. The extreme of this objectivist trend, is, of course, behaviorism which involves the self-conscious denial of the legitimacy of including any references to the subjective aspect of other human beings in any scientific explanation of their reactions. But short of this radical behaviorist position, the general positivistic trend of thought has systematically minimized the importance of analysis in terms of the subjective aspect, and has prevented a clear-cut and self-conscious treatment of the relations of the two aspects to each other.

Of course the results of analysis of human behavior from the objective point of view (that is, that of an outside observer) and the subjective (that of the person thought of as acting himself) should correspond, but that fact is no reason why the two points of view should not be kept clearly distinct. Only on this basis is there any hope of arriving at a satisfactory solution of their relations to each other.

End and value are subjective categories in this sense. Hence it is not surprising that the objectivist bias of positivistic social thought should tend either to squeeze them out altogether or to militate against any really thoroughgoing analysis of them in their bearing on action. For the same reasons the present attempt to present at least the foundations of such an analysis must be couched mainly in subjective terms. The implications of the analysis for the objective point of view can at best be only very briefly indicated.

There seems to be no evading the fact that the subjective analysis of action involves in some form the schema of the means-end relationship. We must be careful to avoid any arbitrary assumption that this schema can exhaust the subjective aspect, but for various reasons it is the most favorable starting-point of such an analysis. [. . .]

It is necessary in following out this program to point out an ambiguity in the concept of "end" which may cause serious confusion. One possible definition would be the following: An end is the subjective anticipation of a desirable future state of affairs toward the realization of which the action of the individual in question may be thought of as directed. The thing to note is that the definition makes the "real" reference of an end — that is, the future state of affairs — a *concrete* state of affairs. But only *some* of the elements in that concrete state of affairs can be thought of as being brought about by the agency of the actor. Part of it consists of a *prediction* of what the future state of affairs will be, independently of his action. Thus, if I say it is an end of my present action to take a vacation in New Hampshire next summer, the concrete state of affairs I anticipate — vacationing in New Hampshire in the summer — will, if the end is realized, only to a certain extent come about through my own agency. The fact that it is *I* who does it will, to be sure, be attributable to that factor — but the geography of New Hampshire and the fact that it is summer will not be my doing — I merely predict, on the basis of my knowledge of the circumstances, that the former will remain substantially the same as now for another year, and that the cycle of the seasons will, by July, have brought summer in place of the present fall weather.

Ends in this sense may be called *concrete* ends. Our concern in this discussion is not, however, with concrete ends, but with ends as a *factor* in action. That is, it is with the prevision of a future state of affairs *in so far as* that future state is to be brought about through the agency of the actor — it is the alterations from what his prediction, if accurate, would yield as the future state without his agency which constitutes the end. Thus I can "see" New Hampshire next summer without my vacationing there. I can also "see" myself at that future time not in New Hampshire, but, for instance, perspiring over my work in Cambridge. It is the peculiar elements of *myself, vacationing* in New Hampshire, which may be considered my end. Thus, ends in this discussion will be used as an analytical category — a *factor* in action, and this sense of the term will be implied throughout unless otherwise stated. It is highly important not to confuse it with the concrete reality I have referred to.

If the means-end relationship involving this sense of the term "ends" is employed in this analysis, it is clear and should be pointed out at the outset that the whole analysis involves a metaphysical position of a "voluntaristic" character. That is, the analysis has empirical significance and is more than a mere exercise in logic only in so far as subjective ends in this sense do actually form an effective factor in action. This postulate a materialistic metaphysics would roundly deny. The metaphysical implication of the analysis is, however, thus far only negative — at the pole of materialism it ceases to have empirical meaning. But on the other hand, short of that pole, the analysis by itself does not beg the question of the quantitative empirical importance of the factor of ends. So long as it is not negligible, we may go ahead with a good conscience. But in so far as positivistic social theory has involved a genuinely materialistic metaphysics (which I believe it very generally has), it has quite rightly shied away from this type of analysis. For it, "ends," in so far as they exist at all, must be epiphenomena. Hence the importance of the foregoing distinction. Some concrete ends *may* be epiphenomena to us also, but to postulate this of the *factor* ends in general is naturally a contradiction in terms.

Before entering on an analysis of the means-end relationship itself, one more preliminary question should be called attention to. The means-end schema is, in type, at the rationalistic pole of the analysis of action. An end is thought of as a *logically formulated* anticipation of certain elements in a future state of affairs, and the relation is thought of as based on knowledge of the inherent connections of things. This is, in its type form, a *scientific* statement couched in the conditional, or, as it is sometimes put, the virtual form. That is, *if* I do certain things, bring about certain conditions, I will achieve my end. But this rational schema of the relation of means and ends is not to be arrived at by empirical generalization from the crude facts of experience. It is not only an analytical schema, but one of a peculiar sort. What it formulates is a *norm* of rational action. Its empirical relevance rests on the view, which I believed to be factually borne out, that human beings do, in fact, strive to realize ends and to do so by the rational application of means to them. This involves what I just called a "voluntaristic" conception of human action. Neither the knowledge of the relation of means and end on which action is based nor the application of that knowledge comes automatically. Both are the result of effort, of the exercise of will. Hence the probability that concrete action will only imperfectly realize such norms. Ignorance, error, and obstacles to the realization of ends which transcend human powers will all play a part in determining the concrete course of events. While on the one hand, the concept of action itself has no meaning apart from "real" ends and a rational norm of means-end relationships (it dissolves into mere "behavior"), on the other hand it equally has no meaning apart from obstacles to be overcome by effort in the realization of the norm. The concpts built up on the basis of the means-end schema or thus not empirical generalizations but, to use Max Weber's term, "ideal types."

But, precisely in so far as this voluntaristic conception of action holds true, they are indispensable to the understanding of concrete human affairs.

I have said that the rational norm of action implied in the means-end schema constitutes a *scientific* statement in conditional form. Indeed, in so far as it has been concerned with the subjective aspect of human action, the whole of modern social theory revolves about the question of the relation of science and action: In what sense and to what extent may action be thought of as guided by scientific knowledge?

It should be clear that the creative, voluntaristic element which we have found to be involved in the factor of ends precludes action ever being *completely* determined by scientific knowledge in the sense of the modern positive sciences. For the business of science is to understand the "given" — its very essence is a certain objectivity, that is, an independence of the "facts" from the will of the scientist. In action, therefore, the element of scientific knowledge may have a place in imparting accurate understanding of the conditions in which action takes place — and in forecasting the results of such conditions whether independent of the actor's agency or not.

But *ends* are not given in this sense — they are precisely the element of rational action which falls outside the schema of positive science. Indeed, many positivistic theorists, by trying to think of rational action as the type *entirely* determined by scientific knowledge, and attempting thus to fit ends into the scientific schema, have in fact squeezed out the *factor* of ends altogether. For concrete ends could only be scientific facts in so far as they constituted scientific predictions from present and past facts. The creative element has no place. But although we must reject this narrow interpretation of rational action, nevertheless the scientific schema is basic to what is historically (in terms of the history of modern thought) the main type of means-end relationship — what I shall call the *intrinsic* relationship. It is that which can be analyzed in terms of scientific knowledge (or its common-sense predecessors), with the one exception of the *determination* of ends.

The factor of ends may be fitted into this schema in the following way. Though what concrete ends should be striven for cannot be determined on the basis of scientific knowledge alone, once the end is given the means to its attainment may be selected on that basis. Moreover, though an end cannot itself be determined by scientific knowledge, the fact or degree of its attainment may, after the time to which it refers has arrived, be verified by scientific observation. In so far as this is true of an end, I shall refer to it as an empirical end. Then action is rational in terms of the intrinsic means-end relationship in so far as, on the one hand, its ends are empirical, and on the other, the relations of means and ends involved in it are the intrinsic relations of things as revealed by scientific knowledge of the phenomena. Once he knows the end. the rationality of such action can be judged by an external observer, both before and after its completion, in terms of his own scientific knowledge. Deviations from the rational norm will be explicable in one or more of three sets of terms: ignorance of intrinsic relationships, lack of effort, or presence of obstacles beyind the power of the actor to remove, whether they be obstacles in the actor's own constitution and character or in his evironment.

But does this type exhaust the logical possibilities of the means-end relationship? By no means! First, as to ends: Here it is necessary to enter into definitely philosophical questions. What is the implication of what I have called the creative character of the factor of ends. and hence of the impossibility of fitting it, for the actor, into the category of facts of the external world? It is, I think, a negation of the positivistic view that the "realities" which can be studied by empirical science are the sole realities significant for human action. I have purposely defined ends in terms of a vague phrase, a future "state of affairs." It is now necessary to define more closely what the phrase means.

It is clear that in so far as an end is, in the foregoing sense, an empirical end, the future state of affairs is to be thought of as a state of the scientifically observable external world. But there is a certain difficulty in thinking if this is alone involved. For the ends of action are not, in fact, to be based on the mere arbitrary whims of a once popular "libertarian" philosophy. Overwhelmingly the realization of the ultimate ends of action is felt to be a matter of moral obligation, to be binding on the individual − not, to be sure, in the sense of physical necessity, but still binding. The ubiquity of the concept of duty is perhaps sufficient proof of this.

But whence this sense of binding obligation? The source of specific moral obligations cannot be derived from the empirical properties of "human nature" as revealed by scientific psychology − for this is part of the same external world as the environment − the subjective point of view is that of the *ego* not of the body, or even the "mind." Psychology may reveal man as a creature who obeys moral obligations − but not as bound by his nature to *one* particular set of such obligations. Moreover, this explanation would violate both the inner sense of freedom of moral choice, which is just as ultimate a fact of human life as any other, and its consequentmoral responsibility. In fact, a psychological explanation of moral obligation really explains away the phenomenon itself. Finally, also there is a very large body of empirical evidence indicating that specific moral values are not completely correlated with "human nature."

If this explanation is rejected, it seems to me that there is only one other avenue left open. The world of "empirical" fact must be only a part, only one aspect, of the universe in so far as it is significant to man. The "external world," i.e., that of science, is as it were an island in a sea the character of which is something different from the island. Our relation to the other aspects of the universe is different from that of scientist to empirical facts. It will be noted that all these characterizations are negative – it is something transcending science.

The ultimate reason, then, for the causal independence of ends in action, the fact that they are not determined by the facts of human nature and environment, is the *fact* that man stands in significant relations to aspects of reality other than those revealed by science. Moreover, the fact that empirical reality can be modified by action shows that this empirical reality, the world of science, is not a closed system but is itself significantly related to the other aspects of reality.

Now it has been stated that the concept of end involves logical formulation. Does this mean that empirical ends are the only possible ones? While our logical formulations of non-empirical reality differ from those of empirical reality – that is, are not *scientific* theories – they exist none the less. They are metaphysical theories, theologies, etc. Now such theories may be thought of in relation to ends in two ways: They may constitute the terms to be used in justifying empirical ends; this is, in fact, an empirically important case. At the same time, however, they may lay down, as desirable, ends of action altogether outside the empirical sphere – that is, ends the attainment of which cannot be verified by empirical observation. Such an end is, for example, eternal salvation. This class, the attainment of a "state of affairs" outside the realm of empirical observability, I should like to call "transcendental ends."

We may then put the situation somewhat as follows: Ultimate empirical ends are justified to the actor in terms, not of scientific but of metaphysical, theories. He may, however, by virtue of his metaphysical theories pursue not merely empirical but also transcendental ends. It is conceivable that there should be a system of empirical ends justified directly by a metaphysical theory without reference to transcendental ends. That is the case, for instance, with the ideal of socialism – it refers to a desired future state of affairs in this world only. But in general such a metaphysical theory at the same time enjoins transcendental ends. Whenever that is the case, empirical ends are also present; otherwise there is no relation to action as an empirical reality. The relation will in general be such that a transcendental end is thought logically to imply as a means to it a given empirical end.

One further distinction in the realm of ends remains to be made. Some empirical ends refer to a state of affairs differing from the merely predicted state by more than a changed state of mind of the actor. On the other hand, one may think of the actor as attempting to attain only a subjective state of mind — happiness, for instance. In these terms I should like to distinguish "objective" empirical ends from "subjective" empirical ends. The attainment of both is verifiable, but in different ways. This is to assume, as we do throughout, the anti-behaviorist position that scientific observation of an individual's subjective state of mind is possible and valid. It is necessary, of course, to distinguish an altered state of mind as a *result* of action from its rôle as an end. "Happiness" or "satisfaction" may be thought of as, in general, a result of the attainment of objective ends — empirical or transcendental. But on occasion it is thought of as an end in itself — whether attainable or not is another question.

The attainment of a transcendental end should not be thought of as that of a state of mind. What is true is that the only empirical evidence we have of its attainment is *through* the statements and the state of mind of the individual actor. Religious persons may state that they are saved, or that they have attained Nirvana. Scientifically, such statements are not verifiable. But we may verify that persons who *believe* they have attained such a transcendental end do *in fact* typically attain certain subjective states of mind. [. . .]

We may now consider the modes in which the ultimate common system of ends is related to action in the intrinsic means-end chain. There are, I think, two modes. Either an ultimate end is also the immediate end of a given train of action or it is not. In the former case the logical situation is very simple — it is merely a matter of an ordinary means-end relationship. Its rationality is to be judged by the ordinary standards of efficiency once the end is given. The standard of efficiency is, of course, applicable only in so far as the end is an empirical end; but this may in turn be derived from a system of transcendental ends. But the strategy, for instance, of a general in a religious war is to be judged in exactly the same terms as though the sole aim of the war were aggrandizement. Such a coincidence of ultimate with immediate ends occurs generally at times of critical decision — for individuals, societies, and social movements.

But most of our action is not directly concerned with critical decisions between conflicting ultimate ends. It is rather a matter of the pursuit of immediate ends which may be removed by a very large number of intermediate links from any system of ultimate ends. The miner mining coal, to smelt iron to make steel to make rails, etc., is contributing to railway transportation, but at a point very far removed from the question of the ultimate value of railway transportation. These very facts of the remoteness of such action from ultimate ends, of the latency of such ends in relation to it, create a problem of control. There would, to be sure, be no such problem were the rationality of action automatic. But such is not the case. This is true neither of the rational formulation which transforms what may be called "value-attitudes" into specific ultimate ends, nor of the knowledge of relation of means to these ends, nor finally of the actual application of this knowledge to action itself. The voluntaristic conception of action implies that there is resistance to the realization of the rational norm − partly the resistance of inertia, partly that of factors which would tend to divert the course of action from the norm. We will not here inquire into what these factors are − merely call attention to their presence.

This problem of control tends to be met by the subjection of action in pursuit of immediate non-ultimate ends to normative rules which regulate that action in conformity with the common ultimate value-system of the community. These normative rules both define what immediate ends should and should not be sought, and limit the choice of means to them in terms other than those of efficiency. Finally, they also define standards of socially acceptable effort. This system of rules, fundamental to any society not in the state of "active religion," is what I call its institutions. They are *moral* norms, not norms of efficiency. They bear directly the stamp of their origin in the common system of ultimate ends.

The question of the modes in which institutional norms become enforced on individual actions is a complex one and cannot be entered into here. Suffice it to say that there are two primary modes, first, by the inherent moral authority of the norm itself due essentially to its derivation from the common system of ends to which the individuals obeying it subscribe. Second, there is the appeal to interest. That is, conformity to the norm may, apart from any moral attitude, be in the given concrete situation a means to the realization of the actor's private ends apart from the common value-system. This type may in turn be divided into two main types − where conformity is due to the positive advantages attached to it − as social esteem, and where it is due to a desire to avoid the unpleasant consequences of non-confomity − its sanctions.

Thus to sum up — the analysis of the intrinsic means-end chain yields the necessity for the existence of a class of ultimate ends which are not means to any further ends in this chain. Partly a priori and partly empirical considerations lead to the view that these ultimate ends do not occur in random fashion, but that both in the case of the individual and of the social group they must be thought of as to a significant degree integrated into a single harmonious *system*. In the case of the social group, which mainly interests us here, this is to be thought of as a system of ultimate ends held in common by the members of the group. In so far as these common ideal ends concern, directly or by logical implication, the relations of members of the group to each other, the norms of what these relationships are thought should be are understandable in terms of the common system of ultimate ends.

This common system may be thought of as related to the rest of the intrinsic means-end chain — above all, the intermediate sector — in two main ways. In the first place the immediate end of a particular concrete complex of actions may be, in this sense, an ultimate end. In the second place the actions in pursuit of non-ultimate immediate ends may be thought of as goverened by normative rules, institutions. Institutions may be classified as technological, economic, and political, according to what elements of the intermediate chain they govern.

Because of the great intricacy and subtlety of the possible relationships between action and moral rules, it is primarily, in connection with the institutional aspect of ultimate ends that the important sociological problems arise. The theory of institutions will indeed form one of the most important, as well as difficult, branches of sociological theory. But in order to see its rôle in perspective, it is necessary to place it in terms of a coherent scheme of the elements of action, as we are attempting to do. It is this which has, more than anything else, been lacking in previous attempts to formulate a theory of institutions.

[. . .]

Recognizing all its limitations, I submit that this [paper] is more than a mere argument for admitting values to a place in social theory. It is not, to be sure, a system of sociological theory embodying the value-factor. It is rather a methodological prolegomena to such a theory, clearing the way and indicating some directions of fruitful analysis. It is, as such, that I should like to have it received by the reader.

In conclusion I should like to say a brief word about science and philosophy. The task of sociology, as of the other social sciences, I consider to be strictly scientific — the attainment of sytematic theoretical understanding of empirical fact. The failure of the positivistic schools of sociology to attain such a goal I do not attribute, as so many do, to the inherent impossibility of the goal, but rather to their own inadequate methods of approaching it. Their inadequacy consists essentially in trying to apply both modes of thought and substantive concepts developed in the study of and suited to one kind of empirical fact — mainly that of the physical world — to quite another, human action in society. It is surely not altogether heterodox to say that the basic conceptions of a science should be developed in connection with a study of its own subject matter — not imported from other sciences.

Part Two

The Parsons¹ Phase

In this Part, the selection represents the range of of concerns which Parsons dealt with in his sociological writings from the publication of *The Structure of Social Action* in 1937, to the immediate post-war period during which he was developing the insights that were to produce the next phase of his theoretical development, and its classic statements such as *The Social System* (1951).

The first reading covers two key aspects of *The Structure of Social Action,* the fully worked-out theoretical statement of the Parsons¹ Phase, and the basis of all his later work: firstly, Parsons's statement of the problem — the failure of utilitarianism to adequately account for the normative orientation of human action — and his belief that its solution lay in the emergent *voluntaristic theory of action* culled from the work of Marshall, Weber, Durkheim and Pareto; secondly, his specification of the fundamental conceptual building block of the voluntaristic theory of action — the *unit act*.

In *The Role of Theory in Social Research* (1938) Parsons is making clear what was in fact a life-long commitment to the necessity of general, analytical theory in sociology.

The next three readings all represent examples of the 'empirical' side of Parsons's work during the early 1940s. In each case they address

— sometimes more abstractly, sometimes more historically — specific socio-political issues. They show a Parsons concerned to comment upon issues of the day, and the world situation; but they are also quite Weberian in tone, and in both *The Sociology of Modern Anti-Semitism* (1942) and *Population and the Social Structure of Japan* (1946) we find Parsons using his extensive reading of Weber's scholarship to good effect, in his discussion of Judaism and Shintoism.

THE STRUCTURE OF SOCIAL ACTION

INTRODUCTORY

The problem

"Who now reads Spencer? It is difficult to realize how great a stir he made in the world. . . . He was the intimate confidant of a strange and rather unsatisfactory God, whom he called the principle of Evolution. His God has betrayed him. We have evolved beyond Spencer." [1] Professor Brinton's verdict may be paraphrased as that of the coroner, "Dead by suicide or at the hands of person or persons unknown." We must agree with the verdict. Spencer is dead. [2] But who killed him and how? This is the problem.

Of course there may well be particular reasons why Spencer rather than others is dead, as there were also particular reasons why he rather than others made such a stir. With these this study is not concerned. But in the "crime," the solution of which is here sought, much more than the reputation of, or interest in, a single writer has been done to death. Spencer was, in the general outline of his views, a typical representative of the later stages of development of a system of thought about man and society which has played a very great part in the intellectual history of the English-speaking peoples, the positivistic-utilitarian tradition. [3] What has happened to it? Why has it died?

The thesis of this study will be that it is the victim of the vengeance of the jealous god, Evolution, in this case the evolution of scientific theory. In the present chapter it is not proposed to present an account either of what has evolved or of what it has evolved into; all that will come later. It is necessary to preface this with a tentative statement of the problem, and an outline of some general considerations relevant to the way the present task is to be undertaken, and how the present study should be judged.

Spencer's god was Evolution, sometimes also called Progress. Spencer was one of the most vociferous in his devotions to this god, but by no means alone among the faithful. With many other social thinkers he believed that man stood near the culminating point of a long linear process extending back unbroken, without essential changes of direction, to the dawn of primitive man. Spencer, moreover, believed that this culminating point was being approached in the industrial society of modern Western Europe. He and those who thought like him were confident that evolution would carry this process on almost indefinitely in the same direction cumulatively.

A good many students have lately become dubious of these propositions. Is it not possible that the future holds in store something other than "bigger and better" industrialism? The conception that, instead of this, contemporary society is at or near a turning point is very prominent in the views of a school of social scientists who, though they are still comparatively few, are getting more and more of a hearing.

Spencer was an extreme individualist. But his extremism was only the exaggeration of a deep-rooted belief that, stated roughly, at least in the prominent economic phase of social life, we have been blest with an automatic, self-regulating mechanism which operated so that the pursuit by each individual of his own self-interest and private ends would result in the greatest possible satisfaction of the wants of all. All that was necessary was to remove obstacles to the operation of this mechanism, the success of which rested on no conditions other than those included in the conception of rational pursuit of self-interest. This doctrine, too, has been subjected to increasingly severe criticism from many quarters, by no means all relevant to the purposes of this study. But another article of faith about the workings of the social world has been breaking down.

Finally, Spencer believed that religion arose from the pre-scientific conceptions of men about the empirical facts of their own nature and their environment. It was, in fact, the product of ignorance and error.

Religious ideas would, with the progress of knowledge, be replaced by science. This was only a phase of a much wider deification of science. Indeed the interest of the Spencerian type of social scientist in religion has thus been virtually confined to primitive man — the question was, how has science developed out of primitive religion? In this field, too, there is increasing skepticism of the Spencerian view.

It has been possible above to cite views on only a few questions. It is, however, enough to indicate that a basic revolution in empirical interpretations of some of the most important social problems has been going on. Linear evolutionism has been slipping and cyclical theories have been appearing on the horizon. Various kinds of individualism have been under increasingly heavy fire. In their place have been appearing socialistic, collectivistic, organic theories of all sorts. The role of reason and the status of scientific knowledge as an element of action have been attacked again and again. We have been overwhelmed by a flood of anti-intellectualistic theories of human nature and behavior, again of many different varieties. A revolution of such magnitude in the prevailing empirical interpretations of human society is hardly to be found occurring within the short space of a generation, unless one goes back to about the sixteenth century. What is to account for it?

It is, of course, very probable that this change is in considerable part simply an ideological reflection of certain basic social changes. This thesis would raise a problem, the answer to which would be difficult to find in terms of Spencerian thought. But to deal adequately with this problem would far transcend the limits of this study.

It is no less probable that a considerable part has been played by an "immanent" development within the body of social theory and knowledge of empirical fact itself. This is the working hypothesis on which the present study has been made. The attempt will be made to trace and evaluate the significance of one particular phase of this process of development which can be discerned and analyzed in detail in the work of a limited group of writers in the social field, mostly known as sociologists. But before entering upon this enterprise it is necessary to make a few preliminary methodological remarks about the nature of a "body of social theory and knowledge of empirical fact." What are the main relations of the principal elements in it to each other, and in what sense and by what kind of process may such a "body" be thought to be undergoing a process of development? Only then can it be stated explicitly what kind of study is here proposed and what order of results may reasonably be expected from it.

[. . .]

[. . .] All empirically verifiable knowledge — even the common-sense knowledge of everyday life — involves implicitly, if not explicitly, systematic theory in this sense. The importance of this statement lies in the fact that certain persons who write on social subjects vehemently deny it. They say they state merely the facts and let them "speak for themselves." But the fact a person denies that he is theorizing is no reason for taking him at his word and failing to investigate what implicit theory is involved in his statements. This is important since "empiricism" in this sense has been a very common methodological position in the social sciences.

[. . .] The general character of the problem of the development of a body of scientific knowledge, [. . .] in so far as it depends on elements internal to science itself, [. . .] is that of increasing knowledge of empirical fact, ultimately combined with changing interpretations of this body of fact — hence changing general statements about it — and, not least, a changing structure of the theoretical system. Special emphasis should be laid on this intimate interrelation of general statements about empirical fact with the logical elements and structure of theoretical systems.

In one of its main aspects the present study may be regarded as an attempt to verify empirically this view of the nature of science and its development in the social field. It takes the form of the thesis that intimately associated with the revolution in empirical interpretations of society sketched above there has in fact occurred an equally radical change in the structure of theoretical systems. The hypothesis may be put forward, to be tested by the subsequent investigation, that this development has been in large part a matter of the reciprocal interaction of new factual insights and knowledge on the one hand with changes in the theoretical system on the other. Neither is the "cause" of the other. Both are in a state of close mutual interdependence.

This verification is here attempted in monographic form. The central focus of attention is in the process of development of one coherent theoretical system, that to be denoted as the *voluntaristic theory of action,* and the definition of the general concepts of which this theory is composed. In the historical aspect the primary interest is in the process of transition from one phase of its development to another, distinctly different, one. Of the first phase Spencer may be regarded as a late, and in some points extreme, but nevertheless a typical representative. For convenience of reference and for no other purpose this has been designated as the "positivistic" system of the theory of action, and its variant, which is most important to the present study, the "utilitarian." Both these terms are used in technical senses in this work and they will be defined in the next chapter, where the main logical structure of the positivistic system is outlined.

It is, however, a striking fact that what is in all essential respects the same system may be found emerging by a similar process of transition from the background of a radically different theoretical tradition which may be designated as the "idealistic." One dominant case of this latter transition, the work of Max Weber, will be dealt with at length. It goes without saying that this convergence, if it can be demonstrated, is a very strong argument for the view that *correct observation and interpretation of the facts* constitute at least one major element in the explanation of why this particular theoretical system has developed at all.

As has been said, interest will be focused in the process of emergence of a particular theoretical system, that of the "voluntaristic theory of action." But the above considerations indicate the great importance of dealing with this in the closest connection with the empirical aspects of the work of the men whose theories are to be treated. So for each major thinker at least a fair sample of the major empirical views he held will be presented, and the attempt made to show in detail the relations of these to the theoretical system in question. In each case the thesis will be maintained that an adequate understanding of how these empirical views were arrived at is impossible without reference to the logical structure and relations of the theoretical concepts employed by the writer in question. And in every case except that of Marshall the attempt will be made to demonstrate that the conspicuous *change in his empirical views* from those current in the tradition with which the writer in question was most closely associated cannot be understood without reference to the corresponding *change in the structure of his theoretical system* from that dominant in the tradition in question. If this can be demonstrated it will have important general implications. It will be strong evidence that he who would arrive at important empirical conclusions transcending common sense cannot afford to neglect considerations of systematic theory.

The choice of writers to be treated here has been dictated by a variety of considerations. The central interest of the study is in the development of a particular coherent theoretical system, as an example of the general process of "immanent" development of science itself. This process has been defined as a matter of the logical exigencies of theoretical systems in close mutual interrelation with observations of empirical fact and general statements embodying these facts. Hence a choice of authors is indicated which will serve to isolate these elements as far as possible from others, such as influence of the general "climate of opinion," irrelevant to the purposes of this study.

The first criterion is actual concern with the theory of action. Among those who are satisfactory in this respect it is desirable to have represented as great a diversity of intellectual tradition, social milieu and personal character as possible. The inclusion of Marshall is justified by the fact that economic theory and the question of its status involve a crucial set of problems in relation to the theory of action in general and the the positivistic system, especially its utilitarian variant.

This question is as will be seen, the most important single link between utilitarian positivism and the later phase of the theory of action. Pareto also was deeply concerned with the same set of problems, but in relation to distinctly different aspects of the positivistic tradition, and in the midst of a strikingly different climate of opinion. The comparison of the two is most instructive.

Durkheim's starting point was also positivistic, indeed by far the most explicitly so of the three. But it was the variant of the positivistic system most radically foreign to that of utilitarian individualism in which Marshall was primarily immersed, and Pareto also, though to a less extent. In personal character and background more violent contrasts are scarcely imaginable than between Marshall, the strongly moralistic middle-class Englishman; Durkheim, the Alsation Jewish, radical, anticlerical, French professor; Pareto, the aloof, sophisticated Italian nobleman; and finally, Weber, a son of the most highly cultured German upper middle class, who grew up on the background of German idealism and was trained in the historical schools of jurisprudence and economics. These intellectual influences wer of no real importance in the formation of the thought of any of the other three. Moreover, Weber's personal character was radically different from any of the other three.

Another point strongly in favor of this choice is that although all four of these men were approximately contemporary, there is with one exception not a trace of direct influence of any one on any other. Pareto was certainly influenced by Marshall in the formulation of his technical economic theory, but with equal certainty not in any respect relevant to this discussion. And this is the only possibility of any direct mutual influence. In fact, within the broad cultural unit, Western and Central Europe at the end of the nineteenth and beginning of the twentieth century, it would scarcely be possible to choose four men who had important ideas in common who were less likely to have been influenced *in developing this common body of ideas* by factors other than the immanent development of the logic of theoretical systems in relation to empirical fact.

[. . .]

THE THEORY OF ACTION

It has already been stated that the aim of this study is to follow in detail a process of fundamental change in the structure of a single theoretical system in the social sciences. [. . .]

For convenience of reference this conceptual scheme will be called the theory of action. The continuity [of the system] consists in the retention, during the whole development, of a basic conceptual pattern which, however much its use and setting may vary with different stages of the process, is maintained in certain essentials unchanged throughout.

The unit of action systems

In the first chapter attention was called to the fact that in the process of scientific conceptualization concrete phenomena come to be divided into units or parts. The first salient feature of the conceptual scheme to be dealt with lies in the character of the units which it employs in making this division. The basic unit may be called the "unit act." Just as the units of a mechanical system in the classical sense, particles, can be defined only in terms of their properties, mass, velocity, location in space, direction of motion, etc., so the units of action systems also have certain basic properties without which it is not possible to conceive of the unit as "existing." Thus, to continue the analogy, the conception of a unit of matter which has mass but which cannot be located in space is, in terms of the classical mechanics, nonsensical. It should be noted that the sense in which the unit act is here spoken of as an existent entity is not that of concrete spatiality or otherwise separate existence, but of conceivability as a unit in terms of a frame of reference. There must be a minimum number of descriptive terms applied to it, a minimum number of facts ascertainable about it, before it can be spoken of at all as a unit in a system.

In this sense then, an "act" involves logically the following: (1) It implies an agent, an "actor." (2) For purposes of definition the act must have an "end," a future state of affairs toward which the process of action is oriented. [4] (3) It must be initiated in a "situation" of which the trends of development differ in one or more important respects from the state of affairs to which the action is oriented, the end. This situation is in turn analyzable into two elements: those over which the actor has no control, that is which he cannot alter, or prevent from being altered, in conformity with this end, and those over which he has such control. [5] The former may be termed the "conditions" of action, the latter the "means." Finally (4) there is inherent in the conception of this unit, in its analytical uses, a certain mode of relationship between these elements. That is, in the choice of alternatives, there is a "normative orientation" of action. Within the area of control of the actor, the means employed cannot, in general, be conceived either as chosen at random or as dependent exclusively on the conditions of action, but must in some sense be subject to the influence of an independent, determinate selective factor, a knowledge of which is necessary to the understanding of the concrete course of action. What is essential to the concept of action is that there should be a normative orientation, not that this should be of any particular type. As will be seen, the discrimination of various possible modes of normative orientation is one of the most important questions with which this study will be confronted. But before entering into the definition of any of them a few of the major implications of the basic conceptual scheme must be outlined.

The first important implication is that an act is always a process in time. The time category is basic to the scheme. The concept end always implies a future reference, to a state which is either not yet in existence, and which would not come into existence if something were not done about it by the actor or is already existent, would not remain unchanged. [6] This process, seen primarily in terms of its relation to ends, is variously called "attainment," "realization," and "achievement."

Second, the fact of a range of choice open to the actor with reference both to ends and to means, in combination with the concept of a normative orientation of action, implies the possibility of "error," of the failure to attain ends or to make the "right" choice of means. The various meanings of error and the various factors to which it may be attributed will form one of the major themes to be discussed.

Third, the frame of reference of the schema is subjective in a particular sense. That is, it deals with phenomena, with things and events *as they appear from the point of view of the actor* whose action is being analyzed and considered. Of course the phenomena of the "external world" play a major part in the influencing of action. But in so far as they can be utilized by this particular theoretical scheme, they must be reducible to terms which are subjective in this particular sense. This fact is of cardinal importance in understanding some of the peculiarities of the theoretical structures under consideration here. The same fact introduces a further complication which must be continually kept in mind. It may be said that all empirical science is concerned with the understanding of the phenomena of the external world. Then the facts of action are, to the scientist who studies them ,facts of the external world — in this sense, objective facts. That is, the symbolic reference of the propositions the scientist calls facts is to phenomena "external" to the scientist, not to the content of his own mind. But in this particular case, unlike that of the physical sciences, the phenomena being studied have a scientifically relevant subjective aspect. That is, while the social scientist is not concerned with studying the content of his own mind, he is very much concerned with that of the minds of the persons whose action he studies. This necessitates the distinction of the objective and subjective points of view. The distinction and the relation of the two to each other are of great importance. By "objective" in this context will always be meant "from the point of view of the scientific observer of action" and by "subjective," "from the point of view of the actor."

A still further consequence follows from the "subjectivity" of the categories of the theory of action. When a biologist or a behavioristic psychologist studies a human being it is an organism, a spatially distinguishable separate unit in the world. The unit of reference which we are considering as the actor is not this organism but an "ego" or "self." The principal importance of this consideration is that the body of the actor forms, for him, just as much part of the situation of action as does the "external environment." Among the conditions to which his action is subject are those relating to his own body, while among the most important of the means at his disposal are the "powers" of his own body and, of course, his "mind." The analytical distinction between actor and situation quite definitely cannot be identified with the distinction in the biological sciences between organism and environment. It is not a question of distinctions of concrete "things," for the organism is a real unit. It is rather a matter of the analysis required by the categories of empirically useful theoretical systems.

A fourth implication of the schema of action should be noted. Certainly the situation of action includes parts of what is called in common-sense terms the physical environment and the biological organism — to mention only two points. With equal certainty these elements of the situation of action are capable of analysis in terms of the physical and biological sciences, and the phenomena in question are subject to analysis in terms of the units in use in those sciences. Thus a bridge may, with perfect truth, be said to consist of atoms of iron, a small amount of carbon, etc., and their constituent electrons, protons, neutrons and the like. Must the student of action, then, become a physicist, chemist, biologist in order to understand his subject? In a sense this is true, but for purposes of the theory of action it is not necessary or desirable to carry such analyses as far as science in general is capable of doing. A limit is set by the frame of reference with which the student of action is working. That is, he is interested in phenomena with an aspect not reducible to action terms only in so far as they impinge on the schema of action in a relevant way — in the role of conditions or means. So long as their properties, which are important in this context, can be accurately determined these may be taken as data without further analysis. Above all, atoms, electrons or cells are not to be regarded as units for purposes of the theory of action. Unit analysis of any phenomenon beyond the point where it constitutes an integral means or condition of action leads over into terms of another theoretical scheme. For the purposes of the theory of action the smallest conceivable concrete unit is the unit act, and while it is in turn analyzable into the elements to which reference has been made — end, means, conditions and guiding norms — further analysis of the phenomena of which these are in turn aspects is relevant to the theory of action only in so far as the units arrived at can be referred to as constituting such elements of a unit act or a system of them.

One further general point about the status of this conceptual scheme must be mentioned before proceeding to the more particular uses of it which will be of interest here. It may be employed on two different levels, which may be denoted as the "concrete" and the "analytical." On the concrete level by a unit act is meant a concrete, actual act and by its "elements" are meant the concrete entities that make it up. Thus by the concrete end is meant the total anticipated future state of affairs, so far as it is relevant to the action frame of reference. For instance, a student may have as his immediate end the writing of a paper on a given subject. Though at the inception of the course of action he will not be in a position to visualize its content in detail (this is true of many concrete ends) he will have a general idea, a forecast of it in general terms. The detailed content will only be worked out in the course of the action. But this visualized product, perhaps being "handed in," is the concrete end. Similarly, concrete means are those things in the situation over which he has an appreciable degree of control, such as books in his possession or in the library, paper, pencil, typewriter, etc. The concrete conditions are those aspects of the situation which he cannot control for the immediate purposes in hand, as the fact that he is limited to books available in his college library, etc. The function of this concrete use of the action schema is primarily descriptive. Facts may be of possible significance to the scientist employing it in so far as they are applicable to entities which have a place in the scheme, to "ends" or other normative elements, "means" or "conditions" of acts or systems of action. But, in this context, it serves only to arrange the data in a certain order, not to subject them to the analysis necessary for their explanation.

For the purpose of explanation a further step in abstraction is generally necessary. It consists in generalizing the conceptual scheme so as to bring out the functional relations involved in the facts already descriptively arranged. The shift can perhaps most clearly be seen by considering that one of the main functions of an analytical as opposed to a concretely descriptive scheme in this context must be to distinguish the role of the normative from that of the non-normative elements of action. The problem is well illustrated by the difficulty one encounters in connection with the concept "end." As so far defined, and end is a concrete anticipated future state of affairs. But it is quite clear that not this total state of affairs but only certain aspects or features of it can be attributed to normative elements, thus to the agency of the actor rather than to features of the situation in which he acts. Thus, to use the previous example, in the process of action leading to the writing of a paper for a course, various aspects of the concrete end cannot be attributed to the agency of the student, such as the fact that there are available given books in the library, and other conditions relevant to the act. An end, then, in the analytical sense must be defined as the *difference* between the anticipated future state of affairs and that which it could have been predicted would ensue from the initial situation *without the agency of the actor having intervened.* Correspondingly, in an analytical sense, means will not refer to concrete things which are "used" in the course of action, but only to those elements and aspects of them which are capable of, and in so far as they are capable of, control by the actor in the pursuit of his end. [7]

A second highly important aspect of the distinction between the concrete and analytical use of the action scheme is the following. The prevalent biological schema of organism and environment has already been mentioned. While the concrete action schema cannot be identified with this it is in certain respects closely analogous to it. That is, a concrete actor is conceived as acting, in the pursuit of concrete ends, in a given concrete situation. But a new logical situation arises when the attempt is made to generalize about total systems of action in terms of the functional interrelations of the facts stated about them. The problem of the discrimination of the roles of normative and non-normative elements may again serve as an example. From the point of view of a single concrete actor in a concrete situation the effects, both present and anticipated, of the actions of others belong in the situation, and thus may be related to the action of the individual in question in the role of means and conditions. But in estimating the role of the normative elements in the total system of action in which this particular actor constitutes a unit, it would obviously be illegitimate to include these elements in the situation for the system as a whole. For what are, to one actor, non-normative means and conditions are explicable in part, at least, only in terms of the normative elements of the action of others in the system. This problem of the relation between the analysis of the action of a particular concrete actor in a concrete, partly social environment, and that of a total action system including a plurality of actors will be of cardinal importance to the later discussion. It forms for instance, one of the principal keys to the understanding of the development of Durkheim's theoretical system. [. . .]

READING 4:

NOTES AND REFERENCES

[1] Crane Brinton, *English Political Thought in the Nineteenth Century,* pp. 226–227.

[2] Not, of course, that nothing in his thought will last. It is his social theory as a total structure that is dead.

[3] This is because Marshall failed to think through implications of his own empirical and theoretical departures from the prevailing system for the logical structure of the system as a whole and, hence, its empirical implications.

[4] In this sense and this only, the schema of action is inherently teleological.

[5] It is especially to be noted that the reference here is not to concrete things in the situation. The situation constitutes conditions of action as opposed to means *in so far as it is not subject to the control of the actor.* Practically all concrete things in the situation are part conditions, part means. Thus in common-sense terms an automobile is a means of transportation from one place to another. But the ordinary person cannot make an automobile. Having, however, the degree and kind of control over it which its mechanical features and our property system lend, he can use it to transport himself from Cambridge to New York. Having the automobile and assuming the existence of roads, the availability of gasoline supply, etc., he has a degree of control of where and when the automobile shall go, and, hence, of his own movements. It is in this sense then

an automobile constitutes a means for the analytical purposes of the theory of action.

[6] While the phenomena of action are inherently temporal, that is, involve processes in time, they are not in the same sense spatial. That is to say, *relations in space* are not as such relevant to systems of action analytically considered. For the analytical purposes of this theory, acts are not primarily but only secondarily located in space. Or to put it somewhat differently, spatial relations constitute only conditions, and so far as they are controllable, means of action. This gives a sense in which the schema of action is always and necessarily abstract. For it is safe to say that there is no empirical phenomenon, no thing or event, known to human experience, which is not in one aspect physical in the sense of being capable of location in space. There is certainly no empirical "self" known which is not an "aspect of" or "associated with" a living biological organism. Hence the events of action are always concretely events in space, "happenings to," physical bodies or involving them. Thus, in one sense, there is no concrete act to which the category of space is inapplicable. But at the same time that category is irrelevant to the theory of action, regarded as an analytical system, which of course implies that the "action" aspect of concrete phenomena never exhausts them. The facts which the theory of action embodies are never "all the facts" about the phenomena in question. On the other hand, there certainly are many concrete phenomena which so far as they are objects of scientific study are exhausted by the "physical," nonaction aspect, such as stones and celestial bodies. This "involvement" of action in the physical world must apparently be taken as one of the ultimates of our experience.

[7] A particular case of this general distinction is of considerable importance. It has already been noted that the actor is an ego or a self, not an organism, and that his organism is part of the "external world" from the point of view of the subjective categories of the theory of action. In this connection it becomes necessary to keep in mind the difference between two distinctions. On the one hand there is that so commonly used by biologists, between the concrete organism and its concrete environment. Thus in the concrete means to a given course of action it is often necessary or useful to distinguish the concrete powers belonging to the actor, that is the strength of his muscles, the manual skills he may have, from means available in his environment, such as tools, etc. But on the analytical level the analogous distinction is clearly different; it is that

between heredity and environment in the sense of biological theory. It is clear that the concrete organism at any given time is not the exclusive product of heredity but of the complex interaction of hereditary and environmental factors. "Heredity," then, becomes a name for those elements influencing the structure and function of the organism which can be considered as determined in the constitution of the germ cells out of whose union the particular organism issues. Equally, in principle, the concrete environment of a developed organism is not to be considered as the exclusive product of environmental factors in the analytical sense, for to the extent that it may be held to have been influenced by the action of organisms upon it, hereditary factors will have played a part. In considering an organism such as man, this is obviously a matter of great importance. Since the biological aspect of man is of such great concrete importance, in dealing with action it is often very convenient to employ such terms as heredity and environment. When doing this it is always of extreme importance to keep clearly in mind which of the two concept-pairs just outlined is applicable and to draw only the inferences appropriate to the one which is relevant.

THE ROLE OF THEORY
IN SOCIAL RESEARCH

Some will perhaps consider it presumptuous for one who has come to be known primarily as a theorist to talk about empirical research, I have done some work in the latter field and hope to make contributions to it before many years. But apart from that I can perhaps but cite a statement of which Max Weber was fond, "In order to understand Caesar it is not necessary to have been Caesar." So perhaps it is possible for one who has not been quite so completely immersed in empirical research as some of you, but who has nevertheless been a good deal concerned with certain of its problems, to help illuminate them.

I should, however, like to make myself clear in advance. The current state of sociological science is not such that anyone is entitled to dogmatize with an air of canonical authority. To my mind the only hope of reaching that fundamental unity of outlook and purpose which I think almost all of us feel should actuate the workers in a field of science, is to attempt seriously, objectively and respectfully to learn each other's work, thought and experience. It is my very strong conviction that, if the current situation be approached in this spirit, and the *trouble* taken to get to the bottom of other people's problems, there

Reprinted, with permission, from *American Sociological Review*, Vol. 3 (1938), pp. 13–20.

will turn out to be far more unity on fundamentals than appears at first sight.

What I can do on an occasion like this seems to me to be to present to you with due humility for your consideration a few of the results of my own thinking about and experience in sociological work.

Practically all competent observers are, I think, agreed that there is a basic difference in the situation in such sciences as physics and chemistry, and those in the social group, particularly sociology. I do not mean to deny that the former group have their crucially important unsolved problems and areas of controversy. These, however, occur either on the frontiers of the technical part of the science itself or in the field of the interpretation of the broad significance of its results as a whole. But there is a very substantial core of material on which there is entirely general agreement. What should go into the more elementary courses in these fields is not in controversy. Moreover this common core is not only a body of discrete miscellaneous facts — it is closely integrated with a logically elaborated body of theory, much of which, like the fundamental equations of dynamics in mechanics, is stated in a highly generalized form.

When we turn to the social field we find a very different situation. Most of our controversial problems seem to be not on the periphery but at the very starting points of the field. There is widespread feeling that we must settle the deepest current controversies before we can do *anything*. This at least seems to be true of those who feel the need to reach high levels of generalization. This feeling of fundamental un-certainty is vividly brought out by the controversial nature of the content of elementary courses.

It is scarcely possible to consider this situation without being struck by what is both one of the most conspicuous and, to me, one of the most disquieting features of the current situation. That is, there is a tendency to the development of a very deep hiatus between the more empirically and the theoretically minded workers in the social science fields.

I do not mean merely that there is a good deal of division of labor, as I am told there is in physics, between men whose work is primarily in the laboratory and those who work only with reports of laboratory results, pencil and complicated mathematical formulae. It is rather the tendency to a complete divorce, a mutual repudiation of the legitimacy of each other's work and interests, which is disquieting. Certain of the empirically minded are not merely not interested in attempting to con-tribute to theory themselves, they are actively anti-theoretical. They consider any work in theoretical fields as positively pernicious and contrary to the canons of science. It is speculation, sterile dialectic, metaphysics or even mysticism.

On the other hand, many of the persons best known as theorists have not only not themselves made distinguished empirical contributions, they have often given the impression of not caring very much at least about the kind of empirical work which the empiricists have done, of having rather a sovereign disdain for the arduous difficulties of the empirical fields.

I do not propose to dwell mainly upon the shortcomings of the empirical schools. A very large part of the difficulty seems to mc to lie on the theoretical side of the controversy. Many features of our theoretical traditions seem to me seriously to have inhibited the potential usefulness of theory for empirical research. One important reason why the empiricists have tended to be anti-theoretical is that they have, often rightly, seen much to object to in the particular brands of theory they have had held up to them.

But before going further into these questions it is necessary to state certain premises which seem to me fundamental, even though they imply a drastic repudiation of certain forms of empiricist position. Sympathy with a person's motives and feelings in a situation does not necessarily imply endorsement of the position he takes.

In these terms I must categorically disagree with the view that any empirical science can be developed to a high point without reference to generalized conceptual schemes, to theory. The process of the growth of scientific knowledge is not a process of accumulation of discrete discoveries of "fact." In the first place our study of fact, however little we may be aware of it, is always guided by the logical structure of a theoretical scheme, even if it is entirely implicit. We never investigate "all the facts" which could be known about the phenomena in question, but only those which we think are "important." This involves a selection among the possible facts. Now if we investigate carefully, though few empiricists do, what is the basis of this selection, it will, I think, uniformly be found that among the criteria of importance and the only ones of strictly scientific status is that of their relevance to the logical structure of a theoretical scheme.

Secondly, few if any empiricists, being as they usually are truly imbued with scientific curiosity, are content simply to state bald, discrete facts. They go beyond this to maintain the existence of relations of interdependence, causal relations. It is stated not merely that the steam railroad was developed and certain kinds of industrial developments took place, but that without the invention of the railroad these developments *could not* have taken place — that the invention of the railroad was a causal *factor* in industrial development.

Now I wish to assert that such an imputation of causal relationship cannot be proved without reference to generalized theoretical categories. If it is asserted, the assertion is logically dependent on these categories whether they are explicit or implicit.

If this be true, the alternative for the scientist in the social or any other field is not as between theorizing and not theorizing, but as between theorizing explicitly with a clear consciousness of what he is doing with the greater opportunity that gives of avoiding the many subtle pitfalls of fallacy, and following the policy of the ostrich, pretending not to theorize and thus leaving one's theory implicit and uncriticized, thus almost certainly full of errors.

This assertion of the inevitability of theory in science naturally cannot be proved on this occasion. The next best thing is to cite authority. Alfred Marshall was an economist who so far as I know has hardly seriously been accused of tender-minded disregard for fact. In an address at the University of Cambridge he made a striking statement which exactly expresses my feeling: "The most reckless and treacherous of all theorists is he who professes to let facts and figures speak for themselves." [1] If Marshall stated this point in a most striking form, I think Max Weber may be said definitely to have proved it. It was one of his greatest methodological contributions definitely to have refuted the claims of German Historical Schools that it is possible to have valid empirical knowledge of causal relationships with no logical implication of reference to generalized theoretical categories.

But if generalized theory is essential to science, it does not follow that anything and everything which goes by that name is of equal value. Quite the contrary, there is much to object to in a great deal of what has gone by the name of sociological theory. Empiricists are, as I have said, right in repudiating much of current theory though that does not justify them in extending this repudiation to all theory in principle simply because it is theory.

Indeed, that there is something wrong with current social theory seems to me to be clearly indicated by the fact that there is such drastic lack of agreement and that most people who write and talk about it feel impelled to divide theorists up into "schools" which, it goes without saying, are mutually incompatible so that a person who agrees with one school in almost any respect, must by definition oppose all other schools in all respects.

This deplorable situation seems to me in large measure due to a failure to distinguish adequately the various conceptual elements which either go to make up, or have become associated with, what are generally called theoretical structures in science, particularly in social science. I should like to distinguish three classes of such elements and put forward the thesis that much of the difficulty is due to modes of conception of and undue emphasis on two of them, resulting in distortion of the significance and role of the third.

1. No science develops in a vacuum, either intellectual or social. The scientific content of an intellectual tradition is always closely interwoven with elements of a different character. So far as these elements are conceptually formulated, they may be called for present purposes philosophical elements. The problem of the relation of scientific and philosphical ideas intermingled in the same body of thought has been a prolific source of trouble in social as in other science.

With regard to this problem thought seems to have tended strongly to get itself into a dilemma: One horn of the dilemma is the view that the scientific and philosophical components of a body of thought must necessarily be bound rigidly together in a single completely determinate system. The inference is that a body of scientific theory, if it is logically coherent, is simply an aspect of a philosophical system and none of it can be accepted without accepting the system as a whole. Thus the critics of classical and neoclassical economic theory have often held that acceptance of the theory for even the most elementary purposes implied the acceptance of the whole rigid philosophical system, extreme rationalism, psychological hedonism, utilitarian ethics and the rest. Conversely it has often been held that it was impossible to be confident of even the most elementary theoretical proposition, such as that the value of money is an inverse function of its quantity, without first settling definitively all the problems of the complete philosophical system on which it supposedly depends.

There is a very widespread and justified feeling that philosophical theories cannot claim the same order of objectivity and verifiability as the propositions of empirical science. Hence it is not surprising that people who dislike these implications should, without questioning the premises on which they rested, attempt to evade them by repudiating theory altogether. After all, to be responsible for a complete philosophical system, once the first innocent step in theoretical reasoning is taken, is a rather terrifying prospect. In this dilemma my sympathies are definitely with the empiricist.

But I cannot accept the dilemma. In my opinion the whole thing rests on a serious misconception of the relation of scientific theory to philosophy. I do not believe either that scientific theory has no philosophical implications, or that it involves no philosophical preconceptions. They cannot, in that sense, be radically divorced. But at the same time it does not follow that they are rigidly bound together in the sense this dilemma implies. On the contrary, though they are interdependent in many subtle ways, they are also independent. Above all it is perfectly possible for a scientist, even a theorist, to get ahead with his work without worrying about a philosophical system in general, but only considering philosophical questions one by one when as they directly impinge on his own scientific problems. Indeed, this false dilemma is the principal source of the charge that theorizing is necessarily "metaphysical" and has no place in science.

Please note, I do not say that scientific theory should never concern itself with philosophical problems. But I do say that its burden can be enormously lightened if it divests itself of unnecessary philosophical concerns; and it can do this to a far greater extent than is generally believed, especially by empiricists.

2. The second type of conceptual element involved in bodies of theory which I wish to discuss is one which falls within the competence of science strictly construed, is hence not philosophical, but has, I think, received quite undue prominence especially in sociology. This is the element of what may be called "broad empirical generalization." Examples are such propositions as "the course of social development as a whole follows a linear evolutionary course," or "social processes are in the last analysis determined by economic (or geographical, or racial, etc., etc.) factors." Such "theories" embody a generalized judgment about the behavior of, or causes in, a hugely complicated class of empirical phenomena. They are analogous to such judgments as "the physical universe as a whole is running down."

Indeed it is in terms of such views, if not their philosophical positions, that sociological theories are usually classified. We have evolutionary vs. cyclical theories, economic, biological, religious interpretations.

Here again we find a dilemma. For we may well ask, how are propositions such as these to be *proved?* Where are the specific observations, the patently rigorous reasoning? If the proof is as cogent as their proponents claim, why the warring schools? Why cannot people be brought to agreement? The empiricist quite understandably begins to suspect it is because there isn't any such evidence, or it is woefully inadequate to the conclusions. Hence so far as theory in general is identified with this kind of thing, it is held to be "speculative," only for people who have not absorbed the discipline of scientific caution, of asserting only what they can demonstrate. Here again my sympathies are with the empiricist. I do not think the great majority of propositions of this order have been or are capable of being rigorously demonstrated.

Critical examination of them will reveal scientific defects of one kind or another.

3. So, if scientific theory in the social field consisted only of these two classes of elements, there would be much reason to follow the empiricist's advice and eschew it altogether. But I am confident that this is not the case, there are other elements as well which the usual empiricist indictment is prone to overlook, what I should like to call generalized analytical theory. This it is which seems to me to be the most important kind of conceptualization in the physical sciences.

Empiricists are often fond of maintaining that they emulate the physical sciences. It is my suspicion that they are able to make this claim partly because analytical theory has in such fields become so completely integrated with empirical research that it is completely taken for granted — no one feels it necessary to talk about its role because it seems obvious. After all, mathematics in its application to physics *is* theory.

Analytical theory in the sense in which I mean the term here, is a body of logically interrelated generalized concepts (logical universals) the specific facts corresponding to which (particulars) constitute statements describing empirical phenomena. Use of this concept in empirical research inherently tends to establish logical relations between them and their particular content (values) such that they come to constitute logically interdependent systems. Correspondingly the phenomena to which they apply come to be viewed as empirical systems, the elements of which are in a state of mutual interdependence.

Much the most highly developed analytical system in this sense in the social field is economic theory. Indeed, economists alone have among social scientists been steeped in an analytical system. But precisely because of the difficulty of clarifying the relation of this analytical system both to empirical reality itself and to the other types of conceptualization just discussed, even economics has not been spared an empiricist revolt, the institutionalist movement, which, though probably now passing, has in this context done a great deal of damage and threatened to do more.

Indeed, one important reason for the apparent backwardness of analytical theory in the social sciences is the greater formidability of these difficulties here as compared with the physical sciences. Those concerned with ordinary biases and with the often difficult distinctions between scientific and philosophical considerations I shall leave aside. But two others are of such great importance that I should like to say a few words about them: (1) Even in mathematical terms it is difficult to handle a system involving more than a very small number of variables.

Where for various reasons mathematical treatment is excluded, as it is in most of the social field, or severely limited as, I think, it is in all, there is a very strong impetus to simplification of problems by dealing with only a few variables in a system.

This inevitably implies that analytical theory in the social field is highly abstract. For the values of the variables of such a system state only a very limited number of facts about the concrete phenomena to which it applies. It is very seldom that other elements are sufficiently constant within any very wide range of variation of these variables so that trustworthy interpretation and prediction can be based on the laws of this analytical system alone. It needs to be supplemented by considerations involving the others as well. This is one of the most important reasons for the unsatisfactoriness of proceeding directly to broad empirical generalization. The case of some of the deductions from economic theory is an extremely vivid one. The facts relevant to any system of analytical theory are *never* all the facts knowable about the phenomenon in question, and only part of these are the values of variables. (2) A variable is a logical universal or combination of them. Its "values" are the particular facts which correspond to this universal. These facts are or can be obtained in one and only one way — by empirical observation. But it is the essence of the ordering function of theory that any old facts, however true, will not do, but only those which "fit" the categories of the system. What facts it is important to know are relative to the logical structure of the theory. This is not to be understood to mean that theory should dictate factual findings, but only the definition of the categories into which the findings are to be fitted.

Precisely here is one of the crucial problems of the relation of theory to empirical research. For theory to be fruitful it is essential that we have research techniques which provide the right kind of facts. There is, indeed, evidence that this is one of the most serious difficulties, that a great deal of current research is producing facts in a form which cannot be utilized by any current generalized analytical scheme. This is a very complex problem. I can comment on only one phase of it.

One important group of social empiricists is particularly partial to measurement. They point out the extreme importance of measurement in physics and conclude that only so far as its facts are the results of measurements can sociology claim the status of a science. I do not wish to depreciate the value of measurement wherever it is possible, but I do wish to point out two things: First, the importance of facts is relative to the way in which they can be fitted into analytical schemes: measurements are fundamental to physics because many of its variables are such that the only facts which make sense as their values are numerical data But numerical data are far less scientifically important until they can be so fitted into analytical categories. I venture to say this is true of the vast majority of such data in the social fields.

Second, measurement as such is not logically essential to science, however desirable. Measurement is a special case of a broader category, classification. It is logically essential that the values of a variable should be reducible to a determinate classification. But the classification they admit of may be far more complex than the single order of magnitude which measurement requires. Where nonmetrical, even nonquantitative data can, with the help of such classification, be made to fit directly the logical structure of an analytical scheme it may be possible to establish relations of crucial importance which any amount of numerical data lacking such analytical relevance could not bring out.

In conclusion I may state schematically what seem to me to be the principal functions of analytical theory in research.

1. In the vast welter of miscellaneous facts we face it provides us with selective criteria as to which are important and which can safely be neglected.

2. It provides a basis for coherent organization of the factual material thus selected without which a study is unintelligible.

3. It provides a basis not only of selection and organization of known facts, but in a way which cannot be done otherwise reveals the *gaps* in our existing knowledge and their importance. It thus constitutes a crucially important guide to the direction of fruitful research.

4. Through the mutual logical implications of different analytical systems for each other it provides a source of cross fertilization of related fields of the utmost importance. This often leads to very important developments within a field which would not have taken place had it remained theoretically isolated.

Finally, it may be asked, have the social sciences outside of economics any analytical theory at all to use? Must we not remain empiricists through sheer lack of anything else to turn to? I do not think so. I believe there is far more analytical theory in use than many of us realize. We have been, like Molière's hero, speaking prose all our lives without knowing it. Moreover, in a work recently published [2] I have traced a process of development of analytical theory of the first magnitude including, I believe, a demonstration of its fruitfulness in empirical research. I am convinced that investigation would show that the ramifications of this development reach far beyond the limited group of workers with whom I have explicitly dealt.

My closing plea is then: Let us take what we already have and both use it to the utmost and develop it as rapidly as we can. Let us not either through failure to understand what it is that we have or through disillusionment with its very real shortcomings, throw it overboard to the tragic detriment of the interests of our science. If it is used and developed through the intimate co-operation of empirical and theoretical work, I am very hopeful for the future of sociological science.

READING 5:
NOTES AND REFERENCES

[1] *Memorials of Alfred Marshall,* Ed. A. C. Pigou, p. 108.
[2] *The Structure of Social Action,* New York, 1937.

THE SOCIOLOGY OF MODERN ANTI-SEMITISM

INTRODUCTORY STATEMENT

In a sense the Jews may be said to form a "minority" group [1] where-ever they live, and as such to constitute a "minority problem." That the Jews do not constitute just "another" minority group is quiet evident from the extraordinary tenacity with which they have maintained their separate identity as a group for well over two thousand years. That "prejudice" against them on the part of the surrounding societies has been a factor of importance in their resistance to assimilation can hardly be doubted; but that this is quite inadequate to explain the broad historical phenomenon becomes apparent to anyone who cares to delve into the problem a little deeper. To find a satisfactory explana-tion of this unique social phenomenon, it is necessary to examine the socioreligious character of the Jewish community in the form it assumed after the Prophetic Period and the Babylonian Exile — that is, its modern form — as well as that of the larger society within which the Jewish community exists.

Reprinted with deletions, with permission from J. Graeber and S. H. Britt (Eds.), *Jews in a Gentile World*, Macmillan, New York (1942), pp. 101–122.

THE CHARACTER OF THE JEWISH PEOPLE[2]

What differentiates the Jewish people more than anything else from others is their strongly religious character. "Israel and the Law are one" is not a mere saying but an actual fact. Without the Law — that is, its religion — Israel — that is, the Jewish people — is inconceivable. To the Jew religion is part of his everyday life; it is inseparable from it. But what is even more important is that this religion is of a very special character. It is a religion specially designed for Israel, a national religion in the fullest sense.

The reason for the importance of religion in the life of the Jews becomes quite obvious when one considers that in their dispersion all over the world their religion served as the strongest unifying force. It was religion that made it possible for them to live as separate entities within larger societies with whom culturally they shared very little. The nations among whom they lived were the "hosts," while they were considered the "guests." Hence, instead of being a people who *had* a religion, they came to be identified *with* their religion. Among the residents of Alexandria or Rome it was only those who adhered to the Jewish religion who were considered Jews. Religious adherence and not nationality or even descent was what defined a Jew. [3]

There are, perhaps, three primary interdependent aspects which must be taken into account in describing the role of religion in the Jewish community: (1) the Jewish God and his peculiar relation to his people, (2) the Law, and (3) the fact that Judaism was, in a sense, the religion of a "people" and not a mere cult of a group of individuals.

Whether Jahweh existed as a deity before he became the God of the People of Israel is not precisely known. In the earlier stages of his existence in that capacity he was apparently the war god of a confederation of seminomadic as well as of settled agricultural tribes living on the borderland of the desert and on the shores of the Mediterranean. It is probable the Jahweh was not, originally, the sole god of these tribes but only the deity who presided over and sanctioned their common military activities.

In this connection their relation to him was conceived as defined by a "covenant," a contractual agreement according to which he had chosen the People of Israel as his instrument in carrying out certain plans of his own, and in return had promised them many good things in a life of plenty and happiness in the "promised land." As a condition for carrying out his promises, however, he had made them agree to "keep his commandments," to order their conduct according to his will, as expressed to his servant Moses. Indeed, Jahweh, as the "Lord of Hosts," was conceived of almost as the actual physical commander of the armed forces of Israel. The relation of the people to him was that of soldiers to their commander; they were, above all, expected to obey orders. Jahweh was, in addition, a rather highly temperamental deity, associated with violence of temper and of action, with the storm. He was quick to anger and difficult to appease.

Two negative aspects of this situation are of peculiar significance. On the one hand, Jahweh was not implicated in the internal social structure of the People of Israel. Above all, he was not bound up with any families or kinship groups in such a way that he had a place in ancestral cults. He was the god of Israel *as a whole* and not of individuals and groups as such. This fact was one of the sources for the later universalistic aspect of the religion of Jahweh. Moreover, in an important sense the Jahweh cult was not a ritualistic cult. He was not primarily the guardian of an order, social, ritual, or even cosmic. He was an active agent with a will and with definite plans. The whole keynote of his being, starting with the creation, was action, the accomplishment of things. Never was it thought possible to "force" Jahweh to do anything by performing the correct ritual acts. On the contrary, the important thing was to know his will. To be sure, this was subject to influence — above all, when he was thought to be angry — but the ritual aspect of his religion took the form of carrying out what were thought to be his specifically ordained wishes — like circumcision and observance of the Sabbath — and of doing things which were thought to be "pleasing in the sight of God," which was the motivation of much of the sacrifice.

In the course of time the People of Israel, favored by the relative quiescence of the two great powers on either side of them, came to be the dominant element of a territorial political entity of some consequence. The kingdom, or kingdoms, since it was split in two later on, was in most respects not unlike other structures of the same era in the Near East. It was, above all, relatively complex in its internal structure, with differentiation of classes and of wealth, tensions between the urban upper classes, and conflicts between the peasant communities and the pastoral and nomadic elements on their fringes. These differences and conflicts became bound up with a partly expressed in differences of religion. Above all, the Prophetic movement was intimately connected with the social tensions of the time.

The second principal element of this peculiar religion is the Law. Its earlier development was greatly influenced by a special priestly class, the Levites. They became the exclusive custodians of religious functions, the most important of which was the sacrificial ritual. The sacrifice, to be sure, was also carried on by the heads of families in houses, but even there it came to be considered a proper thing to have a Levite present. The other principal function of the Levites was to serve as interpreters of the will of Jahweh. The traditional revelation to Moses was scarcely a sufficient basis to meet all the exigencies of life, to explain the sources of the many misfortunes which were thought to be manifestations of Jahweh's displeasure, or to suggest means of appeasing him. To take care of these exigencies there grew up a systematic body of laws, the Torah. In part, like the Ten Commandments out of which it developed, it contained ethical precepts, but much of it concerns ritual and the relation of Israel to his God. In many ways the Torah closely resembled the Egyptian and Babylonian doctrines. What distinguished it was the fact that it was a unified and organized body of rules governing daily conduct. This body of rules, moreover, sanctioned by God as well as by the authority of a highly influential priestly caste, came to be looked upon as a *sine qua non,* as the rules of life. The extent to which the line between the sacred and the profane, between *fas* and *jus,* was obliterated, was in Judaism distinctly unusual.

The main character of the Torah was already established before the Prophetic Age. But the prophetic movement was greatly to accentuate its importance and to give it a unique religious significance. The Prophets altered its content but little. They are called "ethical," not because they introduced a new ethical standard, but because of the new and broader interpretation which they put on the meaning and consequences of conformity or nonconformity to the Law. It involved a devaluation of the sacrificial aspect of religion. It was not "burnt offerings" which were pleasing to God, but scrupulous adherence to the Law, to his commandments.

The tremendous force of the prophetic teaching can be understood only in connection with the precarious position of the people at the time. The political independence of Palestine was in great danger. It had always been precarious, but now it was directly threatened by a career of conquest entered upon by one of the neighbouring great powers, Assyria-Babylonia — a power which was infamous for the ruthlessness and cruelty of its conduct of war. The tiny state was doomed. The prophets' interpretation of this impending disaster as a just chastisement of the people by their God for disregarding the Law had tremendous religious implications. It elevated Jahweh to the position of a universal God. Babylonia and Egypt, the two giants of the ancient world, were instruments of his will as much as was little Israel. Furthermore, it meant that as long as faith was kept Israel remained the hub of the universe, the chosen people, the people who had a mission to perform. The Mission of the People of Israel in time became the central theme of history as a whole, not merely of their own small group. Finally, in all this the Law came to occupy the central place. It was for failure to keep his commandments that God was punishing his people; conversely, it was for obeying his laws that they would be rewarded. The above facts make it understandable why Judaism came to be a religion of a "people." As intimated above, it is probable that Jahweh, like other Near Eastern deities, was originally intimately associated with one or more particular places or localities sacred to him. With the political development and unification of the People of Israel, however, he came to be the god of a nation and eventually, as we have seen, the God of the universe.

In the ancient world people usually worshipped a deity of local significance only; respect for the gods of others was permissible and quite common. The concept of God as the one universal ruler brought about by the teachings of the Prophets was, indeed, revolutionary. Jahweh became the *only* true God. Hence worship of other deities was considered idolatry, a cardinal sin for the Jew. This had the effect of preventing the Jews from going too far in incorporating beliefs of neighbouring peoples or of those among whom they lived in dispersion. The Book of Daniel illustrates very well the attitudes that developed among the Jews as a result. It was primarily as a consequence of this that the Jews could not merge with other peoples and that they could not even form merely a religious sect. On the contrary, they were forced, so to speak, to form a self-contained community whose contacts with the larger society were very limited.

The loss of their territory and national independence and consequent dispersion led the Jews to intensify their tendency to exclusiveness. Greatly increased emphasis was put on the Law and on those ritual elements which served to mark off the Jew from the non-Jew. It was only then that there developed the absolutely rigid prohibition of intermarriage with Gentiles. There was, furthermore, a great elaboration of the food taboos, the result of which was to make it virtually impossible for an observing Jew to eat at the table of a Gentile. Thus the loss of their territory left the Jews in the peculiar position of a people without a country. In time the religion and the culture they grew out of it came to take the place of the territory. Hence, instead of becoming merely a religious sect, the Jews continued to exist as a nation — a most unique social phenomenon.

Owing to their peculiar form of existence, Jews have in the course of time come to share certain characteristics which in the eyes of many came to be associated with them as a group. One of those characteristics commonly associated with them is a certain kind of rationalism or rather intellectualism. Since preoccupation with the Law was an absolute necessity, because it taught the proper conduct in daily life, learning — reasoning — came into very high regard. There is little doubt that this was one of the most potent factors in the evolution of the Jews into the "People of the Book," in their developing intellectual tendencies. Learning was, of course, primarily the occupation of the rabbis, since they were charged with the interpretation of the Law. The rationality, however, which the rabbis cultivated was mainly legalistic in character. It was primarily concerned with reconciling the laws of the past with the exigencies of life, with reconciling, so to speak, the past with the present without discarding any of the holy commandments. Thus, the high prestige of the Law itself, on the one hand, and that of the men who were its trustees, on the other, effected among the people an attitude of high respect for "learning" in general. Such an attitude could readily be extended to cover other fields of study outside that of the Jewish Law, or the Talmud. The strong propensity of Jews to enter the learned professions can certainly, at least in part, be looked upon as a result of the traditional high regard for learning.

Now, the primary emphasis of the Law was on the regulation of relations within the Jewish community itself, which, as intimated, constituted an almost self-sufficient society. Mutual solidarity and helpfulness, including an extraordinary sense of responsibility for coreligionists in distress, were emphasized. It was only natural, however, that the Jews did not feel such responsibilities toward Gentiles. In their relations with Gentiles the Jews felt that some of the stringent laws did not apply. This was merely a transfer of the primitive in-group attitude, where outsiders are outside the law governing the group. Typical is the fact that while the taking of interest from another Jew was prohibited it was permitted in relations with "heathens" or "idolators."

Another characteristic commonly ascribed to the Jew is his business sense. The Jew has, indeed, gone extensively into trade and commerce and been highly successful in them. Being forced to live in urban communities and prohibited from engaging in agriculture and most of the other pursuits, the Jews concentrated in trade — an occupation quite disliked, if not stigmatized, for a long time by the peoples among whom they lived. The nature of their communal life was undoubtedly highly conducive to this type of pursuit. Gentiles, on the one hand, resented but, on the other, welcomed the Jewish trader, for, while looking down upon business of any sort, they felt the need for a middleman. The Jew, owing to his peculiar position, was best adapted for performing the important function of the trader, and hence his concentration in business.

The worldly glory and prestige of peoples of the Western world have been very largely bound up with their political existence and power, with their states. The Jews of the Diaspora were excluded from all this. An analogous function in their history has, however, been performed by the idea of being a chosen people. To be a select people, to feel destined to occupy the place of honor among nations, and at the same time to be condemned to a humble, often humiliating place, could not but create a deep-seated ambivalence of attitudes, a curious combination of humility and pride, which, in the more extreme cases, resulted in arrogance. Indeed, the pride and honor of being a Jew were in a sense the principal source of self-respect; but this self-respect could never be clothed in the accepted symbols of glory and greatness, as in the case of other peoples. It is not surprising, therefore, that the Jews have often displayed a rather extreme sensitiveness in matters touching self-respect and status. So long as their emotional attachments were limited exclusively to the Jewish community and all that mattered to them was the honor in which they had been held in their own community, they remained comparatively free of conflicts. As soon, however, as they were permitted, through emancipation, to participate as members of the larger community, the balance was largely lost and they found themselves torn between two worlds and victims of serious emotional difficulties.

CHIEF CHARACTERISTICS OF WESTERN SOCIETY

A broad general characterization of modern Western society which would correspond to that just given of the Jewish community is a most difficult thing because it involves the problem of the selection and selective ordering of the facts. We know so much factual detail for the United States, for instance, that it is difficult to see the wood for the trees. Nevertheless an attempt will be made here, for without it, as said at the outset of this essay, it is practically impossible to analyze the problem at hand.

Our modern society is highly urbanized and industrialized. It is characterized by high attainments in the technological and economic spheres, by a complex economic and social structure, and by heterogeneity and mobility of population. The latter is especially true of the United States, with which we are primarily concerned here. The complexity of the economic structure is probably responsible for most of the problems faced by individuals. It is the occupational status of the individual responsible for the support of a household, his "job," around which his life, above all, turns. It is particularly important in determining his place of residence and his position in the scale of social stratification. To a tremendous extent his standard of living, his self-respect, and his security, both economic and psychological, revolve about it.

In modern Western society the feeling of nationalism is developed to a high degree. Modern nations are held together by feelings of solidarity, by a sense of "belonging together," rather than by homogeneity of descent. In the United States national solidarity centers primarily around the political act of the achievement of independence from England and the traditions of "liberal democracy" which are associated with that. Underlying that are certain broad social values such as a modicum of "equality of opportunity." We have, formally, a separation of church and state so that religion is a "personal affair." But, comparatively speaking, there exists a certain common religious tradition with no cleavage even approaching that found in some countries, as, for instance, in India. Nevertheless, there exist tremendous cultural and racial differences which have far-reaching results both on the country as a whole and on the individual groups. Certain groups in society, are only partially integrated into the national community. The most clear-cut case is that of the American Negro. The case of the Jews, with significant exceptions, of course, is quite similar, particularly in the instance of the eastern European immigrants and their children. Many of these still move within the narrow circle of their own community, only occasionally breaking through it. They, consequently, consider themselves and are considered by the larger community as outsiders. Of course, as the Jews become acculturated contacts between them and Gentiles increase and the lines marking off the Jew from the general community become less and less rigid. But even when this happens the Jew still finds himself far from constituting a full-fledged member of the general community, and his position remains one of ambivalence. Even the so-called assimilated Jew is not completely a member of the general community, although he may have severed his connection with the Jewish community.

One of the most important reasons for this is in the inherent connection between *Gemeinschaft* [4] structures and birth. It is generally impossible completely to get away from association by birth in the short space of a single life-time.

In the most highly integrated social systems of which we have knowledge it seems that the principal *Gemeinschaft* structures and the appropriate symbols and sentiments have tended to be quite stable and to a large extent traditionalized. [5] Moreover, the other institutions — especially the occupational structure — have been closely integrated with them and, similarly, often highly traditionalized. There is much evidence that this phenomenon has been accompanied by a weakening of family and *Gemeinschaft* ties, which played a tremendous role in former days. We know that when this happens a kind of a "void," or state of *anomie*, may be the result. [6] The whole social structure, in a certain sense, becomes disorganized and as a consequence individuals — some, of course, more than others — are placed under a strain. One consequence of this type of disorganization is susceptibility to the forming of new emotional attachments. There is much evidence that the growth of nationalism since the French Revolution is in good part a result of this process. In extreme cases — namely, with the breaking up of the older traditional *Gemeinschaft* structure — nationalism has actually come close to paranoia. Another manifestation of the same type is to be found in susceptibility to faddism in many spheres, particularly in that of religion. Examples of this type are Father Divine's "Peace" group and Dr. Buchman's "Oxford" movement. Perhaps the classic example is German National Socialism, which, because of its espousal of anti-Semitism, is of particular interest here.

[...]

The question frequently raised these days, in view of the violent form anti-Semitism has taken in many countries of Europe, particularly in Germany, is whether anti-Semitism is likely to become as widespread and as extreme in the United States as in those countries. As just intimated, it is hard to make any definite predictions; but in view of the fact that there are some radical differences in the political and national make-up as well as in the circumstances of the two countries — namely, the United States and Germany — it is safe to say that an anti-Jewish movement will probably not occur here to the same extent as it did there.

It would be very difficult to demonstrate that there are any important differences in anti-Semitism as it is found here and in Germany. It would be equally as difficult to measure the extent to which anti-Semitism, as a latent or potential force, varies in these two countries. It is quite clear, however, that the causes bringing about social disorganization which, in turn, calls forth anti-Semitic feelings are quite different here and in Germany.

The United States, to be sure, has suffered disorganization on a considerable scale, owing to effects of both rapid industrialization and urbanization and the presence of diverse immigrant groups. Germany, while comparatively free of the latter, diverse ethnic groups, has suffered more by the rapid industrialization and urbanization. What is, however, even more important — indeed, what constitutes the crux of the problem faced by it — is the disorganizing effect that the defeat in war and the post-war troubles had upon the country. It brought in its wake a breakdown in its national economy as well as humiliation and insecurity — factors that do not enter at all into the case of the United States. In addition, with the overthrow of the monarchy and the old aristocracy there were lost many of the most important integrating symbols. The nation thus found itself left in a psychologically as well as a structurally very insecure position.

Two factors are particularly responsible for the spread of anti-Semitism in Germany. One is the extreme form of nationalism of the German people, and the other is the Nazi movement. In Germany anti-Semitism is linked up with a peculiarly intense kind of nationalism which has all the earmarks of projection of diffuse aggression on Germany's "enemies." Unquestionably, the postwar regime had seriously neglected to direct the sentiments underlying this nationalism into stabilizing channels. Hence the Nazi party that came into power found it easy to mobilize them to serve its own ends. The aim of the Nazis was to discredit the existing type of government. Since Jews played a prominent role in government, and in the newly emerged social élite, they became a very convenient scapegoat. The second factor, as indicated, was the Nazi movement itself. It is not possible here to go into all the factors responsible for the rise and development of this movement, but they undoubtedly constitute an unusual combination. At least three different factors were involved: (1) effective propaganda, (2) the combination of nationalism, "socialism," and anti-Semitism, and (3) an extraordinarily efficient organization.

In view of the above-said, it seems exceedingly unlikely that nationalism can be brought to such a pitch of intensity in the United States. It is highly doubtful whether we could, in the near future at any rate, be brought to a state of national insecurity comparable to that of Germany. It is also very doubtful whether an appeal to extreme nationalism could be as successful here as in that country. Moreover, our type of liberal, democratic government, which itself would find it difficult to sponsor anti-Semitism on a grand scale, is not, as the German Republic was, burdened with the humiliation of defeat. Hence it is unlikely that a movement with a propaganda appeal similar to that of Germany could attain such proportions here. At least it seems very probable that our form of government is likely to be considerably more resistant to such a movement than was the German. Hence the prediction may be hazarded that it is unlikely that a movement involving anti-Semitism on a scale comparable to that in National Socialist Germany will develop in the United States, or, if it does, will gain such absolute control of government — at least not in the near future. This prediction is made in spite of the fact that most of the basic elements inherent in National Socialism are present in this country.

The attitude expressed in what follows is to be taken only as a personal view, no scientific authority being claimed for it. The author considers anti-Semitism of the type discussed here a pernicious and undesirable phenomenon which should be reduced to a minimum. He has strong moral sentiments regarding the importance and desirability of the universalistic patterns of equality of opportunity, so important in the modern occupational system. This does not, however, mean that these sentiments are ethically absolute in the sense that *no* deviation from them whatever is justified. This would, of course, be incompatible with the prevailing mores underlying our family structure and with the values clustering around it. In other words, in the face of unequal opportunities people will tend to take the ideal of fairness less seriously and to be concerned primarily with improving their and their kin's lot, a practice which involves, of course, discrimination. [. . .]

READING 6:
NOTES AND REFERENCES

[1] The term "minority," is a sociological sense, is scarcely applicable to any subgroup in a society which differs in any respect from the majority. For most purposes the term is probably best confined to a group which can be called a "people," in the sense in which that concept is used below. In this sense it is roughly equivalent to "ethnic group."

[2] The most important single source for the following sketch is Max Weber's study "Das Antike Jodentum," in *Gesammelte Aufsätze zur Religionssoziologie,* Vol. III.

[3] Of course the great majority of Jews in the ancient world, as of other peoples and religious groups, became members of the group by being born and brought up in it. But there was much change, by both loss and proselytism, in the racial composition of the ancient jews, and it was their religion which made them a special and separate group in such a cosmopolitan society as that, for instance, of the Roman Empire.

[4] The word *Gemeinschaft,* in the sense given by Ferdinand Tönnies (in his book *Gemeinschaft und Gesellschaft*), means a type of society characterized by the predominance of tradition, emotion, and instinct; *Gesellschaft* is characterized by the predominance of individuals and intellectualism. — EDITORS.

[5] See Ferdinand Tönnies, *Gemeinschaft und Gesellschaft.* After

having played a prominent part in sociological discussions for a generation or more, Tönnies' dichotomy has turned out to be much too simple for many purposes and to cover up many analytical problems. It is, however, useful in the present context, because it calls attention, in broadly acceptable terms, to the distinction between the predominant institutional character of our occupational system, on the one hand, and, on the other, of such structures as the "nation," "social class," "family," etc.

[6] The fullest exposition of the concept of *anomie* in Durkheim's works is to be found in *Le suicide,* Books II, Chap. V. It is also discussed in the author's *The Structure of Social Action,* Chap. VIII.

AGE AND SEX IN THE SOCIAL STRUCTURE OF THE UNITED STATES

In our society age grading does not to any great extent, except for the educational system, involve formal age categorization, but is interwoven with other structural elements. In relation to these, however, it constitutes an important connecting link and organizing point of reference in many respects. The most important of these for present purposes are kinship structure, formal education, occupation and community participation. In most cases the age lines are not rigidly specific, but approximate; this does not, however, necessarily lessen their structural significance. [1]

In all societies the initial status of every normal individual is that of child in a given kinship unit. In our society, however, this universal starting point is used in distinctive ways. Although in early childhood the sexes are not usually sharply differentiated, in many kinship systems a relatively sharp segregation of children begins very early. Our own society is conspicuous for the extent to which children of both sexes are in many fundamental respects treated alike. This is particularly true of both privileges and responsibilities. The primary distinctions within

Reprinted with deletions, with permission, from T. Parsons (Ed.) *Essays in Sociological Theory*, revised edition, Collier-Macmillan, New York (1954).
© 1954 The Free Press.

the group of dependent siblings are those of age. Birth order as such is notably neglected as a basis of discrimination; a child of eight and a child of five have essentially the privileges and responsibilities appropriate to their respective age levels without regard to what older, intermediate, or younger siblings there may be. The preferential treatment of an older child is not to any significant extent differentiated if and because he happens to be the first born. [. . .] What is perhaps the most important sex discrimination is more than anything else a reflection of the differentiation of adult sex roles. It seems to be a definite fact that girls are more apt to be relatively docile, to conform in general according to adult expectations, to be "good," whereas boys are more apt to be recalcitrant to discipline and defiant of adult authority and expectations. There is really no feminine equivalent of the expression "bad boy." It may be suggested that this is at least partially explained by the fact that it is possible from an early age to initiate girls directly into many important aspects of the adult feminine role. Their mothers are continually about the house and the meaning of many of the things they are doing is relatively tangible and easily understandable to a child. It is also possible for the daughter to participate actively and usefully in many of these activities. Especially in the urban middle classes, however, the father does not work in the home and his son is not able to observe his work or to participate in it from an early age. Furthermore many of the masculine functions are of a relatively abstract and intangible character, such that their meaning must remain almost wholly inacessible to a child. This leaves the boy without a tangible meaningful model to emulate and without the possibility of a gradual initiation into the activities of the adult male role. An important verification of this analysis could be provided through the study in our own society of the rural situation. It is my impression that farm boys tend to be "good" in a sense in which that is not typical of their urban brothers.

The equality of privileges and responsibilities, graded only by age but not by birth order, is extended to a certain degree throughout the whole range of the life cycle. In full adult status, however, it is seriously modified by the asymmetrical relation of the sexes to the occupational structure. One of the most conspicuous expressions and symbols of the underlying equality, however, is the lack of sex differentiation in the process of formal education, so far, at least, as it is not explicitly vocational. Up through college, differentiation seems to be primarily a matter on the one hand of individual ability, on the other hand of class status, and only to a secondary degree of sex differentiation. One can certainly speak of a strongly established pattern that all children of the family have a "right" to be a good education, rights which are graduated according to the class status of the family but also to individual ability. It is only post-graduate professional education, with its direct connection with future occupational careers, that sex discrimination becomes conspicuous. It is particularly important that this equality of treatment exists in the sphere of liberal education since throughout the social structure of our society there is a strong tendency to segregate the occupational sphere from one in which certain more generally human patterns and values are dominant, particularly in informal social life and the realm of what will be called community participation.

Although this pattern of equality of treatment is present in certain fundamental respects at all age levels, at the transition from childhood to adolescence new features appear which disturb the symmetry of sex roles, while still a second set of factors appears with marriage and the acquisition of full adult status and responsibilities.

An indication of the change is the practice of chaperonage, through which girls are given a kind of protection and supervision by adults to which boys of the same age group are not subjected. Boys, that is, are chaperoned only in their relations with girls of their own class. This modification of equality of treatment has been extended to the control of the private lives of women students in boarding schools and colleges. Of undoubted significance is the fact that it has been rapidly declining not only in actual effectiveness but as an ideal pattern. Its prominence in our recent past, however, is an important manifestation of the importance of sex role differentiation. Important light might be thrown upon its functions by systematic comparison with the related phenomena in Latin countries where this type of asymmetry has been far more accentuated than in this country in the more modern period.

It is at the point of emergence into adolescence that there first begins to develop a set of patterns and behavior phenomena which involve a highly complex combination of age grading and sex role elements. These may be referred to together as the phenomena of the "youth culture." Certain of its elements are present in pre-adolescence and others in the adult culture. But the peculiar combination in connection with this particular age level is unique and highly distinctive for American society.

Perhaps the best single point of reference for characterizing the youth culture lies in its contrast with the dominant pattern of the adult male role. By contrast with the emphasis on responsibility in this role, the orientation of the youth culture is more or less specifically irresponsible. One of its dominant features themes is "having a good time" in relation to which there is a particularly strong emphasis on social activities in company with the opposite sex. A second predominant characteristic on the male side lies in the prominence of athletics, which is an avenue of achievement and competition which stands in sharp contrast to the primary standards of adult achievement in professional and executive capacities. Negatively, there is a strong tendency to repudiate interest in adult things and to feel at least a certain recalcitrance to the pressure of adult expectations and discipline. In addition to, but including, athletic prowess the typical pattern of the male youth culture seems to lay emphasis on the value of certain qualities of attractiveness, especially in relation to the opposite sex. It is very definitely a rounded humanistic pattern rather than one of competence in the performance of specified functions. Such stereotypes as the "swell guy" are significant of this. On the feminine side there is correspondingly a strong tendency to accentuate sexual attractiveness in terms of various versions of what may be called the "glamor girl" pattern. Although these patterns defining roles tend to polarize sexually — for instance, as between star athlete and socially popular girl — yet on a certain level they are complementary, both emphasizing certain features of a total personality in terms of the direct expression of certain values rather than of instrumental significance.

[. . .]

It is of fundamental significance to the sex role structure of the adult age levels that the normal man has a "job," which is fundamental to his social status in general. It is perhaps not too much to say that only in very exceptional cases can an adult man be genuinely self-respecting and enjoy a respected status in the eyes of others if he does not "earn a living" in an approved occupational role. Not only is this a matter of his own economic support but, generally speaking, his occupational status is the primary source of the income and class status of his wife and children.

In the case of the feminine role the situation is radically different. The majority of married women, of course, are not employed, but even of those that are a very large proportion do not have jobs which are in basic competition for status with those of their husbands. The majority of "career" women whose occupational status is comparable with that of men in their own class, at least in the upper middle and upper classes, are unmarried, and in the small proportion of cases where they are married the result is a profound alteration in family structure.

This pattern, which is central to the urban middle classes, should not be misunderstood. In rural society, for instance, the operation of the farm and the attendant status in the community may be said to be a matter of the joint status of both parties to a marriage. Whereas a farm is operated by a family, an urban job is held by an individual and does not involve other members of the family in a comparable sense. One convenient expression of the difference lies in the question of what would happen in case of death. In the case of a farm it would at least be not at all unusual for the widow to continue operating the farm with the help of a son or even hired men. In the urban situation the widow would cease to have any connection with the organization which had employed her husband and he would be replaced by another man without reference to family affiliations.

In this urban situation the primary status-carrying role is in a sense that of housewife. The woman's fundamental status is that of her husband's wife, the mother of his children, and traditionally the person responsible for a complex of activities in connection with the management of the household, care of children, etc.

For the structuring of sex roles in the adult phase the most fundamental considerations seem to be those involved in the inter-relations of the occupational system and the conjugal family. In a certain sense the most fundamental basis of the family's status is the occupational status of the husband and father. As has been pointed out, this is a status occupied by an individual by virtue of his individual qualities and achievements. But both directly and indirectly, more than any other single factor, it determines the status of the family in the social structure, directly because of the symbolic significance of the office or occupation as a symbol of prestige, indirectly because as the principal source of family income it determines the standard of living of the family. From one point of view the emergence of occupational status into this primary position can be regarded as the principal source of strain in the sex role structure of our society since it deprives the wife of her role as a partner in a common enterprise. The common enterprise is reduced to the life of the family itself and to the informal social activities in which husband and wife participate together. This leaves the wife a set of utilitarian functions in the management of the household which may be considered a kind of "pseudo-" occupation. Since the present interest is primarily in the middle classes, the relatively unstable character of the role of housewife as the principal content of the feminine role is strongly illustrated by the tendency to employ domestic servants wherever financially possible. It is true that there is an American tendency to accept tasks of drudgery with relative willingness, but it is notable that in middle class families there tends to be a dissociation of the essential personality from the performance of these tasks. Thus, advertising continually appeals to such desires as to have hands which one could never tell had washed dishes or scrubbed floors. Organization about the function of housewife, however, with the addition of strong affectional devotion to husband and children, is the primary focus of one of the principal patterns governing the adult feminine role — what may be called the "domestic" pattern. It is, however, a conspicuous fact that strict adherence to this pattern has become progressively less common and has a strong tendency to a residual status — that is, to be followed most closely by those who are unsuccessful in competition for prestige in other directions.

It is, of course, possible for the adult woman to follow the masculine pattern and seek a career in fields of occupational achievement in direct competition with men of her own class. It is, however, notable that in spite of the very great progress of the emancipation of women from the traditional domestic pattern only a very small fraction have gone very far in this direction. It is also clear that its generalization would only be possible with profound alterations in the structure of the family.

Hence it seems that concomitant with the alteration in the basic masculine role in the direction of occupation there have appeared two important tendencies in the feminine role which are alternative to that of simple domesticity on the one hand, and to a full-fledged career on the other. In the older situation there tended to be a very rigid distinction between respectable married women and those who were "no better than they should be." The rigidity of this line has progressively broken down through the infiltration into the respectable sphere of elements of what may be called again the glamor pattern, with the emphasis on a specifically feminine form of attractiveness which on occasion involves directly sexual patterns of appeal. One important expression of this trend lies in the fact that many of the symbols of feminine attractiveness have been taken over directly from the practices of social types previously beyond the pale of respectable society. This would seem to be substantially true of the practice of women smoking and of at least the modern version of the use of cosmetics. The same would seem to be true of many of the modern versions of women's dress. "Emancipation" in this connection means primarily emancipation from traditional and conventional restrictions on the free expression of sexual attraction and impulses, but in a direction which tends to segregate the elements of sexual interest and attraction from the total personality and in so doing tends to emphasize the segregation of sex roles. It is particularly notable that there has been no corresponding tendency to emphasize masculine attraction in terms of dress and other such aids. One might perhaps say that in a situation which strongly inhibits competition between the sexes on the same plane the feminine glamor pattern has appeared as an offset to masculine occupational status and to its attendant symbols of prestige. It is perhaps significant that there is a common stereotype of the association of physically beautiful, expensively and elaborately dressed women with physically unattractive but rich and powerful men.

The other principal direction of emancipation from domesticity seems to lie in emphasis on what has been called the common humanistic element. This takes a wide variety of forms. One of them lies in a relatively mature appreciation and systematic cultivation of cultural interests and educated tastes, extending all the way from the intellectual sphere to matters of art, music and house furnishings. A second consists in cultivation of serious interests and humanitarian obligations in community welfare situations and the like. It is understandable that many of these orientations are most conspicuous in fields where through some kind of tradition there is an element of particular suitability for feminine participation. Thus, a woman who takes obligations to social welfare particularly seriously will find opportunities in various forms of activity which traditionally tie up with women's relation to children, to sickness and so on. But this may be regarded as secondary to the underlying orientation which would seek an outlet in work useful to the community following the most favorable opportunities which happen to be available.

This pattern, which with reference to the character of relationship to men may be called that of the "good companion," is distinguished from the others in that it lays far less stress on the exploitation of sex role as such and more on that which is essentially common to both sexes. There are reasons, however, why cultural interests, interest in social welfare and community activities are particularly prominent in the activities of women in our urban communities. On the one side the masculine occupational role tends to absorb a very large proportion of the man's time and energy and to leave him relatively little for other interests. Furthermore, unless his position is such as to make him particularly prominent his primary orientation is to those elements of the social structure which divide the community into occupational groups rather than those which unite it in common interests and activities. The utilitarian aspect of the role of housewife, on the other hand, has declined in importance to the point where it scarcely approaches a full-time occupation for a vigorous person. Hence the resort to other interests to fill up the gap. In addition, women, being more closely tied to the local residential community, are more apt to be involved in matters of common concern to the members of that community. This peculiar role of women becomes particularly conspicuous in middle age. The younger married woman is apt to be relatively highly absorbed in the care of young children. With their growing up, however, her absorption in the household is greatly lessened, often just at the time when the husband is approaching the apex of his career and is most heavily involved in its obligations. Since to a high degree this humanistic aspect of the feminine role is only partially institutionalized it is not surprising that its patterns often bear the marks of strain and insecurity. [...]

READING 7:
NOTES AND REFERENCES

[1] The problem of organization of this material for systematic presentation is, in view of this fact, particularly difficult. It would be possible to discuss the subject in terms of the above four principal structures with which age and sex are most closely interwoven, but there are serious disadvantages involved in this procedure. Age and sex categories constitute one of the main links of structural continuity in terms of which structures which are differentiated in other respects are articulated with each other; and in isolating the treatment of these categories there is danger that this extremely important aspect of the problem will be lost sight of. The least objectionable method, at least within the limits of space of such a paper, seems to be to follow the sequence of the life cycle.

POPULATION AND THE SOCIAL STRUCTURE OF JAPAN

The structure and trends of population of an area constitute both an important index to the deeper-lying social structure and situation, and a very important set of conditions which will affect its future development. The population situation of Japan reflects the most fundamental fact about Japanese society: that it has been a society in transition from a "feudal" preindustrial organization — of a very distinctive type — to a modern urbanized industrial society closer to the social type of the great industrial countries of the West than any other Oriental country.

Available evidence indicates that before the Meiji restoration the population of Japan had long been relatively stable at a level of approximately thirty millions. As in practically all other preindustrial societies this stable balance was achieved in terms of a high birth rate balanced by a high morality rate, with all the familiar concomitants of that situation, such as high infant mortality and high disease rates in many fields. The most authoritative recent study states: "The pattern of mortality in Japan . . . was similar to that of mediaeval Europe, or that

Reprinted with deletions, with permission, from T. Parsons (Ed.) *Essays in Sociological Theory*, revised edition, Collier-Macmillan, New York (1954).

of the isolated regions of contemporary China. The ultimate controls of growth were famine and epidemics. . . . Even abortion and infanticide appear to have been techniques that flourished after the great calamities — not techniques . . . to forestall the calamities." [1]

With the dramatic change in Japan's situation in the mid-nineteenth century, there began a rapid process of industrialization and urbanization. As in the corresponding phases of the process in the Western world, it was marked by a rapid increase of population, to a total of over seventy millions in 1940. Only in the latest recorded census period — between 1935 and 1940 — did the rate of increase begin to slacken.

Certain notable facts stand out in the more detailed picture. Apparent increases in death rates are almost certainly explicable in terms of improved registration of deaths. Hence the increase seems almost wholly due to a progressive lowering of death rates without a compensating reduction of birth rates — again typical of the earlier stages of industrialization in the Western world. A further striking fact is that the rural population, as closely as can be ascertained, had remained almost exactly constant during the period. The whole increase has gone to the cities, and until the most recent period to the largest cities. A very large part of this urban increase, however, came from the surplus of rural births. Finally, the process which has marked all Western industrial countries also has set in unmistakably in Japan — the decline in birth rates in urban communities. By 1940 the total rate of growth was beginning to slacken, but it still was very rapid. On the basis of extrapolation of the curve, a stage comparable to the approaching stabilization, or actual decline, in Western countries would not be reached for a long time.

Thus the process of declining rate of increase has probably been setting in more slowly than in the West. But the above are the fundamentals of it. Nothing could better reflect the basic importance of Japan's emergence from rural isolation to industrialism, nor the fact that the social consequences, at the outbreak of the war, were very far from complete.

The population history of the Western world seems to indicate that even a major war does not necessarily change the fundamental course of development of a population. In both Germany and Great Britain the birth and death rates continued to decline after 1918, though the process probably was accelerated by the war. For Japan, however, defeat may mean a profounder population crisis very closely connected with the major problems of her whole society.

The great urban population has not been supported primarily by interchange with the countryside of the home islands; "foreign trade," whether in the free markets of world trade or in a closed imperial system, has played an essential part. The very stability of the rural population seems to indicate great tenacity in a rural standard of living which has risen only gradually during the period of great economic expansion. If Japan is forced back economically upon herself, the rigidity of the whole structure is such that it might force her population balance back into the old pattern of high rural-type birth rates compensated in a correspondingly high death rate — with eventually a new stabilization at a figure probably somewhere between the thirty millions of Tokugawa and the seventy millions of the present. If this happens, however, it will both condition and reflect profound changes in Japanese tendencies of social development — a drastic check to the process of internal change which has dominated the society for the better part of a century.

The recent characteristics of Japanese social structure and its potentialities of adaptation to the consequences of defeat must be understood in terms of the dynamic consequences of this process of industrialization. This process, curiously, has combined features resembling the Western counterpart with striking differences and peculiarities of its own. To understand this in turn it is necessary to sketch briefly the main outline of the older authentically Japanese components and the particular type of Western industrialism which has come into Japan.

The base, and the part which has been changed least fundamentally, is the social structure of the rural villages in which, on the eve of the war, about 70 per cent of the population still lived. In main outline this base has been similar to that of peasant societies in many parts of the world. The basic unit has been the kinship group responsible for the tillage of an agricultural holding. With a good many local variations this still is the common element. The kinship unit is patrilineal, with status inherited by primogeniture, so that the normal household contains three rather than two generations. The eldest son remains in his father's household, brings a wife from outside, and with the retirement or death of the father becomes proprietor and head of the household. Younger sons must find places outside since the holding is passed down intact and undivided. In the last couple of generations much the commonest outlet for younger sons has been migration to the cities, without complete severance of ties with the home village and family. Daughters always go out, either to marry into a similar farm family — perhaps in a neighbouring village — or to migrate to the city. Until she is married a daughter is very strictly under the control of her parental family.

The tradition of continuity of family on the ancestral holdings is very strong. If there is no son to inherit it, it is common practice to adopt a young man to marry a daughter. In this case the usual pattern is reversed. The new son-in-law takes the name of his wife's family and becomes a member of their household. Holdings are so small that doubtless there have been processes of subdivision in the past. Recently, however, the dominant facts are the tenacity with which they are kept together, and the stability of the village community as a group of family units which have held this status for an indefinite period and intend to maintain it indefinitely in the future.

This fundamental pattern has not depended on the extent of independent proprietorship or tenancy. Though varying in different places, the general situation in that regard has been mixed. A very few farmers have owned enough land to rent some of it to others, and there has been a fairly large class who have owned all that they and their families have cultivated. The largest class includes those who have owned some land but have rented the rest in varying proportions. A substantial minority have been entirely tenants with no land of their own. This situation has been facilitated by the fact that most holdings are split up; a family cultivates a number of different plots scattered through the village lands, not a single consolidated "farm" in the American sense.

In spite of the prevalence of tenancy, modern rural Japan is characterized by relative lack of a prominent rural landowning class in the social structure. At first sight this is surprising in view of her feudal history. The explanation lies largely in the fact that the samurai of the Tokugawa period were not a landed gentry in the European sense, but were attached to the court of the *daimyo* who owned the land and paid them "rice stipends" out of the proceeds. Continuity of status bound to specific holdings of land thus applied to the peasantry and the high feudal nobility, but not to the gentry class.

In modern Japan there are landowners in the villages who are "gentlemen" rather than cultivators. But they are not decisively important to the social structure. Of the rural land owned by non-cultivators, town- or city-dwelling landlords probably hold a larger proportion. A certain prestige seems to attach to landownership as compared to other sources of income, but by no means a decisive one when compared to China or "county" England. On the whole, owners of rural land tend to merge with the larger middle class of people of business and professional status, which, though much smaller and weaker, is very similar to our own in basic characteristics.

The most distinctive feature of rural Japanese social organization, which it shares with the rest of the society, is the family council. The most important structural implication of this is the solidarity of a considerable number of household units which are related by kinship on both the paternal and maternal sides, though the former tends to predominate. All major decisions — such as the purchase or sale of land, marriage of a child, unusual steps in education, a new business venture — must be referred to the family council. The prestige of seniority or other high status works effectively in attaining unanimity within the family council.

Through the mechanism of the family council, kinsmen whose places of residence have become scattered are kept close together in mutual support. Property is managed in the light of common interest. The most promising youths of the various collateral lines may be picked for united backing in getting higher education or in a business venture. In particular the branches of rural families that have migrated to the cities are kept closely bound to relatives in their native villages. This pattern has certainly done a great deal to preserve the older patterns of life in the urban population and to slow up the process of social change which urbanization inevitably sets in motion. Finally it should be noted that the system of family councils produces an interlocking network of overlapping kinship groups. There is a slightly different council for each household. Members who are central for one will be peripheral for another. This seamless web binds every individual in a very tight system of traditional obligations.

On top of this peasant base in preindustrial Japan was erected a highly stratified class system based on rigid primogeniture and continuity of kinship groups in their hereditary status. The family council system and the sharp subordination of the individual have been at least as marked on this level as on that of the peasantry. The two most important elements of this higher structure were the *daimyo* nobility and the samurai gentry.

The most important features of these older upper classes for the understanding of modern Japan account both for the surprising lack of resistance to "modernization" in the Meiji period, and for certain peculiar features of the society which emerged as a result. The Tokugawa regime was a unique kind of feudal dictatorship. Though built up on a decentralized feudal structure of society, it did not in fact put the *daimyo* class in a very firm position in the total society, largely because the principle of the regime was that of divide and rule. The "inner lords" (*fudai daimyo*) who were directly integrated with the regime were made so heavily dependent on it that their position was inherently weak. At the same time they were set over against the "outer lords" (*tozama*) who were kept impotent by exclusion and isolation from each other. The initiative for the restoration came from the latter; but the situation did not encourage a new equilibrium on a feudal basis. Having upset the delicate balance of the Tokugawa regime itself, they set up a highly centralized structure in which the socially dominant classes and the government were bound up closely with each other.

The samurai class, as noted above, were in a slightly different position, the dominant characteristic of which was their lack of independent roots in the land and the local community, with corresponding direct dependence on the *daimyo* to whom each was bound by ties of personal loyalty. One consequence was sharp differentiation in the power and wealth of different samurai. The most prominent and powerful were those who held positions of trust and influence at the courts of outstanding *daimyo*, especially the outer lords. In the restoration these men were in fact more influential than the *daimyo* themselves, though each acted in his lord's name. Already they constituted a kind of higher civil service group.

With the success of the political overturn it was natural that the nobility — including the *kuge* or court nobility — should be amalgamated with these ambitious and influential samurai to form a new centralized national nobility. Outside their traditional loyalty to their particular *daimyo* the samurai had no vested interest to bind them to their local community. The position of the *daimyo* was weak, so it did not prove very difficult to deprive them of their special feudal status, to buy out their rights, and set up almost overnight one of the most highly centralized political structures of modern times.

One additional important group was involved. In the absence of modern technology, transportation, and communications, there had been little organization of production in Japan beyond the handicraft level. But, as is common in such societies, an upper class with considerable wealth and everything that was to be found in the capital of a centralized regime in Yedo had produced a situation favorable to a considerable growth of mercantile trade and finance. This was further favored by the long period of internal peace of the Tokugawa regime. As a result mercantile houses of very considerable wealth and extensity of interests grew up. Even the *daimyo,* especially the outer lords, engaged in manufacturing and commerce — at first surreptitiously, then openly.

Here was an extreme example of such a new "bourgeois" class having to fit into the interstices of the existing social structure. "Feudal"

Japan was dominated by aristocratic classes of the type which idealized the military virtues and a corresponding code of honor and looked with extreme contempt on the merchant and tradesman. Traditionally even the humble peasant ranked higher in the social scale than the merchant. In fact considerable wealth and influence developed, but in a setting which promoted maximum dissatisfaction with the existing regime.

The wealthier merchant classes thus were naturl allies of the rebellious elements and played a prominent part in financing and otherwise facilitating the restoration. They were rewarded by admission to the new national aristocracy, with seats in the House of Peers, patents of nobility for many of the most prominent, and a general tendency to intermarry and fuse with the older families. This, however, was very different from the "bourgeois revolutions" which took place in much of Europe. In various respects the older aristocratic groups remained dominant; it was their values and patterns of life which set the principal tone for the new Japan. Important as the mercantile elements were as the direct vehicle of Japan's economic modernization, it was only for brief periods, as in the 1920's, that they acquired anything like the upper hand.

Japan thus made the transition to modernization with minimum immediate disturbance of her preindustrial social structure. The peasant base remained essentially intact. The old upper classes faced greatly altered conditions, but on the whole as a group remained in the top positions of prestige, wealth and power. The military values and code of the samurai had an opportunity for a new field of expression in the form of the armed forces of a modern nation, supported by a nationalistically tinged system of universal education.

With these older patterns and values there also remained intact the Japanese family system with its rigid system of obligations subordinating all individual interests to those of family units. Through long centuries of conditioning by a hierarchical social system, these patterns of subordination of the individual to his larger family, of the young to the old, or women to men, shaded almost imperceptibly into a subordination of people of lower to those of higher status in a highly crystalized class system, and of general predisposition to accept legitimate authority. The imperial institution — master symbol of this highly hierarchized and integrated system — not only remained intact but was also exalted to a new position of prestige which was exploited systematically by the new ruling group.

The dynamic significance of this older component of Japanese social structure is greatly heightened by its exceedingly close integration with the magico-religious tradition of Shinto. It is important to understand the radical difference of this from the Christian tradition in its relation to social obligations. The rather sharp segregation of spiritual from temporal affairs which is characteristic of the Occident is unknown to Japan. From the highest pinnacle of government in the person of the emperor to the humblest household, virtually every status has at the same time a magico-religious and a secular aspect. The obligations of everyday social life are not merely derived ultimately from religious authority, they are immediately and directly ritual obligations. The pressure to conformity which inheres in every well-integrated system of social relationships is greatly heightened by this situation as long as general acceptance of the whole pattern of Shinto remains untouched.

While much of ordinary social obligation in Japan carries a directly sacred character unknown to Occidentals, at the same time it involves an attitude toward these sacred sanctions quite different from our own. The Western emphasis is on the individual's own responsible conscience; social pressures are minimized and submission to them is felt to be unworthy. Our concept of moral heroism idealizes the person who stands up for his convictions *against* others and against tradition. The predominant feeling of the individual who transgresses his obligations is that of guilt — while that of others is one of moral indignation.

In Japan the emphasis is quite different. Obligations are not imposed by a principle in which one "believes" but by specific acts of oneself or others in traditionally defined situations, or by the accepted patterns of one's status. "Responsibility" is the willingness to accept the implications of these obligations and carry them out regardless of personal cost. The individual's own emotional reaction to transgression is shame that the honor due to his status is besmirched, while that of others is that he has disgraced the *group* with which he is identified — the consequences are not personalized in his *own* character. Moral idealism is to take responsibility in the above sense, not to stand out for principles. Moral conflict is a matter of being caught between conflicting obligations, not of conflict between principle and pressure of practical necessity as it is predominantly with Occidentals.

This mode of incidence of sacred sanctions in a "moral" context is an indispensable background for understanding Japanese behaviour in the situations presented by the social structure. Though highly formalistic it is a system characterized by a moral rigor in many respects greater than in Western societies.

There is every reason to believe that the rigor is so great that, even apart from the special insecurity introduced by the consequences of Westernization, it does not operate without severe strains on most individuals. Whatever these may be there is no doubt that they are intensified by the juxtaposition with radically different Occidental values.

There is a good deal of evidence that, with all its outward stability, the Tokugawa system had been accumulating tensions over a long period and in fact was far from completely static. However that may have been, the new society was inherently dynamic. It not only grew rapidly in population, in industrial organization and productive facilities, in foreign trade and political prestige — emerging as the only Oriental unit in the system of great powers — but it also underwent a rapid and drastic internal social transformation. Many of the tensions generated by this internal change were certainly expressed in heightened nationalistic feeling and thus formed the popular basis of Japanese expansionism.

The new regime speedily created a highly centralized organization into which all the most influential social elements were drawn. Second only to consolidation of its own power, it was dedicated to a program of swift modernization of the country through adoption of Western patterns of organization and technology, both industrial and military. The combination of centralization and modernization set the fundamental pattern of those aspects of recent Japanese society which most closely resemble the West.

[...]

The Japanese society which was caught up into the war thus was undergoing a highly dynamic process of change and was in a state of unstable equilibrium. The fundamental components of that situation certainly are still present. The question of the future is in large part the question of what are the principal possibilities of re-structuring which the new situation will allow, and what kinds of further dynamic change may be expected under the conditions which probably will exist. Obviously there are so many unknown factors that there can be no question of an attempt at "prediction." The best that can be done is to make a contribution to clarification of the problems which will have to be faced by all who deal with policy toward Japan. This includes the humblest American citizen who by his vote and expressed opinion exercises influence even as an individual.

Clearly there is no formula by which measures taken in the immediate future — short of extermination — could remove, certainly and permanently, the possibility of revival of a Japanese militarism which might become a future threat to American security. There seem to be three major possibilities of the direction Japanese social development might take. All three have the potentiality either of making the Japanese more amenable to adjustment in a peaceful world order, or of their again becoming truculently aggressive and, in the absence of adequate repressive controls, acquiring the means to make themselves unpleasant. In all three cases, the alternative that works out will depend substantially on the international environment of Japan rather than on her internal development alone.

The first of the three major possibilities is reversion to an essentially preindustrial agrarian society in which an overwhelming majority are peasants. In this case the structures with higher integrative functions might vary within a wide range of alternatives. Secondly, it is conceivable that power should be secured by a revolutionary regime of the communist type which, within a relatively short period, would drastically liquidate the older traditional patterns. What might emerge from such a situation in positive terms is exceedingly difficult to foresee. Finally, it is possible that the fundamental trend of development since the Meiji restoration should be continued, but that the nationalistic-militaristic element should be prevented from predominating. Then the general evolution should take the direction of approximation to the Western "democratic" type of society with emphasis on either its individualistic or its socialistic version.

Certain fundamental features of the situation, relevant to selection among those possibilities, can be taken for granted. First is the fact that, whatever the losses resulting from the war and from immediate postwar economic and social chaos, the fundamental factors making for rapid increase in population would still operate. The only immediate alleviations of this tendency to be expected involve the incidence of higher death rates from disease, malnutrition, and the like, and the kind of decline in birth rates associated with chaotic social conditions in which levels of insecurity are exceedingly high. Even if such conditions should lead to an absolute decline the prospect is that with restoration of order and a minimum of security an upward tendency would be resumed immediately — unless held in check by very nearly absolute limitations of resources.

Secondly, there may be a very serious crisis in the economic sphere — not merely a cyclical depression — caused by the interruption of foreign trade and the cutting off of the islands from the foreign raw materials and markets on which the economy has been dependent. The problems of this crisis are beyond the scope of this paper. The present concern is only with its social consequences. It will mean a considerable period of economic contraction, lowering the standards of living, diminishing fields of individual opportunity, and insecurity.

Finally it may be assumed that there will be rather thorough demilitarization. This includes not only removal of armaments and certain potential facilities for their production, but also complete demobilization of the armed forces, prohibition of the renewal of universal military service, and elimination of the privileged constitutional position of the service ministries. The principal specific social mechanisms which in prewar Japan were instrumental in tipping the balance in favor of aggressive militarism will thus be eliminated from the picture − at least for as long as control is effective.

The combination of the first two factors is certain to mean that there is a heightened state of general insecurity and, for a considerable period, a contracting rather than expanding field of opportunity for the majority of individuals. There also will be an initial revulsion associated with the disastrous defeat. Whether this is of long-run significance will depend on the subsequent development of the situation. The case of Germany after the last war should not be forgotten.

If Japan is permitted to stew in her own juice after demilitarization by being virtually cut off from international trade and cultural relations, it will almost certainly serve to consolidate the traditional indigenous patterns more firmly than ever. The urban and industrial sector of the society has provided the main focus of the forces making for their weakening, and this sector would be diminished greatly in relative significance. Millions of urban people would be forced back into the villages and absorbed into the traditional kinship groupings.

Such a situation would produce many explosive tensions, starting with sheer overcrowding of the land. Perhaps the most important, however, would result from the system of inheritance. The powerful tradition of primogeniture would inhibit subdivision of holdings; but at recent rates of population growth − which, as noted, are likely to be resumed − there would be no satisfactory status available in the rural community structure for the surplus − to say nothing of food. The system certainly could give here and there, but it is sufficiently rigid so that one or two major outcomes is probable. On the one hand the lid may be kept on, i.e., discipline might be maintained in terms of the old patterns and the explosive tensions mastered. The result of these pressures then would be to bring population into balance, presumably on a partly preindustrial basis with reduced rate of increase through higher death rates rather than fewer births. Presumably some reduction through postponement of marriage is also possible. On the other hand the lid may blow off and some kind of internal revolution occur which would break up the traditional peasant system.

Which of these possibilities is actually realized and what the consequences may be will not depend mainly on the social structure of the masses of the population, but on the higher integrative structures. In this respect the situation is such that a stable situation in a sense favorable to the United States is not likely. A foundation for a revival of aggressive tendencies would probably be laid which could be kept in check only by an external system of political order so strong that any challenge to it would be suicidal. [. . .]

READING 8:
NOTES AND REFERENCES

[1] Irene B. Taeuber and Edwin G. Beal, "The Dynamics of Population in Japan," *Demographic Studies of Selected Areas of Rapid Growth* (New York: Milbank Memorial Fund, 1944), p. 6.

Part Three

The Parsons² Phase

During this phase, Parsons's work came to represent a virtually para-digmatic form of structural-functionalism. It is a phase which also saw the incorporation of Freudian concepts into Parsons's action and system theories — the first reading, on *Psychoanalysis and the Social Structure* (1951), representing the analytical basis on which Parsons connects his own version of functional analysis of action systems to the psychoanalytic concepts.

The extracts from *The Social System* (1951) deal essentially with Parsons's specification of the *pattern variables,* which formed the basis of his famous AGIL schema (*Adaptation, Goal-attainment, Integration* and *Latency*) which came to be so central to his development of action theory. It is interesting to note that there were originally *five* pattern variables in Parsons's specification of the alternative of normative orientation to the action situation.

Parsons's discussion of *Illness and the Role of the Physician* (1951) has become a sociological classic. It is reprinted here because it indicates how the highly abstract and general conceptual scheme outlined in *The Social System* could be directly applied to a specific social setting.

Finally, the extract from *Economy and Society* (1956) shows Parsons (with the collaboration of Neil Smelser) returning to an interest in economic theory, but seen through the eyes of an action theory concerned primarily with the interchanges and boundary maintenance characteristics of subsystems of action, and social systems. The book provides a bridge between Parsons² and Parsons³ theories, and in it Parsons is increasingly interested in the media of interchange between action systems.

PSYCHOANALYSIS AND THE SOCIAL STRUCTURE

THE BASIC COMMON FRAME OF REFERENCE

Both psychoanalytic theory and the type of sociological theory which is in process of developing a new type of analysis of social structure and its dynamics go back to the same basic conceptual scheme or frame of reference which it is convenient to call the theory of action. This theory conceives the behaving individual or actor as operating in a situation which is given independently of his goals and wishes, but, within the limits of that situation and using those potentialities which are subject to his control, actively oriented to the attainment of a system of goals and wishes. Studying the processes of action, the scheme takes the point of view of the meaning of the various elements of the system to the actor. Meaning may be of several different types, of which, perhaps, the most important are the cognitive and the affective or emotional. Finally, the mutual orientation of human beings to each other, both as objects of meaning and as means to each other's goals, is a fundamental aspect of the scheme. Though it is logically possible to treat a single individual in isolation from others, there is every reason to

Reprinted with deletions, with permission, from T. Parsons *Essays in Sociological Theory* revised edition, Collier-Macmillan, New York (1954), pp. 336–347.

believe that this case is not of important empirical significance. All concrete action is in this sense social, including psychopathological behavior.

There are two main foci of theoretical organization of systems within the broad framework of this conceptual scheme. One is the individual personality as a system, and the other is the social system. The first is, according to this point of view, the primary focus of the subject matter of the science of psychology; the second that of social science in the specific sense. The same fundamental conceptual components are involved in the treatment of both, and on a broader level whatever theories exist in both are part of the same fundamental theoretical system. Nevertheless, it is extremely important to differentiate the various levels and ways in which these conceptual components are involved or combined. It is dangerous to shift from the one level to the other without taking adequate account of the systematic differences that are involved.

THE SOCIAL SYSTEM AS A STRUCTURAL-FUNCTIONAL SYSTEM OF ACTION

It is essential from the point of view of social science to treat the social system as a distinct and independent entity which must be studied and analyzed on its own level, not as a composite resultant of the actions of the component individuals alone. There is no reason to attribute any fundamental logical or ontological priority to either the social system or the personality. In treating the social system as a system, structural categories have proved to be essential in the same sense as in the biological sciences, and presumably also in psychology. [1] In the present state of knowledge of social systems, it is not possible to treat a total social system directly as a dynamic equilibrium of motivational forces. It is necessary to treat motivational problems in the context of their relation to structure, and to raise dynamic problems in terms of the balance of forces operating to maintain or alter a given structure. At this point, however, psychological categories in social science play a fundamental role which is in some respects analogous to biochemistry in biological sciences. In this context what is meant by social structure is a system of patterned expectations of the behavior of individuals who occupy particular statuses in the social system. Such a system of patterned legitimate expectations is called by sociologists a system of roles. In so far as a cluster of such roles is of strategic significance to the social system, the complex of patterns which define expected behavior in them may be referred to as an institution. For example, in so far as the behavior of spouses in their mutual relationships is governed by socially sanctioned legitimate expectations in such a sense that departure from these patterns will call forth reactions of moral disapproval or overt sanctions, we speak of the institution of marriage. Institutional structures in this sense are the fundamental element of the structure of the social system. They constitute relatively stable crystallizations of behavioral forces in such a way that action can be sufficiently regularized so as to be compatible with the functional requirements of a society.

From the psychological point of view, institutionalized roles seem to have two primary functions. The first is the structuring of the reality situation for the action of the individual. They define the expectations of behavior which are generalized in the attitude patterns of other individuals with whom he may come into contact. They tell him what the probable consequences of various alternative forms of action are likely to be. Second, they structure the 'superego content' for the individual. It is fundamentally the patterns institutionalized in role structure which constitute the moral standards which are introjected in the process of socialization and become an important part of the personality structure of the individual himself, whether he conforms to them or not. It may be stated as a fundamental theorem of social science that one measure of the integration of a social system is the coincidence of the patterns which are introjected in the average superego of those occupying the relevant social status with the functional needs of the social system which has that particular structure.

THE DISCREPANCY BETWEEN PERSONALITY STRUCTURE AND INSTITUTIONAL MOTIVATION

One of the most important reasons why it is dangerous to infer too directly from the psychological to the social structure level and vice versa is the extremely important fact that there is not a simple correspondence between personality structure and institutional structure. On the level of clinical diagnosis, the persons occupying the same well-defined status in the social system will be found to cover a wide range of personality types. It is true that seen in sufficiently broad perspective there will be modal types which differ from one society to another, but this is a statistical correspondence and not one of the social pattern to the personality pattern of each individual. This means that there must be mechanisms by which the behavior of individuals is motivated to conform with institutional expectations, even though personality structure as such does not give an adequately effective background for it.

It is convenient to refer to the fundamental mechanism involved here as the 'structural generalization of goals'; thus there is a level of the structuring of motivational forces which is essentially a function of the institutional situations in which people are put, rather than of their particular personality structures. It may be said to operate within the range of flexibility which personality structures permit, and, of course, to involve a greater or less amount of strain to carry out that conformity. This, however, is one area of the analysis of motivation where the relation of psychology to social structure is particularly important. To cite just one example, most attempts at a direct psychological attack on the problem of so-called economic motivation, or the profit motive, have proved to be singularly unfruitful. The essential reason for this is that the uniformities of social behavior do not directly correspond to uniformities on the psychological level independent of the institutional context. Anything like the profit motive of modern Western society is not a psychological universal, and the corresponding behavior would not be found in many, for instance, nonliterate and other societies.

THE PROBLEM OF THE USE OF MOTIVATIONAL CATEGORIES IN DYNAMIC EXPLANATIONS ON THE SOCIOLOGICAL LEVEL

The most notable direct contributions of psychoanalytic theory to the empirical understanding of behavior would seem to fall in the dynamic theory of motivation of the individual in the context of the structure of personality. The most important problem of the relation of psychoanalysis to social structure from the point of view of the sociologist is how these categories can be used for explanatory purposes on the level of the analysis of social structure and its changes as such. This is a field in which it is particularly dangerous to attempt too direct an explanation. The lack of correspondence between personality structure and social structure should make this clear.

The sociologist is, in the first instance, concerned with behavior and attitudes which are of strategic significance to the social system. In the terms stated, this means tendencies which either support the structure of an existing social system or tend to alter it in specific ways. The judgments of significance on which the statements of sociological problems of motivation are based must therefore be couched in terms of the frame of reference of the social system, not of personality, though of course they must be compatible with established knowledge of personality.

Such problems must in turn be approached in terms of constructs of typical motivation, typical of the persons occupying given statuses in the social structure. The most obvious of the ingredients of such constructs will of course be derived from the situation in which a given incumbent of such a status is placed — a situation principally compounded of the behavior and attitudes of others. But psychoanalytic theory shows that these alone are not sufficient; certain typical elements of structure of the particular personality, such as superego and ways in which the instinctual components are organized, are also involved. It is furthermore often necessary to link these elements in a developmental sequence so that the motivational structures resulting from an earlier situation in the life cycle become elements in shaping the situations of a later stage.

There is involved throughout this procedure a peculiar process of abstraction from the frame of reference of personality as a functioning system. Psychologists and psychoanalysts tend to take this frame of reference for granted and thus find it difficult to accept the sociologist's mode of abstraction. They feel it is psychologically inadequate, as indeed it is. But adequacy is not an absolute; it is relative to the problems which facts and conceptual schemes can help to solve. The typical problems of the psychologist and the sociologist are different and therefore they need to use the same concepts at different levels of abstraction and in different combinations.

In general it may be said that psychological analysis is oriented to the explanation of the concrete acts, attitudes, or ideas of individuals. Both motivational elements and the social structure come into this, the latter as describing the situation in which the individual must act or to which he has been exposed. Adequacy is judged in terms of the completeness of accounting for one given act, attitude, or idea as compared to another. The frame of reference is, as has been said, the personality of the relevant individual treated as a system.

The sociologist's problems are different. They concern the balance of motivational forces involved in the maintenance of, and alteration in, the structure of a social system. This balance is a peculiar sort of resultant of very complex interaction processes. It can only be successfully analyzed by abstracting from the idiosyncratic variability of individual behaviors and motivations in terms of strategic relevance to the social system. Conversely the psychologist abstracts from what are to him the equally idiosyncratic variations of social situations in reaching psychological generalizations about such matters as the relations of love and security.

If we had a completely adequate dynamic theory of human motivation it is probable that this difference of levels of abstraction would disappear. Then the use of structural categories, on the levels of either personality or the social system, would be unnecessary, for such categories are only empirical generalizations introduced to fill the gaps left by the inadequacy of our dynamic knowledge. In the meantime, however, we must put up with the complications involved in the diversity of levels.

It follows from these considerations, if they are accepted, that the motivational constructs needed for the solution of any sociological problem will generally turn out to be adequate to explain the action of any particular individual involved in the very concrete events being studied. They will be concerned with certain elements in this motivation, but the combinations of these elements with others, and hence what will be the order of their strategic significance to the psychological problem, cannot be inferred from the sociological analysis.

Conversely, psychologists, whether they are aware of it or not, categorize the social structure. But by the same token, the conceptualizations they find adequate for their purposes will generally turn out to be inadequate to the explanation of a single process of change in a social structure in which the same concrete persons and action-sequences were involved.

It is, in my opinion, neglect of the indispensability of distinguishing these levels of abstraction which, more than errors or differences of opinion about facts, has accounted for the difficulties. These difficulties, from the sociologist's point of view, have been prominent in much of what may be called psychologically (psychoanalytically) oriented sociology which attempts to generalize about societies from *Totem and Taboo* to Geoffrey Gorer's *American People*. In the absence of very careful discrimination of these levels it was almost inevitable that the analyst would 'extrapolate' directly from what he found in the personalities he had studied in the clinical situation. He would then necessarily categorize social structures *ad hoc* in the light of these references without systematic reference to the social system as a conceptual scheme and the criteria of relevance inherent in such a reference. [2] Certain sociologists likewise indulge in *ad hoc* psychological constructions without reference to technical psychological considerations. [3]

[...]

Psychoanalytic theory can make a crucially important contribution to the problems of the sociologist, though not, of course, to the exclusion of other traditions of psychological theory. This contribution is, however, likely to be much more fruitful if it is made in the form of the adaptation of psychoanalytic concepts and analyses of motivation to the technical needs of sociological theory in terms of problems stated in sociological terms.

This way of using psychoanalytic theory, it has been pointed out, involves putting it into a frame of reference, the social system, which is not usually familiar to the clinical analyst and which is not reducible to terms of his own critical experience and standards of expectation, couched as these are, implicitly or explicitly, in terms of the frame of reference of personality. To make the transition requires such a shift in perspective and problems that it must be held that the analyst, no matter how well trained, is not per se competent to apply psychoanalytic theory to sociological problems. To do this he must be a trained sociologist, he must learn to think in terms of social systems, and he does not automatically learn this from clinical experience as an analyst but only from studying sociology as such.

But if the sociologist is to utilize the potential contributions of psychoanalysis to his problems, he can only do so competently by going to the authentic sources, by learning psychoanalysis himself, as far as possible by the regular training procedures. To some important degree the same people must have real competence in both fields. Only from such a solid base is the diffusion of psychoanalytic knowledge into such a neighbouring field possible without distortion.

If the general position here taken is sound, there is a further implication which may be briefly noted in conclusion. If psychoanalytic theory is as important to sociology as it certainly seems to be, the converse relationship should also be important. This is indeed strongly indicated by the fact that analytical theory has laid so much emphasis on the psychological importance of social relationships — of the child to parents, of the adult to love objects, etc.

Concretely, these relationships are aspects of social systems; the family, for example, is a small-scale social system. The sociological aspects of the family as a social system have, understandably, not been explicitly considered by psychoanalysts because they have concentrated on the particular relations of each patient to each of the members of his family in turn. There has been little occasion to consider the total family as a social system, though this might well yield insights not derivable from the 'atomistic' treatment of each relationship in turn.

Unfortunately the sociologists as yet have not provided as much help as they might. The science is in general very immature (but then, psychoanalysis is not yet very old) and the principal preoccupation of sociologists has so far been with 'macroscopic' social systems. But the evidence is strong that the same fundamental conceptual scheme, the social system, is applicable all the way from the largest-scale societies (like the United States) to groups of such small size as the family. But the sociological study of small groups is in its barest beginnings and, paradoxically, only suggestions of the technical analysis of the family as a social system exist.

But in relation to the family the problem for the psychoanalyst is the obverse of that outlined above for the sociologist. Supposing that in the near future we attain something which could respectably be called a sociology of the family; this would no more as such solve the analyst's problems about family structure than a psychoanalytic theory of personality solves the sociologist's problems of motivation. But such a theory would contain the essential conceptual bases on which the analyst could construct a theory of family structure adapted to his needs.

The sociologist must face the problems of human motivation whether he wants to or not. If he does not acquire a genuinely competent theory, he will implicitly adopt a series of *ad hoc* ideas which are no less crucial because they are exempted from critical analysis. Turning to psychoanalysis with the proper adaptations can provide him with a way out of the dilemma. Perhaps the situation is not altogether incomparable in reverse. The analyst is in fact dealing with social systems. His ideas about them have tended to be *ad hoc* and common sense. Such ideas may be adequate for many empirical purposes but tend to break down as subtler levels of generalization by the products of genuinely technical analysis. Originating as they do in another frame of reference, to be useful to the analyst these would have to be adapted to his problems and needs. But can he in the long run do without them any more than the sociologist can do without the insights of psychoanalysis?

READING 9:
NOTES AND REFERENCES

[1] *Cf*. Cannon, Walter B. and Higginson, George: *The Wisdom of the Body;* Second Edition, New York: W. W. Norton & Co., 1939; Freud: *The Ego and the Id*. London: Hogarth Press, 1927.

[2] In extreme instances, the history of social change has tended to be interpreted as the simple consequence of the collective 'acting out' of the emotional tensions observed in personalities.

[3] In essence this is what Max Weber did on a high level in his construction of ideal types of motivation. *Cf*. Parsons, Talcott: Introduction to: *The Theory of Social and Economic Organization* (Sec. 2) by Max Weber. New York: Oxford University Press, 1947.

THE SOCIAL SYSTEM:
THE PATTERN VARIABLES

[...]

THE PATTERN-ALTERNATIVES OF VALUE-ORIENTATION AS DEFINITIONS OF RELATIONAL ROLE-EXPECTATION PATTERNS

The role-partner in a social relationship is a social object. To develop a systematic scheme of points of reference for the analysis of orientations in roles it is then essential first to analyze those basic alternatives of selection which are particularly significant in defining the character of relations to such a good object, and which are constitutive of the character of the relationship pattern itself rather than of its "content" in interest terms, its cultural or motivational aspects in any sense other than as constitutive of relational patterns. In other words the analysis of the differentiation of a social structure must start with the patterns which enter into its relational institutions. The following discussion is posited on the view that there is on a given level of generality a strictly limited and defined set of such alternatives, and that the relative primacies given to choices between them can be treated as constitutive of the patterning of relational institutions.

Reprinted with deletions, with permission from T. Parsons *The Social System*, Macmillan, New York (1951), pp. 58–59, 66–67, 101–112.
© 1951 Talcott Parsons.

It should be made as clear as possible exactly what the following discussion is attempting to do. We are concerned with the patterning of the collectively-integrative sub-type of the moral type of evaluative action-orientation. [. . .] Within this we are concerned with analyzing the structure of an actor's relations to social objects in order to identify the points of reference which define the strategically significant limits of variability of this category of orientations. We will bring out a limited number of such ranges which, in their simplest form, can be defined as polar alternatives of possible orientation-selection. These alternatives will be defined in terms of relative primacies among the types of orientation possibilities which have been discussed in previous sections.

It should again be emphasized that we are here dealing with the foci for the patterning of relational institutions. We are therefore concerned with primacy relations among the possibilities of evaluative action-orientations and the correlative modes of value-orientation, not with the types of interest or with culture-pattern types as such. The first problem then is that of primacy relations as between instrumental, expressive and moral orientations (including the sub-types of the latter). In motivational terms it may be presumed that the "ultimate" interest of any actor is in the optimization of gratification. The most *direct* path to gratification in an organized action system is through expressive orientations; hence relative to the expressive, both the instrumental and the moral modes of orientation impose renunciations or discipline. The social object is always actually and potentially to some degree an object of cathexis.

[. . .]

If the derivation of these five alternative pairs [*which are constitutive of relational patterns,* Ed.] from possibilities of the combination of the basic components of the action system has been correct, if they are in fact all on the same level of generality and are exhaustive of the relevant logical possibilities on that level, they may be held to constitute a system. Then, on the relevant level which, as we shall see is *only one* which needs to be considered, their permutations and combinations should yield a system of types of possible role-expectation patterns, on the relational level, namely defining the pattern of orientation to the actors in the role relationship. This system will consist of thirty-two types, which may in turn be grouped into a smaller number of more fundamental ones. [. . .]

For the convenience of the reader these five concept-pairs, which will be called the *pattern variables* of role-definition, may be schematically outlined as follows:

I. The Gratification-Discipline Dilemma
   Affectivity vs. Affective Neutrality
II. The Private vs. Collective Interest Dilemma
   Self-Orientation vs. Collectivity-Orientation
III The Choice Between Types of Value-Orientation Standard
   Universalism vs. Particularism
IV. The Choice between "Modalities" of the Social Object
   Achievement vs. Ascription
V. The Definition of Scope of Interest in the Object
   Specificity vs. Diffuseness.

That these five pattern variables are focused on the relational aspect of the role structure of the social system does not mean that they are irrelevant to the definition of the patterns of regulative and of cultural institutions. They cannot be, if only because of the element of consistency of pattern which must run throughout a system of value-orientations in a cultural tradition. But for us the system of relational institutions is the core of the social structure and it will facilitate development of the analysis to start from this core and work out from there.

[. . .]

TYPES OF SOCIAL VALUE-ORIENTATION

The main thread of the organization of material of this chapter has been the pattern variables and their context of applicability to the different modes of organization of the components of relational systems. In conclusion we may bring together this material by showing how all five of the variables can be used to set forth a classification of value pattern types defining role-orientations. This is done in Tables 1 and 2. The organization of these tables of classification requires some comment.

When the pattern variables are seen in the context of the general action scheme, they fall into a pattern of mutual interrelations; they do not, that is, simply constitute a list, but they have important systematic interrelations. There is a certain symmetry in the scheme which revolves about an axis which has two primary aspects of significance. This axis is that of the polarity between motivational orientation on the one hand, and cultural orientation on the other. In the presently relevant sense, as will be evident from the above analysis, it is the value-orientation aspect of culture which is of crucial significance here.

This polarity of the reference points of actions systems in general

is reflected on the next level of derivation "down" toward their concrete structure, that is, in the pattern variables, in that two of them
are of particular relevance to one pole of the reference system, two to
the other, and the fifth is, as it were, "neutral" between them. These
relations are diagrammatically represented in Chart I.

TABLE 1
Types of combination of Value-Orientation Components†
Major Social Value-Orientations

	UNIVERSALISM	PARTICULARISM
	A. Universalistic Achievement Pattern	B. Particularistic Achievement Pattern
Achievement	Expectation of active achievement in accord with universalized standards and generalized rules relative to other actors.	Expectation of active achievements relative to and/or on behalf of the particular relational context in which the actor is involved.
	C. Universalistic Ascription Pattern	D. Particularistic Ascription Pattern
Ascription	Expectation of orientation of action to a universalistic norm defined either as an ideal state or as embodied in the status-structure of the existing society.	Expectation of orientation of action to an ascribed status within a given relational context.

The first section of the present chapter built up certain elementary
types of social sub-system from the organization of types of action-
orientation in different relational systems. This analysis started out
from the pole of motivational orientations. It used them, not on the
most elementary level, but on that of organization *with* cultural elements which was called [. . .] evaluative *action* orientation. The two
pattern variables of affectivity-neutrality and specificity-diffuseness
were the ones most directly relevant to that motivational focus and
may be said to be the keynote of value-orientation relevance on that
level. The universalism-particularism variable was then brought in as

†For simplicity the pattern variable of self vs. collectivity orientation is omitted
from these tables. Because of its symmetrical relation to the whole scheme it can
be used to subdivide any cell in the tables.

TABLE 2

Types of Value Orientation Components of Social Role Expectation
Universalism

	AFFECTIVITY	NEUTRALITY
Universalistic Achievement Patterns →		
Specificity	**1** Expectation of specific affective expressions toward a class of objects designated on basis of achievement.	**2** Expection of specific disciplined action in relation to a class of objects designated on basis of achievement.
Achievement		
Diffuseness	**3** Expectation of diffuse affective expression towards class of objects on basis achievement.	**4** Expectation of diffuse disciplined action toward classes objects on basis of achievement.
Specificity	**9** Expectation of specific affective expression toward class of objects on basis of qualities.	**10** Expectation of specific disciplined action toward class of objects on basis of qualities;
Ascription		
Diffuseness	**11** Expectation of diffuse affective expression toward class of objects on basis of qualities.	**12** Expectation of diffuse disciplined action toward class objects on basis of qualities.
Universalistic Ascriptive Patterns →		

introducing further specification into the structuring of these orientations, above all because of its relevance to the primacy of cognitive elements in instrumental orientations, once goals are assumed as given.

This consideration, combined with their relevance to the structure of personality [. . .] justifies putting this pair of variables together. They may, indeed, be considered as the major axes of the organization of action with reference to the needs of personality, that is, in the *first* context of the problems of functional prerequisites of social systems discussed [as] the Hobbesian problem of order. They formulate the necessity of balances in two fundamental respects. On the one hand the actor must have gratifications; without them he can neither subsist nor be adequately motivated for the performance of social roles. On the other hand he must also accept discipline, both in the interest of his own longer run gratification-deprivation balance, and in the social interest, that of his role-performance. Secondly in its psychological reference the specificity-diffuseness variable in the first place formulates

Table 2 – *(Continued)*
Types of Value-Orientation Components of Social Role-Expectation Particularism

AFFECTIVITY	NEUTRALITY	
		Particularistic Achievement ← Patterns
5 Expectation of specific affective expression vis-à-vis a particular object or one in particular relationship on basis of performance.	6 Expectation of specific disciplined action toward an object in particularistic relation to ego on basis of performances.	Specificity
		Achievement
7 Expectation of diffuse affective expression toward object in particularistic relation to ego on basis of performance.	8 Expectation of diffuse disciplined action toward object in particularistic relation to ego on basis of performance.	Diffuseness
13 Expectation of specific affective expression toward object in particularistic relation to ego on basis of qualities.	14 Expectation of specific disciplined action toward object in particularistic relation to ego on basis of qualities.	Specificity
		Ascription
15 Expectation of diffuse affective expression toward object in particularistic relation to ego on basis of qualities.	16 Expectation of diffuse disciplined action toward object in particularistic relation to ego on basis of qualities.	Diffuseness Particularistic Ascriptive ← Patterns

CHART 1

Grouping of Pattern Variables

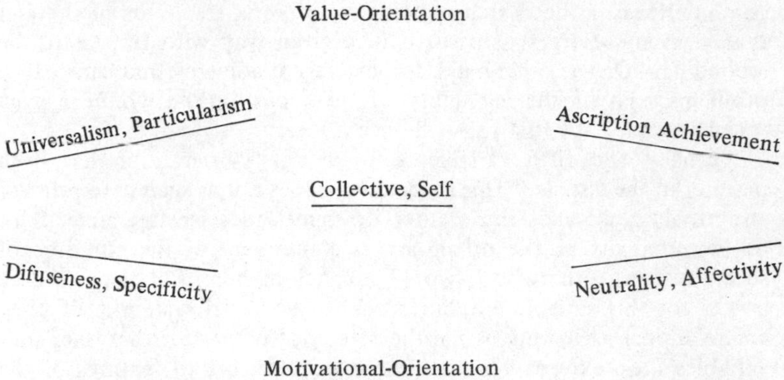

Value-Orientation

Universalism, Particularism

Ascription Achievement

Collective, Self

Difuseness, Specificity

Neutrality, Affectivity

Motivational-Orientation

the significance of diffuse loyalties, but at the same time conversely the necessity of limitations on such loyalties, in the interest of instrumental performances and kinds of gratification which cannot be integrated with attachments. In relation to collectivities solidarity with its diffusion of responsibility to the collectivity, involving diffuseness, is the institutionalized counterpart of loyalty between individuals without institutionalization.

We must keep in mind that we are here dealing with the social system context, not with action in general. Hence these two variables for us concern the mechanisms which mediate between the needs and capacities of the personalities which as actors compose social systems, and the structure of the social systems themselves.

The other pair of variables is universalism-particularism and ascription-achievement. These variables have, by contrast with the other pair, reference to the social system as such. They are concerned, as we have seen, respectively with the type of value-norms which enter into the structure of the social system, and with the ways in which the characteristics of actors as objects of orientation are "taken account of" in the selective processes through which social structures are built up. *Both* pairs of variables are constitutive of the structure of the relational system, otherwise they would not be relevant to the present analysis. But the second pair is concerned more with the social-system pole of functional reference. There is a sense in which the motivational adequacy of a social system to the needs of individuals can be more nearly accounted for in terms of the first pair, ignoring the second. But this is not true of the bases of *structural* differentiation and variability of social systems. In a sense, therefore, the second pair will have primacy for analysis of the variability of social systems as structural types, the combinations of the first pair being, as it were, resultants of the fact that a given society is structured in a given way with respect to the second pair. On the other hand, for analysis of adjustive and personality problems, and of the variability of these phenomena *within* a given social structure, the first pair will have primacy.

Finally the fifth variable, self-collectivity-orientation has been placed "in the middle." This is because it does not as such have primary structural significance, but rather its significance is integrative. It is, to be sure, just as the others are, a component of the structure of social systems, otherwise it would not belong here. But the reference points for this variable are "internal" to the social system itself, they are relational as it were, while the reference points for the other four variables are "external" in the sense of referring to features of the action-components which are logically prior to their organization in social systems.

For these reasons, in Table 1 and 2 the fourfold table of possible combinations of the variables, universalism-particularism and ascription-achievement are given primacy as yielding a classification of four *major* types of *social* value-orientation. Each of the cells of this first part of the table may, however, be regarded not as a single cell but as a summary designation for a "block" of eight cells of the full table which details all the thirty-two possibilities of combination of polar values of the five variables. However, for most purposes of classification of social structure, it seems justified to regard these latter as "sub-types" of the four major types. This point should not, however, be overemphasized. The most important thing is the classification itself, and the possibility of deriving a systematic classification of this sort from the most general considerations of the structure of action and its elaboration in social systems. It constitutes the *fundamental starting point* for a classification of possible types of social structure and eventually of societies. It should, however, be *quite* clear that *as such* it does not constitute such a classification because it includes only the value-orientation element and does not account for the rest of the components of the social system.

A very brief comment on each of the four major types is in order to give the classification some kind of concrete relevance; [. . .] Cell 1, the "Universalistic Achievement Pattern" is best exemplified in the dominant American ethos. The combination of universalism and achievement-orientation puts the primary emphasis on universalistically defined goal-achievement and on the dynamic quality of continuing to achieve particular goals. It does not emphasize a "final" goal-state, which once achieved is to be maintained in perpetuity. The combination of universalism with achievement values puts the primary universalistic accent on process, that is, on means-choice and particular goal-choice, leaving the goal-system fluid. In some such sense the Philosophy of Pragmatism epitomizes this orientation.

When universalism is combined with an ascriptive emphasis in Cell 3 on the other hand, to constitute the "Universalistic Ascriptive Pattern"

TABLE 2 – (*Continued*)
Major Types of Value-Orientation of Personal Attitudes

	AFFECTIVITY	NEUTRALITY
	A. Receptiveness-Responsiveness Attitude	B. Approval Attitude
Specificity	Disposition to be receptive to and respond to alter's attitude of expectation of mutual gratifications within a specific sphere or context.	Disposition to approve alter's action within a specific sphere conditional on his performances in terms of a standard.
	C. Love Attitude	D. Esteem Attitude
Diffuseness	Disposition to be receptive to and to reciprocate a diffuse affective attachment to alter and accept the obligation of loyalty accompanying it.	Disposition to evaluate alter as a total personality relative to a set of standards.

the primary relevance of unrivalistic standards shifts to the validation of the quality-ideal. The focus is on the attainment of an ideal state of affairs, which once attained is considered to be permanently valid. But the universalistic element introduces a factor of strain since, in its main lines, it is scarcely possible to maintain that any status quo of a social system conforms with any sharply defined ideal state. Hence a tendency to a dualism of ideal and real. Broadly the philosophy of "idealism" and the German cultural ideal seem to conform with this pattern.

When we move to Cell 2, the combination of particularism and achievement which is called the "Particularistic Achievement Pattern"

TABLE 2 – (*Continued*)
Types of Value-Orientation Components of Need-Dispositions
(Attitudes) of Personality

Affectivity

	UNIVERSALISM	PARTICULARISM
Receptiveness-Responsiveness Block →		
Ascription	1 Disposition to receive and give specific gratifications vis-à-vis any member of a class of quality-selected objects.	2 Disposition to receive and give specific gratifications in reciprocal relation with a particular object possessing special qualities.
Specificity		
Achievement	3 Disposition to receive and give specific gratifications to any object in a class characterized by a type of performance.	4 Disposition to receive and give specific gratifications in interaction with a particular object on the basis of mutual performances.
Ascription	9 Disposition to love and be loved by any person belonging to a class defined by specified qualities.	4 Disposition to love and be loved by a particular object by virtue of specific qualities.
Diffuseness		
Achievement / Love Block →	11 Disposition to love and be loved by any object conforming to standards of performance.	12 Disposition to love and be loved by a particular object by virtue of its specific permance record or prospects.

there is a great mitigation of this tension between ideal and real, for the focus is no longer on an absolutely ideal state, but on a *given* dynamic relational system. But with the accent on achievement the actor's relation to this is "dynamically" conceived. It is not something which "comes automatically," but which must be achieved, and may, if not enough care is taken, deteriorate and have to be re-achieved. An

TABLE 2 – (*Continued*)
Types of Value-Orientation Components of Need-Disposition
(Attitudes) of Personality

Neutrality

UNIVERSALISM	PARTICULARISM	
		Approval ← Block
5 Disposition to approve and be approved by object possessing or on a basis of specific qualities.	6 Disposition to approve and be approved in reciprocal relation to particular object on basis of specific qualities.	Ascription
		Specificity
7 Disposition to approve and be approved by any of class of objects with specific performance records or capacities.	8 Disposition to approve and be approved in reciprocal relationship with particular object on basis of mutual specific performances.	Achievement
13 Disposition to esteem and want to be esteemed by any object possessed of certain qualities.	14 Disposition to esteem and want to be esteemed by a particular object by virtue of possession of specific qualities.	Ascription
		Diffuseness
15 Disposition to esteem and want to be esteemed by any object conforming to given standards.	16 Disposition to esteem and want to be esteemed by a particular object on basis of given performances or prospects.	Achievement
		Esteem ← Block

excellent example seems to be the Classical Chinese cultural pattern, with its concept of a harmonious order for the maintenance or restoration of which men are held to be responsible. There is truth in the common saying that the Confucian Chinese were above all concerned with morality, namely responsibility for the maintenance of a given social structure as a going concern. But, by contrast with both universalistic types of pattern this is, as Max Weber said, a doctrine of "adaptation *to* the world" not of "mastery *over* the world."

Finally the combination of ascription and particularism yields what may be called the "Particularistic Ascriptive Pattern." Here the order is conceived as given in a more radical sense, in that man is thought of as adapting his action within an order for which he cannot be held responsible. The accent, therefore, is on "making the most" of expressive opportunities, using the social order as a kind of "stage" for the play. The Spanish-American pattern seems to be a close approximation to this type.

One or two interesting relations between these four types may be called to attention. First they involve an order of "tension" which may be put roughly as Cells 3, 1, 2, 4 from high to low. This order is changed, however, when the focus is on responsibility for the social system, as such, that is, the accent is on collectivity-orientation. Here it seems that there are two pairs. Cells 2 and 3 place a strong accent on such responsibility because a *system* as such is in the center of attention. Cells 1 and 4 on the other hand tend to be much more "individualistic" but of very different types in the two cases. In the first case it is a kind of "goal-achievement" individualism which is not bound into a particularistic nexus as in Cell 2, in that the accent on achievement tends to preclude subordinating the achieving unit to a system in any sense, and the ascriptive focus on an absolute ideal is lacking. In the case of cell 4, on the other hand, the individualism has an expressive focus, because it has to take place within a framework treated as given. [. . .]

[. . .]

Next, however, it is essential to place these cultural ideal patterns in their *adaptive* context in relation to the functional problems of social systems. In a very broad way the differentiations between types of social system do correspond to this order of cultural value pattern differentiation, but *only* in a very broad way. Actual social structures are not value-pattern types, but *resultants* of the integration of value-patterns with the other components of the social system.

[. . .]

ILLNESS AND THE ROLE OF THE PHYSICIAN: A SOCIOLOGICAL PERSPECTIVE

The present paper will attempt to discuss certain features of the phenomena of illness, and of the processes of therapy and the role of the
therapist, as aspects of the general social equilibrium of modern Western
society. This is what is meant by the use of the term "a sociological
perspective" in the title. It is naturally a somewhat different perspective
from that usually taken for granted by physicians and others, like
clinical psychologists and social workers, who are directly concerned
with the care of sick people. The are naturally more likely to think in
terms of the simple application of technical knowledge of the etiological
factors in ill health and of their own manipulation of the situation in
the attempt to control these factors. What the present paper can do is
to add something with reference to the social setting in which this
more "technological" point of view fits.

Undoubtedly the biological processes of the organism constitute
one crucial aspect of the determinants of ill health, and their manipulation one primary focus of the therapeutic process. With this aspect of
"organic medicine" we are here only indirectly concerned. However, as

Reprinted, with permission, from *American Journal of Orthopsychiatry*, Vol 2
(1957), pp. 452–460.
†Initially presented at a meeting in 1951.

the development of psychosomatic medicine has so clearly shown, even where most of the sympotomatology is organic, very frequently a critically important psychogenic component is involved. In addition, there are the neuroses and psychoses where the condition itself is defined primarily in "psychological" terms, that is, in terms of the motivated adjustment of the individual in terms of his own personality, and of his relations to others in the social world. It is with this motivated aspect of illness, whether its symptoms be organic or behavioral, that we are concerned. Our fundamental thesis will be that illness to this degree must be considered to be an integral part of what may be called the "motivational economy" of the social system and that, correspondingly, the therapeutic process must also be treated as part of that same motivational balance.

Seen in this perspective illness is to be treated as a special type of what sociologists call "deviant" behavior. By this is meant behavior which is defined in sociological terms as failing in some way to fulfill the institutionally defined expectations of one or more of the roles in which the individual is implicated in the society. Whatever the complexities of the motivational factors which may be involved, the dimension of conformity with versus deviance or alienation from the fulfillment of role expectations is always one crucial dimension of the process. The sick person is, by definition, in some respect disabled from fulfilling normal social obligations, and the motivation of the sick person in being or staying sick has some reference to this fact. Conversely, since being a normally satisfactory member of social groups is always one aspect of health, mental or physical, the therapeutic process must always have as one dimension the restoration of capacity to play social roles in a normal way.

We will deal with these problems under four headings. First something will have to be said about the processes of genesis of illness insofar as it is motivated and thus can be classed as deviant behavior. Secondly, we will say something about the role of the sick person precisely as a social role, and not only a "condition"; third, we will analyze briefly certain aspects of the role of the physician and show their relation to the therapeutic process and finally, fourth, we will say something about the way in which both roles fit into the general equilibrium of the social system.

Insofar as illness is a motivated phenomenon, the sociologist is particularly concerned with the ways in which certain features of the individual's relations to others have played a part in the process of its genesis. These factors are never isolated; there are, the constitutional and organically significant environmental factors (e.g., bacterial agents), and undoubtedly also psychological factors internal to the individual personality. But evidence is overwhelming as to the enormous importance of relations to others in the development and functioning of personality. The sociologist's emphasis, then, is on the factors responsible for "something's going wrong" in a person's relationships to others during the processes of social interaction. Probably the most significant of these processes are those of childhood, and centering in relations to family members, especially, of course, the parents. But the essential phenomena are involved throughout the life cycle.

Something going wrong in this sense may be said in general to consist in the imposition of a strain on the individual, a strain with which, given his resources, he is unable successfully to cope. A combination of contributions from psychopathology, learning theory and sociology makes it possible for us to say a good deal, both about what kinds of circumstances in interpersonal relations are most likely to impose potentially pathogenic strains, and about what the nature of the reactions to such strains is likely to be.

Very briefly we may say that the pathogenic strains center at two main points. The first concerns what psychiatrists often call the "support" a person receives from those surrounding him. Essentially this may be defined as his acceptance as a full-fledged member of the group, in the appropriate role. For the child this means, first of all, acceptance by the family. The individual is emotionally "wanted" and within considerable limits this attitude is not conditional on the details of his behavior. The second aspect concerns the upholding of the value patterns which are constitutive of the group, which may be only a dyadic relationship of two persons, but is usually a more extensive group. Thus rejection, the seducibility of the other, particularly the more responsible, members of the group in contravention of the group norms, the evasion by these members of responsibility for the enforcement of norms, and, finally, the compulsive "legalistic" enforcement of them are the primary sources of strain in social relationships. It is unfortunately not possible to take space here to elaborate further on these very important problems.

Reactions to such strains are, in their main outline, relatively familiar to students of mental pathology. The most important may be enumerated as anxiety, production of fantasies, hostile impulses and the resort to special mechanisms of defense. In general we may say that the most serious problem with reference to social relationships concerns the handling of hostile impulses. If the strain is not adequately coped with in such ways as to reduce anxiety to manageable levels, the result will, we believe, be the generating of ambivalent motivational structures. Here, because intrinsically incompatible motivations are involved, there must be resort to special mechanisms of defense and adjustment. Attitudes towards others thereby acquire the special property of compulsiveness because of the need to defend against the repressed element of the motivational structure. The ambivalent structure may work out in either of two main directions: first, by the repression of the hostile side, there develops a compulsive need to conform with expectations and retain the favorable attitudes of the objects; second, by dominance of the hostile side, compulsive alienation from expectations of conformity and from the object results.

The presence of such compulsive motivation inevitably distorts the attitudes of an individual in his social relationships. This means that it imposes strains upon those with whom he interacts. In general it may be suggested that most pathological motivation arises out of vicious circles of deepening ambivalence. An individual, say a child, is subjected to such strain by the compulsive motivation of adults. As a defense against this he himself develops a complementary pattern of compulsive motivation, and the two continue, unless the process is checked, to "work on each other." In this connection it may be especially noted that some patterns of what has been called compulsive conformity are not readily defined as deviant in the larger social group. Such people may in a sense be often regarded as "carriers" of mental pathology in that, though themselves not explicitly deviant, either in the form of illness or otherwise, by their effects on others they contribute to the genesis of the kinds of personality structure which are likely to break down into illness or other forms of deviance.

Two important conclusions seem to be justified from these considerations. The first is that the types of strain on persons which we have discussed are disorganizing both to personalities and to social relationships. Personal disorganization and social disorganization are, in a considerable part, two sides of the same concrete process. This obviously has very important implications both for psychiatry and for social science. Secondly, illness as a form of deviant behavior is not a unique phenomenon, but one type in a wider category. It is one of a set of alternatives which are open to the individual. There are, of course, reasons why some persons will have a psychological make-up which is more predisposed toward illness, and others toward one or other of the alternatives; but there is a considerable element of fluidity, and the selection among such alternatives may be a function of a number of variables. This fact is of the greatest importance when it is seen that the role of the sick person is a socially structured and in a sense institutionalized role.

The alternatives to illness may be such as to be open only to the isolated individual, as in the case of the individual criminal or the hobo. They may also involve the formation of deviant groups as in the case of the delinquent gang. Or, finally, they may involve a group information which includes asserting a claim to legitimacy in terms of the value system of the society, as in joining an exotic religious sect. Thus to be a criminal is in general to be a social outcast, but in general we define religious devoutness as "a good thing" so that the same order of conflict with society that is involved in the criminal case may not be involved in the religious case. There are many complex and important problems concerning the genesis and significance of these various deviant patterns, and their relations to each other, which cannot be gone into here. The most essential point is to see that illness is one pattern among a family of such alternatives, and that the fundamental motivational ingredients of illness are not peculiar to it, but are of more general significance.

We may now turn to our second main topic, that of the sense in which illness is not merely a "condition" but also a social role. The essential criteria of a social role concern the attitudes both of the incumbent and of others with whom he interacts, in relation to a set of social norms defining expectations of appropriate or proper behavior for persons in that role. In this respect we may distinguish four main features of the "sick role" in our society.

The first of these is the exemption of the sick person from the performance of certain of his normal social obligations. Thus, to take a very simple case, "Johnny has a fever, he ought not to go to school today." This exemption and the decision as to when it does not apply should not be taken for granted. Psychiatrists are sufficiently familiar with the motivational significance of the "secondary gain" of the mentally ill to realize that conscious malingering is not the only problem of the abuse of the privileges of being sick. In short, the sick person's claim to exception must be socially defined and validated. Not every case of "just not feeling like working" can be accepted as such a valid claim.

Secondly, the sick person is, in a very specific sense, also exempted from a certain type of responsibility for his own state. This is what is ordinarily meant by saying that he is in a "condition." He will either have to get well spontaneously or to "be cured" by having something done to him. He cannot reasonably be expected to "pull himself together" by a mere act of will, and thus to decide to be all right. He may have been responsible for getting himself into such a state, as by careless exposure to accident or infection, but even then he is not responsible for the process of getting well, except in a peripheral sense.

This exemption from obligations and from a certain kind of responsibility, however, is given at a price. The third aspect of the sick role is the partial character of its legitimation, hence the deprivation of a claim to full legitimacy. To be sick, that is, is to be in a state which is socially defined as undesirable, to be gotten out of as expeditiously as possible. No one is given the privileges of being sick any longer than necessary but only so long as he "can't help it." The sick person is thereby isolated, and by his deviant pattern is deprived of a claim to appeal to others.

Finally, fourth, being sick is also defined, except for the mildest cases, as being "in need of help." Moreover, the type of help which is needed is presumptively defined; it is that of persons specially qualified to care for illness, above all, of physicians. Thus from being defined as the incumbent of a role relative to people who are not sick, the sick person makes the transition to the additional role of patient. He thereby, as in all social roles, incurs certain obligations, especially that of "cooperating" with his physician − or other therapist − in the process of trying to get well. This obviously constitutes an affirmation of the admission of being sick, and therefore in an undesirable state, and also exposes the individual to specific reintegrative influences.

It is important to realize that in all these four respects, the phenomena of mental pathology have been assimilated to a role pattern which was already well established in our society before the development of modern psychopathology. In some respects it is peculiar to modern. Western society, particularly perhaps with respect to the kinds of help which a patient is felt to need; in many societies magical manipulation have been the most prominent elements in treatment.

In our society, with reference to the severer cases at any rate, the definition of the mental "case" as sick has had to compete with a somewhat different role definition, namely, that as "insane." The primary difference would seem to center on the concept of responsibility and the mode and extent of its application. The insane person is, we may say, defined as being in a state where not only can he not be held responsible for getting out of his condition by an act of will, but where he is held not to be responsible in his usual dealings with others and therefore not responsible for recognition of his own condition, its disabilities and his need for help. This conception of lack of responsibility leads to the justification of coercion of the insane, as by commitment to a hospital. The relations between the two role definitions raise important problems which cannot be gone into here.

It may be worth while just to mention another complication which is of special interest, namely, the situation involved when the sick person is a child. Here, because of the role of child, certain features of the role of sick adult must be altered, particularly with respect to the levels of responsibility which can be imputed to the child. This brings the role of the mentally sick child in certain respects closer to that of the insane than, particularly, of the neurotic adult. Above all it means that third parties, notably parents, must play a particularly important part in the situation. It is common for pediatricians, when they refer to "my patient," often to mean the mother rather than the sick child. There is a very real sense in which the child psychiatrist must actively treat the parents and not merely the child himself.

We may now turn to our third major problem area, that of the social role of the therapist and its relation to the motivational processes involved in reversing the pathogenic processes. These processes are, it is widely recognized, in a certain sense definable as the obverse of those involved in pathogenesis, with due allowance for certain complicating factors. There seem to be four main conditions of successful psychotherapy which can be briefly discussed.

The first of these is what psychiatrists generally refer to as "support." By this is here meant essentially that acceptance as a member of a social group the lack of which we argued above played a crucial part in pathogenesis. In this instance it is, above all, the solidary group formed by the therapist and his patient in which the therapist assumes the obligation to do everything he can within reason to "help" his patient. The strong emphasis in the "ideology" of the medical profession on the "welfare of the patient" as the first obligation of the physician is closely related to this factor. The insistence that the professional role must be immune from "commercialism," with its suggestion that maximizing profits is a legitimate goal, symbolizes the attitude. Support in this sense is, so long as the relationship subsists, to be interpreted as essentially unconditional, in that within wide limits it will not be shaken by what the patient does. As we shall see, this does not, however, mean that it is unlimited, in the sense that the therapist is obligated to "do anything the patient wants."

The second element is a special permissiveness to express wishes and fantasies which would ordinarily not be permitted expression in normal social relationships, as within the family. This permissiveness must mean that the normal sanctions for such expression in the form of disapproval and the like are suspended. There are of course definite limits on "acting out." In general the permissiveness is confined to verbal and gestural levels, but this is nonetheless an essential feature of the therapeutic process.

The obverse of permissiveness, however, is a very important restriction on the therapist's reaction to it. In general, that is, the therapist does not reciprocate the expectations which are expressed, explicitly or implicitly, in the patient's deviant wishes and fantasies. The most fundamental wishes, we may presume, involve reciprocal interaction between the individual and others. The expression of a wish is in fact an invitation to the other to reciprocate in the complementary role, if it is a deviant wish, an attempt to "seduce" him into reciprocation. This is true of negative as well as positive attitudes. The expression of hostility to the therapist in transference is only a partial gratification of the wish; full gratification would require reciprocation by the therapist's becoming angry in return. Sometimes this occurs; it is what is called "countertransference"; but it is quite clear that the therapist is expected to control his countertransference impulses and that such control is in general a condition of successful therapy. By showing the patient the projective character of this transference reaction, this refusal to reciprocate plays an essential part in facilitating the attainment of insight by the patient.

Finally, fourth, over against the unconditional element of support, there is the conditional manipulation of sanctions by the therapist. The therapist's giving and withholding of approval is of critical importance to the patient. This seems to be an essential condition of the effectiveness of interpretations. The acceptance of an interpretation by the patient demonstrates his capacity, to the relevant extent, to discuss matters on a mature plane with the therapist, who shows his approval of this performance. It is probably significant that overt disapproval is seldom used in therapy, but certainly the withholding of positive approval is very significant.

The above four conditions of successful psychotherapy, it is important to observe, are all to some degree "built into" the role which the therapist in our society typically assumes, that of the physician, and all to some degree are aspects of behaviour in that role which are at least partially independent of any conscious or explicit theory or technique of psychotherapy.

The relation of support to the definition of the physician's role as primarily oriented to the welfare of the patient has already been noted. The element of permissiveness has its roots in the general social acceptance that "allowances" should be made for sick people, not only in that they may have physical disabilities, but that they are in various ways "emotionally" disturbed. The physician, by virtue of his special responsibility for the care of the sick, has a special obligation to make such allowances. Third, however, the physician is, by the definition of his role, positively enjoined not to enter into certain reciprocities with his patients, or he is protected against the pressures which they exert upon him. Thus giving of confidential information is, in ordinary relationships, a symbol of reciprocal intimacy, but the physician does not tell about his own private affairs. Many features of the physician-patient relationship, such as the physician's access to the body, might arouse erotic reactions, but the role is defined so as to inhibit such developments even if they are initiated by the patient. In general the definition of the physician's role as specifically limited to concern with matters of health, and the injunction to observe an "impersonal," matter-of-fact atitude without personal emotional involvement, serve to justify and legitimize his refusal to reciprocate his patient's deviant expectations. Finally, the prestige of the physician's scientific training, his reputation for technical competence, give authority to his approval, a basis for the acceptance of his interpretations.

All of these fundamental features of the role of the physician are given independently of the technical operations of psychotherapy; indeed they were institutionalized long before the days of Freud or of psychiatry as an important branch of the medical profession. This fact is of the very first importance.

First, it strongly suggests that in fact deliberate, conscious psychotherapy is only part of the process. Indeed, the effective utilization of these aspects of the physician's role is a prominent part of what has long been called the "art of medicine." It is highly probable that, whether or not the physician knows it or wishes it, in practicing medicine skillfully he is always in fact exerting a psychotherapeutic effect on his patients. Furthermore, there is every reason to believe that, even though the cases are not explicitly "mental" cases, this is necessary. This is, first, because a "psychic factor" is present in a very large proportion of ostensibly somatic cases and, secondly, apart from any psychic factor in the etiology, because illness is always to some degree a situation of strain to the patient, and mechanisms for coping with his reactions to that strain are hence necessary, if the strain is not to have psychopathological consequences. The essential continuity between the art of medicine and deliberate psychotherapy is, therefore, deeply rooted in the nature of the physician's function generally. Modern psychotherapy has been built upon the role of the physician as this was already established in the social structure of Western society. It has utilized the existing role pattern, and extended and refined certain of its features, but the roles of the physician and of the sick person were not created as an application of the theories of psychiatrists.

The second major implication is that, if these features of the role of the physician and of illness are built into the structure of society independent of the application of theories of psychopathology, it would be very strange indeed if they turned out to be isolated phenomena, confined in their significance to this one context. This is particularly true if, as we have given reason to believe, illness is not an isolated phenomenon, but one of a set of alternative modes of expression for a common fund of motivational reaction to strain in the social system. But with proper allowances for very important differences we can show that certain of these same features can also be found in other roles in the social system. Thus to take an example of special interest to you, there are many resemblances between the psychotherapeutic process and that of the normal socialization of the child. The differences are, however, great. They are partly related to the fact that a child apparently needs two parents while a neurotic person can get along with only one psychiatrist. But also in the institutions of leadership, of the settlement of conflicts in society and of many others, many of the same factors are operative.

We therefore suggest that the processes which are visible in the actual technical work of psychotherapy resemble, in their relation to the total balance of forces operating within and upon the individual, the part of the iceberg which protrudes above the surface of the water; what is below the surface is the larger and, in certain respects, probably still the more important part.

It also shows that the phenomena of physical and mental illness and their counteraction are more intimately connected with the general equilibrium of the social system than is generally supposed. We may close with one rather general inference from this generalization. It is rather generally supposed that there has been a considerable increase in the incidence of mental illness within the last generation or so. This is difficult to prove since statistics are notably fragmentary and fashions of diagnosis and treatment have greatly changed. But granting the fact, what would be its meaning? It could be that it was simply an index of generally increasing social disorganization. But this is not necessarily the case. There are certain positive functions in the role of illness from the social point of view. The sick person is isolated from influence upon others. His condition is declared to be undesirable and he is placed in the way of reequilibrating influences. It is altogether possible that an increase in mental illness may constitute a diversion of tendencies to deviance from other channels of expression into the role of illness, with consequences less dangerous to the stability of society than certain alternatives might be. In any case the physician is not merely the person responsible for the care of a special class of "problem cases." He stands at a strategic point in the general balance of forces in the society of which he is a part.

Reading 12

ECONOMY AND SOCIETY:
THE ECONOMY AS A SOCIAL SYSTEM

In the last chapter we took two steps toward demonstrating our principal thesis that economic theory is a special case of the general theory of social systems. (1) We attempted to show logical parallels between the categories of the general theory of social interaction and some central economic concepts. We chose three examples: the supply-demand schema is an instance of the performance-sanction paradigm, the goods-services classification as a case of the distinctions between physical and social objects and between qualities and performances, and the similar sociological and economic conceptions of the mutual advantage in exchange. (2) We introduced the general concept of *social system* and showed that the concept of an economy — as defined by Harrod, for instance — can be treated as a social system. [1] Specifically, the economy can be regarded first as meeting the *adaptive* exigencies of the society as a whole by means of the production of utility, and second as having goal-attainment, adaptive, integrative and pattern-maintenance exigencies of its own. In the latter connection we suggested treating the factors of production and shares of income as classes of input into and

Reprinted with deletions, with permission, from T. Parsons and N. Smelser *Economy and Society* (1956), pp. 39–51, Macmillan, New York.

output from the economy, respectively, corresponding to the four fundamental system problems. Furthermore, we noted that the economic distinction between real and monetary cost refers to evaluations of inputs into the economy, first from the standpoint of the society and second from that of the economy. And finally, we tried to make clear, though without extensive development, that the ways in which the conception of the economy as a social system can be spelled out empirically depend on variations in the concrete structures of different societies, on their levels of general social differentiation and the more specific ways in which the economy is conceived to fit with the other aspects of the total society.

Now we must further develop the theme of the economy as a social system and its relation to its situation — including the rest of society. Then we should be able to relate the general theory of social interaction not only to frames of reference and concepts of economic theory, but more importantly, to some central dynamic propositions of economic theory. [. . .] we will incorporate some propositions about the general nature of social systems without providing full justifications for them here.

As we have noted, a social system tends to differentiate with respect to all four of the basic functional dimensions. Before we discuss these dimensions extensively, we must clarify the special status of the economy's value pattern and the processes of pattern maintenance. One aspect of the value pattern concerns the modes in which it is incorporated into *institutions*, the primary function of which is to regulate certain classes of activity. This is what we mean by "institutionalized" value patterns. We will inquire into the institutional structure of the economy in some detail in the next chapter, when we examine the institutions which govern most closely the exchanges between the economy and the other sectors of society.

But another context in which the institutionalization of value patterns is important for the economy *as a system* concerns the economy's own pattern-maintenance exigencies. For the economy the most important implication of the institutionalization of its value pattern is a relatively stable pattern of *control* over the "rent factors" in the productive process. This means that (1) on the cultural and social levels a given "state of the arts" and organization of the social system in non-economic respects, (2) on the physical level a given supply of physical resources, and (3) on the motivational level of a given set of commitments to productive functions are given (within limits) independently of changes in the current level and patterns of sanctions (prices).

These "givens" are a society's *economic commitments*. From a sociological point of view these commitments reflect the direct implications of the societal value system for the performance of the adaptive or economic function. On the one hand, they specify the relative importance of economic production compared to other social system goals; on the other hand, they imply the segregation of certain of the society's resources for economic production.†

To say that these social commitments are in a certain sense "given" is not to say that they operate without the mediation of "mechanisms." In the utilization of rent factors, however, the mechanisms operating are of a *different* character from those operating in the other boundary processes of the economy. This proposition is a special statement of the sociological principle that "pattern-maintenance" functions are in some sense qualitatively different from other performance-sanction interaction systems. The difference in the economic case lies in the segregation of these commitments from the operation of ordinary price mechanisms, i.e., the insulation of supply from fluctuations of demand. This is what the term "commitment" implies. At the same time, once the commitment is made, the specific allocation of the "given" elements within the economy *does* become an integral part of ordinary economic processes. This system of economic commitments is, therefore, *interdependent* with the differentiated sub-systems of the economy.

These institutionalized value commitments guarantee the availability of a certain quota of resources for economic production. In this way, however, only the pattern-maintenance exigencies of the economy are met. As a system, it still faces goal-attainment, adaptive and integrative exigencies. As we have defined it, the *goal* of the economy is to provide goods and services for consumption. If the wants relative to these goods and services were quantitatively and qualitatively stable, and if the conditions of production were completely determined by the above "givens," then production processes could be completely routinized. Production would be a function of two sets of "givens": the commitments on the resource side, and the schedules of wants. Once an allocation of resources relative to the wants had been established, there would be no need for *economic* analysis. [2]

But in fact both the state of demand and conditions of production change continuously, and adjustments must be made within the limits

† These resources include, of course, the physical, cultural and organizational components we have mentioned; they also include that aspect of concrete labour services which Marshall referred to as involving the "science of activities" as distinguished from that of "wants."

left open by the institutionalized commitments. Relative to the body of given commitments, therefore, a set of processes in the economy differentiates in order to accommodate specific expected consumers' demand for particular quantities of particular goods and services. This differentiated aspect of the economy — which includes sales and distribution — is the "production" sub-system in a narrower sense. Within this sub-system the *goal* of the economy is implemented. This implementation involves continuous mutual adjustment between changing states of demand and changing processes of production. The latter depend partly upon the demand conditions, but partly upon changes originating in the conditions of production themselves.

Next, the *adaptive* specialization of the economy concerns the allocation of consumable resources between ultimate consumption and further productive use. It is impossible to assume that from the point of view of the economy this allocation will automatically be stable. Specialization therefore develops in this area of investment for productive purposes; the distinctive exigency to be adapted to is the need for procurement of capital funds.

Finally, the area of *integration* of the economy itself is inherently stable. New opportunities arise, and changes in the situation force internal changes. Hence there is specialization in the adjustment of the organization of the factors of production. The entrepreneur is the specialist in this area.

These four — economic commitments, production-distribution, provision of capital, and entrepreneurship — are the primary *functional* bases of differentiation of the economy as a system. They are schematically represented in Figure 1. [. . .]

By themselves, these functional bases are not adequate to account for the *concrete structure* — the firms, banks, plants, etc. — of the economy. For this purpose we must consider, besides the value system and the functional bases, at least two other sets of exigencies: (1) adaptive exigencies to which concrete units in the economy are subjected; (2) integrative exigencies, or the consequences of the fact that the economy must be integrated on an institutional level, both within itself and with the non-economic sub-systems of the society. The second set is the subject-matter for the next chapter. We will discuss the first set briefly here.

The adaptive exigencies confronting concrete economic structures may be classified according to our four-problem scheme: (1) in connection with the land factors — physical, cultural, and motivational commitments — certain non-economic conditions operate as adaptive exigencies; (2) in connection with the economy's production sub-system, conditions governing labour supply and demand for consumption goods are adaptive exigencies; (3) at the capital boundary non-economic conditions of capital supply and various political regulations upon capitalization are exigencies; and (4) in the case of the entrepreneurial function, the conditions on which entrepreneurial service is available to the economy and the forms of the "profit motive" among actual and potential entrepreneurs are adaptive exigencies.

Exigencies such as these, in manifold combination, account for the modes and levels of *segmentation* of the economy, i.e., its division into *concrete* units of organization such as firms and the aggregation of firms to form industries. They are also relevant to the relation between size of firm and form of business organization, problems of

Figure 1

FUNCTIONAL DIFFERENTIATION OF
THE ECONOMY AS A SYSTEM

A		G
Capitalization and Investment Sub-system.	Production Sub-system— including Distribution and Sales.	
Economic Commitments: Physical, Cultural and Motivational Resources.	Organizational Sub-system: Entrepreneurial Function.	
L		I

location of industry, and similar questions.

We may distinguish two main aspects of these adaptive exigencies. The first is *technological and ecological,* referring to supply and location of natural resources, size and geographical distribution of the population, etc., in relation to the technical problems of organizing production. The second aspect is *socio-cultural*, which deals with non-economic aspects of the social system and its culture. Under this heading are many elements of the motivation to productive work, consumers' wants, attitudes toward risk, control of economic enterprise, definition of the entrepreneurial and managerial roles, etc.

The differentiation of the economy by industries derives primarily from one complex of these exigencies. On the sociocultural side is the specific composition of consumers' wants; on the technological side are the requirements for materials and labour for the process of production itself.

Segmentation into firms and plant units involves other combinations of the exigencies. Within the determinants of any particular firm or plant, we may isolate three sets of conditions: (1) Market conditions at the consumers' end — the market or markets for the particular products, actual want structure and purchasing power of consumers, accessibility of markets, retail outlets, etc. (2) Market conditions at the producers' end — access to materials, labour supply, capital funds, etc. (3) Complex social exigencies in the actual organization of production — the technological conditions determining the economies of scale, the conditions of the organization of labour and its effective supervision, etc.

The productive organization, e.g., a plant, is a *concrete* social system in itself. Its *goal* is defined by its place in the economy, but it is not only an economic entity. It has a political system with loyalties and institutionalized authority; it is subject to internal integrative exigencies like any other social system, and it must have its own institutionalized values and cultural tradition. Therefore, the general type of analysis by means of which we treat the economy as a social system can be repeated on the appropriate levels for each of its concrete units. [3] It goes almost without saying that at these levels the most important ranges of variation in concrete forms of economic organization are found. The economic historian and the student of comparative problems must therefore devote particularly intensive attention to this problem area.

The concrete structure of the economy thus presents many challenges for sociological analysis. It is not, however, possible to develop them here. What follows is confined to the primary *functional* differentiation within the economy and between the economy and other social sub-systems. This differentiation is closely related to what we have called boundary processes. We have referred to these processes in connection with the classifications of the factors of production and the shares of income, but we have not yet examined the boundaries from all sides. That is to say, we have not attempted a direct analysis of the *structure of the situation* in which the economy functions. We must now turn to this task.

THE FUNCTIONAL DIFFERENTIATION OF SOCIETY

As we have pointed out repeatedly, the economy is a subsystem of a larger system — the society; furthermore, the economy is differentiated from other sub-systems on a primary-function level. These other subsystems are the most essential part of the situation in which the economy functions. [. . .] A theory of social systems is abstract in its own right; when this is applied to the relations between the economy and other social systems, reasoning becomes compounded in its complexity. We feel it worth while to generalize these relations as far as possible, however, both to develop general theory and to provide the reader with the widest possible scope fo interpreting our subsequent analyses.

Any social system must, as a condition of equilibrium, reach a relatively satisfactory solution of the four basic system problems. Maximization with respect to all four — and probably any two — at once is possible. Put in a slightly different way, the social system is subject to these four dimensions as primary functional exigencies.

[. . .]

Our most general proposition is that total societies *tend* to differentiate into sub-systems (social structures) which are specialized in each of the four primary functions. Where concrete structures cannot be identified. as is often the case, it is still often possible to isolate types of processes which are thus specialized.

The economy is the primary sub-system specialized in relation to the *adaptive* function of a society. If this proposition is correct, three other cognate sub-systems in a differentiated society should correspond to the other three functional problems. The sub-system goal of each of the three should be defined as a primary *contribution* to the appropriate functional need of the total society. For instance, the goal of the economy is the production of income which is at the disposal of the society. In these terms, the other three societal sub-systems cognate with the economy are: (1) a goal-attainment sub-system, (2) an integrative sub-system, and (3) a pattern-maintenance and tension-management sub-system — all three of which possess the characteristics of social systems. Let us discuss each in turn.

The goal-attainment sub-system focuses on the political (in a broader sense) functions in a society. Since these functions are not coterminous with the governmental structure, it seems appropriate to term this sub-sector the "polity," parallel with the economy. The goal of the economy, as we have noted, is to *produce* generalized facilities, as means to an indefinite number of possible uses. The important feature of this production is not only the quantity of such facilities (in a "physical" sense), but their *generalizability,* i.e., their adaptability to these various uses. The goal of the polity, however, is the *mobilization* of the necessary prerequisites for the *attainment* of given system goals of the society. Wealth is *one* of the indispensable prerequisites, but as we shall see, there are other equally important ones.

To put it in a slightly different way, the goal of the polity is to maximize the capacity of the society to attain its system goals, i.e., collective goals. We define this capacity as *power* as distinguished from wealth. We will discuss wealth as an ingredient of power presently; suffice it to say that the use of wealth for collective goals means a sacrifice of the *general* disposability of wealth, and hence its availability for other sub-systems than the polity.

The polity is related to government in approximately the same way that the economy is to "business." The analytical system does not coincide with concrete organization but political goals and values tend to have primacy over others in an organ of government, much the same as economic goals and values tend to have primacy in a business organization.

For present purposes we will not analyse the internal differentiation of the polity or of the other two remaining systems. We will specify only those functions in each of these three sub-systems which impinge directly on the economy. It is possible, however, to analyse the internal differentiation of the polity, the integrative sub-system and the pattern-maintenance sub-system in much the same way as we have analysed the economy above. [. . .]

The integrative sub-system of the society relates the cultural value-patterns to the motivational structures of individual actors in order that the larger social system can function without undue internal conflict and other failures of co-ordination. These processes maintain the institutionalization of value patterns which define the main structural outline of the society in the first instance. Sociologists refer to specialized integrative mechanisms primarily as mechanisms of social control [4].

The integrative system of the society is the "producer" of another generalized capacity to control behaviour analogous to wealth and power. Some sociologists, notably Durkheim, refer to his capacity as "solidarity." [5] Wealth, therefore, is a generalized capacity to command goods and services, either as facilities or as reward objects for any goal or interest at any level in society. Power is the generalized capacity to mobilize the resources of the society, including wealth and other ingredients such as loyalties, "political responsibility," etc. to attain particular and more or less immediate collective goals of the system. Correspondingly, solidarity is the generalized capacity of agencies in the society to "bring into line" the behaviour of system units in accordance with the integrative needs of the system, to check or reverse disruptive tendencies to deviant behaviour, and to promote the conditions of harmonious co-operation.

Wealth or income is an output of the economy *to* other subsystems of the society. Thus only in a secondary sense should we describe an economy as "wealthy";the appropriate adjective is "productive." The *society* is wealthy or not wealthy. Similarly, a polity is not powerful, but a society is. The polity is more or less effective in the "production of power." Finally, the society has a high level of solidarity, but the integrative sub-system itself does not. The integrative system "contributes" solidarity to the social system. In the case of all three, "factors" analogous to the factors of production combine to produce the appropriate output or contribution; similarly, the output itself is distributed by shares among the different sub-systems of the society.

The pattern-maintenance and tension-management sub-system stands relative to the society as the land complex stands relative to the economy. At the societal level, this sub-system focuses on the institutionalized culture, which in turn centres on patterns of value orientations. [6] Such patterns are relevant to all social action. For any system, however, they are most nearly constant and relatively independent of the urgency of immediate goal needs the exigencies of adaptive and integrative problems imposed on the system.

This relative constancy and insulation from exigencies does not mean that pattern maintenance occurs "automatically," i.e., without mechanisms. On the contrary, such patterns are institutionalized only through organization of potentially very unstable elements (in the process of socialization), and to be successful this organization requires complex "maintenance operations."

Pattern maintenance and tension management differ from the integrative problem in the sense that they focus on the *unit* of the system, not the system itself. Integration is the problem of *inter*unit relationships, pattern maintenance of *intra*unit states and processes. Of course such a distinction depends on the degree of differentiation between system units. In the present context the distinction raises questions of the importance of the differentiation of the economy from other subsystems in any given case. The differentiation is very clear in the modern industrial case. Hence it is essential to discriminate between the processes by which the basic economic commitments are *maintained* and the processes by which the boundary relations between the economy and other social sub-systems are *adjusted*. To take a specific case, a sharp fall in production occasioned by a deficit in consumer spending (a Keynesian depression) differs vastly from a fall occasioned by a breakdown in the fundamental motivation to work productively. In the latter case "pump-priming" measures are irrelevant; it is a problem of maintaining patterns of value.

The functioning of a unit in an interaction system ultimately depends on the motivation of the individual actors participating in the unit. The "tension-management" aspect of the pattern-maintenance sub-system concerns this motivation. The primary adaptive exigencies *of this sub-system* lie on those personality elements which maintain adequate motivation to conform the cultural values. The tension which is managed is individual motivation, in actual or potential conflict with the fulfilment of behaviour expectations in institutionally defined roles. Unless controlled or managed, such tension disorganizes the relevant unit and thereby interferes with its functioning in the system.

The pattern-maintenance sub-system also has a type of "product" or contribution of generalized significance throughout the total social system. This is a type of "respect" accorded as rewards for conformity with a set of values. In cases when degrees of this respect are compared to others, we might call it *prestige*. Prestige, therefore, is the "product" of successful pattern maintenance or tension management in the interest of pattern conformity; it is a *capacity* to act in such a way as to implement the relevant system of institutionalized values.

The exact mechanisms of tension management and pattern maintenance vary from system to system. The primary function of the latency sub-system is always relative to a given superordinate system reference. It defines the conditions of stability of the units of this superordinate system, whatever the units happen to be. But the units themselves, at the next level down in an analytical breakdown, have the properties of systems. The definition of the conditions of stability therefore depend empirically on the system level in question.

READING 12:
NOTES AND REFERENCES

[1] We do not wish to claim that the conception of the economy as a social system is entirely original with us. The closest approaches to it will probably be found in the Marx, Sombart, Weber line of continental European students of "capitalism." The first two of these writers do not, we feel, adequately distinguish economy and polity especially with reference to the problems we will treat below in connection with the input of capital as a factor of production. Weber probably came closest to our conception of any previous writer, especially in his clear distinction between "economic action" and

"economically relevant action," the former belonging to the economy as a system, the latter not (cf. Weber, *Theory of Social and Economic Organization,* Chap. II, Sec. 1; see also 1st German Edition, Pt. II, Chap. I, pp. 181—183). He defines an economy (*Wirtschaft*) as "an autocephalous system of economic action." It is, we believe, much more difficult to find precursors of this view in the English-language literature though we think at times Marshall came close to it. It seems likely that this possibility of theoretical development has been mainly blocked by the (often implicit) assumptions of utilitarian individualism which we criticized in the last chapter.

[2] An approximation to such a state of affairs does, in fact, exist in highly traditional "underdeveloped" economies; this is the primary reason why economic theory is not very helpful in the study of such cases. See, for instance, Firth, R., *Primitive Polynesian Economy,* 1939.

[3] Perhaps the most extensive recent analysis of the factors in the adaptive structuring of the units of the economy is found in P. Sargant Florence, *The Logic of British and American Industry,* 1953;

[4] Cf. Parsons, *The Social System,* Chap. VII.

[5] Another term is "cohesion."

[6] For the general theoretical background, cf. *Toward a General Theory of Action, The Social System,* and *Working Papers in the Theory of Action.*

Part Four

The Parsons³ Phase

In the final stages of his theoretical development, Parsons's interests were increasingly focused on the *cybernetic* notion of a hierarchy of control determining the relationships among action systems. The cybernetic analogy is used to describe relations within the whole range of action systems — organism, personality, social system, and culture — and is focused on description of a set of *generalized media of interchange* which include money, power, influence, intelligence and affect. The first two selections represent an early (1961) and a late (1975) stage in the specification of the key elements of this last stage in Parsons's elaboration of action theory.

The extract from *Death in the Western World* (1978) represents Parsons's concerns with a final elaboration of action theory to the consideration of those systems which constitute the *environment* of action — at one level, the sources of cultural values themselves beyond the cultural system, and at a more basic level, the physico-medical system which represents the final, bottom level of energic conditions in the hierarchy of control.

Reading 13

A PARADIGM FOR THE ANALYSIS
OF SOCIAL SYSTEMS

[...]

Let us now turn to a more detailed discussion of our conception of a social system. First, the concept of interpenetration implies that, however important *logical* closure may be as a theoretical ideal, *empirically* social systems are conceived as *open* systems, engaged in complicated processes of interchange with environing systems include, in this case, cultural and personality systems, the behavioral and other subsystems of the organism, and, through the organism, the physical environment. The same logic applies internally to social systems, conceived as differentiated and segmented into a plurality of subsystems, each of which must be treated analytically as an open system interchanging with environing subsystems of the large system.

The concept of an open system interchanging with environing systems also implies *boundaries* and their maintenance. When a set of interdependent phenomena shows sufficiently definite patterning and stability over time, then we can say that it has a "structure" and that it is fruitful to treat it as a "system." A boundary means simply that a theoretically and empirically significant difference between structures

Reprinted with deletions, with permission, from T. Parsons (*et al.*) (Eds.), *Theories of Society*, The Free Press, Glencoe (1961), pp. 36–41.

and processes internal to the system and those external to it exists and tends to be maintained. In so far as boundaries in this sense do not exist, it is not possible to identify a set of interdependent phenomena as a system; it is merged in some other, more extensive system. It is thus important to distinguish a set of phenomena not meant to constitute a system in the theoretically relevant sense — e.g., a certain type of statistical sample of a population — from a true system.

Structural and Functional Modes of Analysis. Besides identifying a system in terms of its patterns and boundaries, a social system can and should be analyzed in terms of three logically independent — i.e., cross-cutting — but also interdependent, bases or axes of variability, or as they may be called, bases of selective abstraction.

The first of these is best defined in relation to the distinction between "structural" and "functional" references for analysis. However relative these two concepts may be, the distinction between them is highly important. The concept of structure focuses on those elements of the patterning of the system which may be regarded as independent of the lower-amplitude and shorter time-range fluctuations in the relation of the system to its external situation. It thus designates the features of the system which can, in certain strategic respects, be treated as constants over certain ranges of variation in the behavior of other significant elements of the theoretical problem.

Thus, in a broad sense, the American Constitution has remained a stable reference point over a period of more than a century and a half. During this time, of course, the structure of American society has changed very greatly in certain respects; there have been changes in legal terms, through legislation, through legal interpretations, and through more informal processes. But the federal state, the division between legislative and executive branches of government, the independent judiciary, the separation of church and state, the basic rights of personal liberty, of assembly, and of property, and a variety of other features have for most purposes remained constant.

The functional reference, on the other hand, diverges from the structural in the "dynamic" direction. Its primary theoretical significance is integrative; functional considerations relate to the problem of *mediation* between two fundamental sets of exigencies: those imposed by the relative constancy or "givenness" of a structure, and those imposed by the givenness of the environing situation external to the system. Since only in a theoretically limiting case can these two be assumed to stand in a constant relation to each other, there will necessarily exist a system of dynamic processes and mechanisms.

Concepts like "structure" and "function" can be considered as either concrete or analytical. Our present concern is with their analytical meaning; we wish to state in a preliminary way a fundamental proposition about the structure of social systems that will be enlarged upon later — namely, that their structure as treated within the frame of reference of action *consists* in institutionalized patterns of normative culture. It consists in components of the organisms or personalities of the participating individuals only so far as these "interpenetrate" with the social and cultural systems, i.e., are "internalized" in the personality and organism of the individual. I shall presently discuss the problem of classifying the elements of normative culture that enter into the structure of social systems.

The functional categories of social systems concern, then, those features in terms of which systematically ordered modes of adjustment operate in the changing relations between a given set of patterns of institutionally established structure in the system and a given set of properties of the relevant environing systems. Historically, the most common model on which this relationship has been based is that of the behaving organism, as used in psychological thinking. From this point of view, the functional problem is that of analyzing the mechanisms which make orderly response to environmental conditions possible. When using this model in analyzing social systems, however, we treat not only the environment but the structure of the system as problematical and subject to change, in a sense which goes farther than the traditional behavior psychologist has been accustomed to go.

In interpreting this position, one should remember that the immediately environing systems of a social system are not those of the physical environment. They are, rather, the other primary subsystems of the general system of action — i.e., the personalities of its individual members, the behaviorally organized aspects of the organisms underlying those personalities, and the relevant cultural systems in so far as they are not fully institutionalized in the social system but involve components other than "normative patterns of culture" that are institutionalized.

"Dynamic" Modes of Analysis. The importance of the second basis or axis of empirical variability, and hence of theoretical problem formulation, follows directly. A fundamental distinction must be made between two orders of "dynamic" problems relative to a given system. The first of these concerns the processes which go on under the assumption that the structural patterns of institutionalized culture are given, i.e., are assumed to remain constant. This is the area of problems of *equilibrium* as that concept has been used by Pareto, Henderson, and others, and of homeostasis as used by Cannon. The significance of

such problems is directly connected with both the concept of system and the ways in which we have defined the relation between structure and function.

The concept of equilibrium is a fundamental reference point for analyzing the processes by which a system either comes to terms with the exigencies imposed by a *changing* environment, without essential change in its own structure, or fails to come to terms and undergoes other processes, such as structural change, dissolution as a boundary-maintaining system (analogous to biological death for the organism), or the consolidation of some impairment leading to the establishment of secondary structures of a "pathological" character. Theoretically, the concept of equilibrium has a normative reference in only one sense. Since the structure of social systems consists in institutionalized normative culture, the "maintenance" of these normative patterns is a basic reference point for analyzing the equilibrium of the system. However, whether this maintenance actually occurs or not, and in what measure, is entirely an empirical question. Furthermore, "disequilibrium" may lead to structural change which from a higher-order normative point of view, is desirable.

The second set of dynamic problems concerns processes involving change in the structure of the system itself. This involves, above all, problems of interchange with the cultural system, however much these may in turn depend upon the internal state of the social system and its relations to other environing systems. Leaving distinctions within the category of internal adjustive processes aside for the moment, one can say that, with respect to its external interchanges, problems of equilibrium for the social system involve primarily its relations to its individual members as personalities and organisms, and, through these, to the physical environment. Problems of structural change, on the other hand, primarily involve its relations to the cultural systems affecting its patterns of institutionalized normative culture.

However fundamental the distinction between dynamic problems which do and do not involve structural change may be, the great importance of an intermediate or mixed case should be emphasized. This is the problem of change involving the structure of subsystems of the social system, but not the over-all structural pattern. The most important case in this category is that of processes of structural differentiation. Structural differentiation involves genuine *reorganization* of the system and, therefore, fundamental structural change of various subsystems and their relations to each other. Its analysis therefore presents problems of structural change for the relevant subsystems, but not in the same sense for the system as a whole. The problems involved concern the organization of the structural components of social systems, particularly the hierarchical order in which they are placed. Further discussion will have to await clarification of these problems.

The Hierarchy of Relations of Control. The third of the three essential axes of theoretical analysis may be defined as concerning a hierarchy of relations of control. The development of theory in the past generation in both the biological and the behavioral sciences has revealed the primary source of the difficulty underlying the prominent reductionism of so much earlier thought. This was the reductionist tendency to ignore the importance of the ways in which the organization of living systems involved structures and mechanisms that operated as agencies of control — in the cybernetic sense of control — of their metabolic and behavioral processes. The concept of the "behavioral organism" put forward above is that of a cybernetic system located mainly in the central nervous system, which operates through several intermediary mechanisms to control the metabolic processes of the organism and the behavioral use of its physical facilities, such as the motions of limbs.

The basic subsystems of the general system of action constitute a hierarchical series of such agencies of control of the behavior of individuals or organisms. The behavioral organism is the point of articulation of the system of action with the anatomical-physiological features of the physical organism and is its point of contact with the physical environment. The personality system is, in turn, a system of control over the behavioral organism; the social system, over the personalities of its participating members; and the cultural system, a system of control relative to social systems.

It may help if we illustrate the nature of this type of hierarchical relationship by discussing the sense in which the social system "controls" the personality. There are two main empirical points at which this control operates, though the principles involved are the same in both cases. First, the situation in which any given individual acts is, far more than any other set of factors, composed of *other* individuals, not discretely but in ordered sets of relationship to the individual in point. Hence, as the source of his principal facilities of action and of his principal rewards and deprivations, the concrete social system exercises a powerful control over the action of any concrete, adult individual. However, the *patterning* of the motivational system in terms of which he faces this situation also depends upon the social system, because his own personality *structure* has been shaped through the internalization of systems of social objects and of the patterns of institutionalized culture. This point, it should be made clear, is independent of the sense in which individuals are concretely autonomous or creative rather than "passive" or "conforming," for individuality and creativity are, to a considerable extent phenomena of the institutionalization of expectations. The social system which controls the personality is here conceived analytically, not concretely. [. . .]

Control Relations within the Social System. The same basic principle of cybernetic hierarchy that applies to the relations between general subsystems of action applies again *within* each of them, notably the social systems, which is of primary concern here. The principle of the order of cybernetic priority, combined with primacy of relevance to the different boundary-interchange exigencies of the system, will be used as the fundamental basis for classifying the components of social systems. The relevance of this hierarchy applies, of course, to all the components distinguished according to the first of our three ranges of variation, to structures, functions, mechanisms, and categories of input and output.

The most strategic starting point for explaining this basic set of classifications is the category of functions, the link between the structural and the dynamic aspects of the system. I have suggested that it is possible to reduce the essential functional imperatives of any system of action, and hence of any social system, to four, which I have called pattern-maintenance, integration, goal-attainment, and adaptation. These are listed in order of significance from the point of view of cybernetic control of action processes in the system type under consideration.

The Function of Pattern-Maintenance. The function of pattern-maintenance refers to the imperative of maintaining the stability of the patterns of institutionalized culture defining the structure of the system. There are two distinct apsects of this functional imperative. The first concerns the character of the normative pattern itself; the second concerns its state of "institutionalization." From the point of view of the individual participant in a social system, this may be called his motivational *commitment* to act in accordance with certain normative patterns; this, as we shall see, involves their "internalization" in the structure of his personality.

Accordingly, the focus of pattern-maintenance lies in the structural category of *values*, which will be discussed presently. In this connection, the essential function is maintenance, at the cultural level, of the stability of institutionalized values through the processes which articulate values with the belief system, namely, religious beliefs, ideology, and the like. Values, of course, are subject to change, but whether the empirical tendency be toward stability or not, the potentialities of disruption from this source are very great, and it is essential to look for mechanisms that tend to protect such order — even if it is orderliness in the process of change.

The second aspect of this control function concerns the motivational commitment of the individual — elsewhere called "tension-management." A very central problem is that of the mechanisms of socialization of the individual, i.e., of the processes by which the values of the society are internalized in his personality. But even when values have become internalized, the commitments involved are subject to different kinds of strain. Much insight has recently been gained about the ways in which such mechanisms as ritual, various types of expressive symbolism, the arts, and indeed recreation, operate in this connection. Durkheim's analysis of the functions of religious ritual may be said to constitute the main point of departure here.

Pattern-maintenance in this sense plays a part in the theory of social systems, as of other systems of action, comparable to that of the concept of inertia in mechanics. It serves as the most fundamental reference point to which the analysis of other, more variable factors can be related. Properly conceived and used, it does not imply the empirical predominance of stability over change. However, when we say that, because of this set of functional exigencies, social systems show a *tendency* to maintain their structural patterns, we say essentially two things. First, we provide a reference point for the orderly analysis of a whole range of problems of variation which can be treated as arising from sources *other* than processes of structural change in the system, including, in the latter concept, its dissolution. Second, we make it clear that when we do analyze structural change we are dealing with a different kind of theoretical problem than that involved in equilibration. Hence, there is a direct relation between the function of pattern-maintenance — as distinguished from the other three functional imperatives — and the distinction between problems of equilibrium analysis, on the one hand, and the analysis of structural change on the other. The distinction between these two types of problems comes to focus at this point in the paradigm.

The Function of Goal-Attainment. For purposes of exposition it seems best to abandon the order of control set forth above and to concentrate next upon the function of goal-attainment and its relation to adaptation. In contrast to the constancy of institutionalized cultural patterns, we have emphasized the variability of a system's relation to its situation. The functions of goal-attainment and adaptation concern the structures, mechanisms, and processes involved in this relation.

We have compared pattern-maintenance with inertia as used in the theory of mechanics. Goal-attainment then becomes a "problem" in so far as there arises some discrepancy between the inertial tendencies of the system and its "needs" resulting from interchange with the situation. Such needs necessarily arise because the internal system and the environing ones cannot be expected to follow immediately the changing patterns of process. A goal is therefore defined in terms of equilibrium. It is a directional change that tends to reduce the discrepancy between the needs of the system, with respect to input-output interchange, and the conditions in the environing systems that bear upon the "fulfilment" of such needs. Goal-attainment or goal-orientation is thus, by contrast with pattern-maintenance, essentially tied to a specific situation.

A social system with only one goal, defined in relation to a generically crucial situational problem, is conceivable. Most often, however, the situation is complex, with many goals and problems. In such a case two further considerations must be taken into account. First, to protect the integrity of the system, the several goals must be arranged in some scale of relative urgency, a scale sufficiently flexible to allow for variations in the situation. For any complex system, therefore, it is necessary to speak of a system of goals rather than of a single unitary goal, a system, however, which must have some balance between integration as a system and flexible adjustment to changing pressures.

For the social system as such, the focus of its goal-orientation lies in its relation as a system to the personalities of the participating individuals. It concerns, therefore, not commitment to the values of the society, but motivation to contribute what is necessary for the functioning of the system; these "contributions" vary according to particular exigencies. For example, considering American society, one may suggest that, given the main system of values, there has been in the cold-war period a major problem of motivating large sectors of the population to the level of national effort required to sustain a position of world leadership in a very unstable and rapidly changing situation. I would interpret much of the sense of frustration expressed in isolationism and McCarthyism as manifestations of the strains resulting from this problem. [1]

The Function of Adaptation. The second consequence of plurality of goals, however, concerns the difference between the functions of goal-attainment and adaptation. When there is only one goal, the problem of evaluating the usefulness of facilities is narrowed down to their relevance to attaining this particular goal. With a plurality of goals, however, the problem of "cost" arises. That is, the same scarce facilities will have *alternative* uses within the system of goals, and hence their use for one purpose means sacrificing the gains that would have been derived from their use for another It is on this basis that an analytical distinction must be made between the function of effective goal-attainment and that of providing disposable facilities independent of their relevance to any particular goal The adaptive function is defined as the provision of such facilities.

Just as their is a pluralism of lower order more concrete goals there is also a pluralism of relatively concrete facilities Hence there is a parallel problem of the organization of such facilities in a system. The primary criterion is the provision of flexibility, so far as this is compatible with effectiveness; for the system this means a maximum of generalized disposability in the processes of allocation between alter native uses Within the complex type of social system this disposability of facilities crystallizes about the institutionalization of money and markets. More generally, at the macroscopic social-system level, the function of goal-attainment is the focus of the political organization of societies while that of adaptation is the focus of economic organization. [2]

The most important kinds of facilities involve control of physical objects, access to the services of human agents and certain cultural elements. For their mechanisms of control to be at all highly generalized, particular units of such resources must be "alienable," i.e., not bound to specific uses through ascription. The market system is thus a primary focus of the society's organization for adaptation. Comparable features operate in less differentiated societies, and in more differentiated subsystems where markets do not penetrate, such as the family. [3]

Within a given system, goal-attainment is a more important control than adaptation. Facilities subserve the attainment of goals, not vice-versa — though of course the provision or "production" of facilities may itself be a goal, with a place within the more general system of goals. There are, however, complications in the implications of this statement.

The Function of Integration. The last of the four functional imperatives of a system of action — in our case, a social system — is that of integration. In the control hierarchy, this stands between the functions of pattern-maintenance and goal-attainment. Our recognition of the significance of integration implies that all systems, except for a limiting case, are differentiated and segmented into relatively independent units, i.e., must be treated as boundary-maintaining systems within an environment of other systems, which in this case are other subsystems of the same, more inclusive system. The functional problem of integration concerns the mutual adjustments of these "units" or subsystems from the point of view of their "contributions" to the effective functioning of the system as a whole. This, in turn, concerns their relation to the pattern-maintenance problem, as well as to the external situation through processes of goal-attainment and adaptation.

In a highly differentiated society, the primary focus of the integrative function is found in its system of legal norms and the agencies associated with its management, notably the courts and the legal profession. Legal norms at this level, rather than that of a supreme constitution, govern the *allocation* of rights and obligations, of facilities and rewards, between different units of the complex system; such norms facilitate internal adjustments compatible with the stability of the value system or its orderly change, as well as with adaptation to the shifting demands of the external situation. The institutionalization of money and power are primarily integrative phenomena, like other mechanisms of social control in the narrower sense. These problems will be further discussed in later sections of this essay.

For any given type of system — here, the social — the integrative function is the focus of its most distinctive properties and processes. We contend, therefore, that the problems focusing about the integrative functions of social systems constitute the central core of the concerns of sociological theory.

READING 13:
NOTES AND REFERENCES

[1] Cf. the paper, Parsons, "McCarthyism and American Social Tension," *Yale Review*, Winter, 1955. Reprinted as Chap. 7, *Structure and Process in Modern Societies*, Glencoe: The Free Press, 1960.

[2] It should be noted that the above formulation of the function of adaptation carefully avoids any implication that "passive" adjustment is the keynote of adaptation. Adaptation is relative to the values and goals of the system. "Good adaptation" may consist either in passive acceptance of conditions with a minimization of risk or in active mastery of conditions. The inclusion of active mastery in the concept of adaptation is one of the most important tendencies of recent developments in biological theory. An important relation between the two functional categories of goal-attainment and adaptation and the old categories of ends and means should be noted. The basic discrimination of ends and means may be said to be the special case, for the personality system, of the more general discrimination of the functions of goal-attainment and adaptation. In attempting to squeeze analysis of social behaviour into this framework, utilitarian theory was guilty both of narrow-

ing it to the personality case (above all, denying the independent analytical significance of social systems) and of overlooking the independent significance of the functions of pattern-maintenance and of integration of social systems themselves.

[3] The importance of adaptive flexibility for the functioning of families as systems is well illustrated in the study of Robert Angell, *The Family Encounters the Depression* (New York: Chas. Scribner's Sons, 1936).

SOCIAL STRUCTURE AND THE SYMBOLIC MEDIA OF INTERCHANGE

In response to Peter Blau's invitation to me to participate in this major symposium on the theory of social structure, it seemed to me that it would be appropriate to take as a subtopic within that field an outline of a development which has been of very great importance to me and a few other associates for a number of years now. This is the analysis of what we have been calling generalized symbolic media of interchange as components of social systems and other systems of action.

THE PROPERTIES OF MEDIA

For me, the primary model was money, [1] but another which has been conspicuous in recent years and has recently been much further studied by Victor Lidz, [2] is language. There has, however, been a tendency to treat each of these phenomena as unique in itself and not related to other phenomena in the action system. This postulate of the uniqueness of money on the one side, language on the other, is one of

Reprinted with permission of Macmillan Publishing Co., Inc., from *Approaches to the Study of Social Structure*, edited by Peter M. Blau (New York: The Free Press, 1975), pp. 94–120. Copyright © 1975 by The Free Press, A Division of Macmillan Publishing Co., Inc. Reprinted also with permission of Open Books Publishing Ltd., London the traditions which some of us have been challenging. Our attempt has been to treat each of them as members of a much more extensive family of media. So far we have explored intensively the family, which is anchored in the social system, where, in addition to money, we have dealt at some length with political power, influence, and value-commitments as such media. [3] We have also extended the analysis to the level of a general system of action where the anchor concept has been intelligence, unconventionally conceived not as a trait of personality but as a generalized medium. We have tentatively worked out a four-fold scheme for the general action level. We have also made beginnings with respect to the personality of the individual, but this is only the beginning and will need much further work.

The foundations of this development lay in two major steps of my own theoretical development, specifically, of the four-function scheme. Its first version was published in *Working Papers in the Theory of Action,* [4] in which I collaborated with Robert Bales and Edward Shils. The second, somewhat later foundation was the substantially revised version of my views of the relation of economic and sociological theory which was published in the small book *Economy and Society,* [5] in collaboration with Neil Smelser. Subsequent to these works, however, the development of the idea of generalized media took a few years. The first venture beyond money was the analysis of the concept of political power [6] and the second was the concept of influence. [7] It was in connection with the latter that I first encountered James Coleman in this context, when at the meeting of the Association for Public Opinion Research at which I presented my paper he was one of the main commentators. [8]

With respect to money, three of its functions which were clearly stated by the classical economists relatively early in the last century stood out as salient. Money, that is to say, was (1) a medium of exchange which had value in exchange, but in the pure type case, no value in use. (2) Money functioned as a measure of value, as they put it, in that it makes goods and services and factors of production, which in other respects such as physical properties are incomparably heterogeneous, comparable in terms of an economic measure, that of utility. And (3) money served as a store of value in that if it were accepted in exchange for possession of concrete commodities or access to concrete services, apart from phenomena of inflation, retaining possession of money does not lead to loss over time; on the contrary, it leads to gain in the form of interest.

The endeavour in extending the theoretical model of money as medium to other media was to match these traits with cases which, though formally similar, had a different content. The first criterion or property of a medium was the symbolic character which was stated by the classical economists for money in the proposition that it had value in exchange, but not value in use. Such a criterion applies to linguistic symbols, e.g., the word "dog," though signifying a species of mammalian quadruped, can neither bark nor bite, though the concrete dog can do both. Under this general rubric of symbolic character, we have stressed four further properties of such a medium as money. First comes *institutionalization*, especially in relation to property. We thus held such a medium to be characterized by a state of institutionalization, one aspect of which for the case of money is its backing by governmental authority through the status that is technically called legal tender. In the case of power this criterion led us to focus on what Weber [9] calls legitimate use of power as distinguished from a Hobbesian capacity to gain one's ends through having "what it takes," [10] Money can, of course, be used illegitimately through such channels as political bribery, and similarly power and influence can be used illegitimately; but these are special cases rather than constitutive criteria of the phenomena.

Second, there must be *specificity* of meaning and efficaciousness in both evaluation and interchange. As we put it in the case of money, it is the medium which can operate in economic exchanges, but many other interchange relations among humans cannot be mediated by money.

The third property may be called *circulability*. Money, like possession of commodities, changes hands. Any other medium should be subject to transfer of control from one acting unit to another in some kind of interchange transactions.

A fourth property, which proved of particular importance in bringing political power within this context, was the contention that a medium *could not have a zero-sum character* attributed to it in all contexts. Most political scientists dealing with political power had either explicitly stated or tacitly assumed that it was a zero-sum phenomenon, that is, that an increase in the amount of power held by one group in a system *ipso facto* entailed a corresponding decrease in the amount held by others. [11] This patently was not the case with money because of the phenomenon — well known to economists — of credit creation. And we went to considerable trouble to show that it need not be assumed to be a characteristic of power systems. [12]

THE INSTITUTIONAL CONTEXTS OF MEDIA

It is an exceedingly important point that the theoretical articulation of social system media with the social structure should be conceived at what I should call the institutional, precisely as distinguished from the collective, level. Unfortunately, sociological terminology has almost from the beginning tended to confuse the two. We speak of organizations and other collectivities as institutions, (not McGill University or the Université de Montreal), but we also speak of property, contract, and authority as institutions. In the collective sense, of course, the concept of membership in an institution makes sense; in the latter context, membership is simply nonsensical — one simply cannot speak of being a member of the institution of property. Institutions in the latter sense, the one relevant here, are complexes of normative rules and principles which, either through law or other mechanisms of social control, serve to regulate social action and relationships — of course, with varying degrees of success. Each medium then is conceived to be articulated in a functionally defined institutional complex.

For the economic case, it would seem that the central institution is that of property. The underlying concept of property rights centers on rights of possession, which in turn can be broken down into disposal-acquisition, control, and use. In legal history there has been endless discussion and analysis of the nature of property. The objects of rights of possession are broadly classifiable into the three categories of (1) commodities of physical objects; (2) services, that is, human performances evaluated as having utility in the economic sense; and (3) financially significant assets where the economic value is abstracted from any particular characteristics in other respects, such as corporate or government securities, bank accounts, or insurance policies, all of which constitute rights to money payments under specifiable conditions.

The other principal economic institutions are occupation and contract. I conceive occupation essentially to be the institutionalized rubric under which rights to services as an output of the economic process, as distinguished from goods or commodities, are, as rights, transferable from performers to recipients. Seen in this context, a commodity is a physical object of output, possession in which can be transferred without the involvement of human agency beyond the settlement of terms; whereas services require that the performer stand in continuing relation to the recipient throughout the duration of the process.

We think it exceedingly important to make a distinction between services and their occupational organization as categories of economic output on the one hand and labor as a factor of production in the sense of economic theory on the other hand. Labor becomes service only when it has been combined with the other factors of production, and thereby its value has been added to.

Contract we conceive to be the primary integrative reference of the institutionalization of the economic complex. It is the institutional nexus which defines the conditions of legitimate exchange and possession in a sociological as distinguished from either a specifically economic or legal context. I would consider Durkheim [13] to be the preeminent sociological theorist of the nature of contract.

Other media, of course, function in complexes of institutional norms which are different from those of primarily economic significance. In the political context the paramount institutional complex is what we call authority. This may be defined as the legitimized capacity to make and to contribute to the implementation of decisions which are binding on a specifiable collective unit or class of them, where the holder of authority has some kind of right of speaking in the name of the collectivity. A typical case is that of a duly legitimized official of a unit of government. The principal modes of institutionalization under authority are the familiar executive, legislative, and judicial categories.

Even within the restricted framework outlined so far, it can, I think, be seen that the conception of generalized media and their articulation with structural components at the institutional level introduces an element of dynamic into the analysis of social relationships and processes. The broadest formula is that, in sufficiently highly differentiated systems of interchange, the principal processes, whether they be those of equilibration or of structural change, are mediated by the interchange of media for intrinsic outputs and factors and conversely of intrinsically significant outputs and factors for media. In this process the media provide or perform regulatory and integrative functions in that the rules governing their use define certain areas of legitimacy and the limits of such areas within which extension of systems of transaction can develop and proliferate. The introduction of a theory of media into a kind of structural perspective I have in mind goes far, it seems to me, to refute the frequent allegations that this type of structural analysis is inherently plagued with a static bias, which makes it impossible to do justice to dynamic problems. Let me, then, again insist that under the category of dynamic I mean to include both equilibrating processes and processes of structural change.

Having reviewed certain features of money as a medium and its institutionalization, let us now say something about the first major extension beyond money which we undertook, namely fitting a revised concept of political power into the idea of media of interchange. This was substantially more difficult than the analysis of money because in the latter case we were aided by the fact that the economic theorists have handed us a monetary concept which, with certain adaptations, could be treated as ready-made for sociological purposes. As I have noted, this has not been the case for the concept of political power, most conspicuously owing to the explicit or implicit assumption of a zero-sum condition. There are, however, also certain other difficulties. One of the most important of them has been the lack of specificity of the concept of power. This goes back to the great tradition of Hobbes, which most political theorists have follwed, as have such sociologists as Max Weber. Hobbes' [14] famous definition will be remembered: "The power of a man . . . is his present means to obtain some future apparent good." Power, this is to say, is *any* capacity for an acting unit in a social system to "get what it wants," as Weber [15] said, with or without opposition, in a nexus of social relationships. By this definition, money clearly is a form of power, as also are influence and a number of other entities.

A theoretically satisfactory solution of this problem proved difficult, but I think it was finally arrived at. Two essential features of this solution are its collective reference and its rooting of power in legitimacy. It is first our contention that the concept of political power should be used essentially in a collective context to designate capacities to act effectively with reference to the affairs of a collective system, not necessarily of government. The Hobbesian version of individualism, to talk about relations among individuals independent of their collective affiliations, has been one source of lack of specificity.

The second essential ingredient is the concept of *bindingness*. [16] This bindingness definitely rests on a conception of legitimacy. That is, people who have power have legitimated rights to make and implement collectively binding decisions. The role of coercion can be dealt with from this point of view in that coercive sanctions are important in the follow-up of binding decisions. The most general formula is that in the case of a decision which is politically binding in the present sense, noncompliance on the part of those to whom it applies will in general evoke coercive sanctions. Physical force is not so much the prototype of such sanctions as the limiting case whereby the symbolic elements of social interaction are reduced to a minimum in favor of measures which either compel or strongly motivate to submission independent of questions of legitimacy.

It is assumed throughout this analysis that the category "political" is analytically defined and not the label for a concrete set of phenomena. In this respect it is parallel to that of "economic," which deals, at a technical theoretical level, with an analytically defined set of aspects of concrete behavior, and not, except secondarily, with a concrete type of behavior. Thus, to cite an example, Chester Barnard's famous book

The Functions of the Executive [17] deals overwhelmingly with action in business firms. This, however, does not make it a theoretical treatise in economics; I would consider it one of the classics of political theory. The firm as collectivity, that is to say, performs political functions in the analytical sense, even though, since it is a firm, these functions are subordinated to economic organization, purposes, and goals — in Barnard's case, the purveying of telephone service under the imperative of financial solvency and profit.

Before leaving the subject of political power, a few further words should be said about the zero-sum problem in that context. As I mentioned, there was a particularly sharp difference of opinion between economic theorists dealing in the monetary area and political theorists dealing in that of power to the effect that, of course, money was not subject to zero-sum conditions, whereas power almost "of course" was. This dichotomy did not seem to make sense, and I think the claim can be made that the issue has been resolved, at least in principle, in favor of the economic non-zero-sum model, as generalizable to the power case. [18] The essential question seems to me to be whether there are processes, and what they are, by which power, as defined, can be newly introduced into a power system without a corresponding diminution of the power in the hands of other elements.

In the case of money the classical instance is the creation of new money in the form of credit by banks. This is to say that bankers lend funds which are the property of their depositors to borrowers on terms that involve an inherent risk to the depositors' financial interest but are nonetheless both legally legitimized and relatively safe under "ordinary" circumstances. There is a fundamental asymmetry in the relations of a bank to its depositors, on the one hand, and its borrowers, on the other. Depositors are entitled to the return of their deposits in full on demand; the bank, however, makes loans which are not payable before the expiration of the stated terms of the loans. In a certain technical sense, therefore, any normally operating bank is inherently "insolvent," but entering this condition of insolvency is a condition of its being an economically productive institution in a sense other than being only a custodian of deposited funds.

We would contend that the — or one — political analogue of the banking function in the lending context is to be found in that of political leadership. Political leadership will make promises, fulfillment of which is dependent on the implied consent of the constituencies of the political leaders who have given them a grant of power under institutionalized authority, most obviously in cases of election to office. Once in office, however, such power holders may introduce extended plans which can be implemented only through new political power. As in the case of bank loans regarded as funds for investment, it is expected that they will pay off over time, but any immediate stringency which calls for immediate repayment can ordinarily not be met. Essentially, what this type of leadership is doing in our opinion is to use its fiduciary position to extend credit to politically significant enterprises which are not at the time of these decisions in a position to present complete pay-off in political effectiveness. We think that this is a process which is rather strictly analogous to that of credit creation on the part of bank executives.

In the case of credit creation through the legal bindingness of loan contracts, power is mobilized in support of economic investment. similarly in the case of power creation, the influence of leadership may be mobilized in support of the expansion of power. In both cases this support comes from calling on the medium next higher in the cybernetic order. It need not, however, follow that *only* this next higher medium is involved in such cases. it seems more likely that various cybernetically higher forces, in combinations that vary from case to case, are mobilized in such a way that the total effect is "funnelled" through the next higher medium.

The next step beyond establishing, in what seemed to us to be a relatively satisfactory theoretical manner, a status of the concept of political power as a symbolic medium, was to explore the possibilities of finding still other members of the family of media anchored in social system functions. The obvious focus of this next step concerned a medium which was primarily anchored in integrative functions of the system. This led into a complex set of ramifications of considerations of sociological theory. The paths were even less clearly marked than in the case of political power. An index of this indeterminancy was the fact that there was no obvious single term such as power, to say nothing of that of money. We, however, thought that the use of the concept influence in much sociopolitical discussion made it worth exploring as a possible symbolic label appropriate to this particular context. [19] As the crucial differentiating criterion between power and influence, we took that of collective bindingness in the one case and its absence in the other. The essential problem was what was going on in the context of a unit or class of units trying to get something of collective significance "done," and what, if anything, was the difference between the two cases. In the case of power we used the criterion of the bindingness of their decisions on the collectivity as a whole as the primary criterion. If, however, they were using influence, their decisions and recommendations would not in this sense be binding, that is, noncompliance with them would not result in coercive sanctions. We have treated influence as a medium of *persuasion*.

Persuasion here should be regarded as only a partially adequate term. The place assigned to it in the sanction paradigm [20] is to our mind clearly justified by the contrast with the relevance of the two categories of negative sanctions, namely, deterrence and activation of commitments.

The mode of persuasion that is particularly relevant for influence entails invoking collectively relevant *justifications* of the course of action recommended by the agent of influence. This in general invokes considerations of *collective* interest transcending those of the particular units involved and usually includes the call to what is at some level defined as a matter of moral obligation.

There are a number of different contexts of social interaction in which this problem could be worked through. One that has turned out to be particularly important to me and my colleagues is that of the performance of professional services, which for us came to a head in the medical world. When, however, such a term as "doctor's orders" is used, it clearly is not binding on the patient to comply with those orders at the penalty of some kind of coercive negative sanctions. The penalty will probably be health disadvantages to the patient, but he can make his own decision without exposing himself to "punishment" for noncompliance, that is, punishment administered by the physician or by some collective agency of health care which he represents. Thus a heart attack is not imposed by the medical profession on patients who disregard warnings about overexertion.

At the same time, it was difficult to clarify the implications of the fundamental distinction about media that influence should not be interpreted to be a matter of conveying specific information but rather of using a position of prestige which might be based, among other things, on specialized knowledge and experience, to persuade objects of interaction, in the medical case patients, that it was in their interest and that of the relevant collective groups to accept what was often called the "advice" of a physician. [21] The costs of such non-acceptance, however, would be assumed directly by the patient and not imposed through the means of coercive sanction. We came to feel that influence in this sense is a deeply important mode of the regulation of communication in systems where neither economic interests nor politically binding considerations are paramount.

A particularly significant empirical finding came in some of the work on academic systems in which I have participated. [22] We felt that we were able to make a pretty clear discrimination between positions or the components predominantly involving power in our technical sense and involving influence within the academic context. For example, in an as yet fragmentarily published study of academic roles, we used the question whether the respondent would prefer to function as a department chairman or as an influential senior member of the department. [23] We found our respondents, on the whole, highly sensitive to this distinction and, especially at the institutions of higher prestige, a substantial majority preferred to be influential members of their departments. We thought we could draw the line between the fact that the chairman, by virtue of his office, exercises certain capacities to make power decisions binding on the department and that fact that an influential member cannot do this except through the collective process of departmental decision-making through voting or "persuading" the chairman and other colleagues. We suggest, therefore, that independently of specific expertise, which, after all, cannot be generalized in a highly differentiated system, persons occupying positions of prestige in the system could function effectively to persuade their colleagues and the collectivity without having coercive sanctions at their disposal.

Parallel to property and authority we conceive prestige to be the primary institutional category focussing on the integrative system, or societal community. It operates primarily under the legitimation of the value-pattern of solidarity, similar to utility in the economic sphere and collective effectiveness in the political.

Under the authorization of relative prestige, then, we postulate the institutionalization of capacity, through influence, to mobilize commitments of units to what we have called valued association, and to regulate the interplay between political support and identification through membership in (plural) solidary involvements.

INTELLIGENCE AND AFFECT

The roster of primary media anchored in the social system is conceived to consist of the three that have been briefly discussed, namely, money, political power, and influence, and a fourth we have called value-commitment, which is anchored in the fiduciary system. [24] It has, however, become increasingly evident that the same general mode of analysis ought to be extended to other systems of action than the social. The example that has been most fully worked out is that of what we have been calling the general system of action. This is interpreted to comprise the social system, the cultural system, the personality or motivational system of the individual, and what currently I have started to call the behavioral system, omitting earlier reference to the organism. (This change has been under the influence of a paper by Victor and Charles Lidz which relates the conception to the cognitive psychology of Jean Piaget.) [25]

To my mind, an important line of development of the theory, which has occurred essentially since my original book. *The Structure of Social Action,* [26] has sought to clarify the nature of the general action system. The first major step in this direction was achieved in the volume *Toward A General Theory of Action.* [27] A particularly significant distinction − on a strictly analytical level, of course − is that between the social system and the cultural system, in our technical sense of terms. The recent program of study on the university in which I have collaborated with Gerald Platt [29] involves these problems, because one cannot deal theoretically with the university without taking into account systematically both its characteristics as a social system and its involvement with a cultural system.

The focus of the university's involvement in the cultural system lies especially in its concern with knowledge. This concerns the transmission of knowledge, notably from faculty members to students through the processes of teaching and learning, but also the advancement of knowledge which is particularly concentrated in the research function. From the point of view of researchers and their collaborators, research is also a learning process since a research program whose outcome is known in advance would be pointless. The researcher has to *learn* the answers to the problems posed in a research project.

Knowledge we have treated as the primary cultural component of a larger complex involving all of the subsystems of the general system of action. In this connection we have treated rationality as predomi-. nantly a phenomenon of the social system, as competence is anchored in the personality system; and we have adapted the concept of intelligence to the role of a generalized symbolic medium as anchored in what Lidz and Lidz [30] call the behavioural system. The most important link between the cultural and social systems we treat as the commitment of the university as a whole to the value of cognitive rationality. Rationality, as noted in this context, we conceive to be basically a social category, whereas the term "cognitive" formulates the relation of rationality to the prevailing concern with knowledge in the two primary modes of transmission and advancement just mentioned. The individual's capacity to handle cognitive problems we have called competence, which we conceive as established in the personality through processes of socialization which constitute an essential part of the experience of participation in academic communities, especially, though far from exclusively, in the role of student, whether graduate or undergraduate.

Let me now elucidate a bit how we have tried to adapt the concept of intelligence to the rubric of generalized medium of interchange. The simplest definition we would give is that intelligence may be considered to be the capacity of an acting unit, usually an individual, effectively to mobilize the resources requisite to the solution of cognitive problems. This definition is conventional enough. The unconventionality of our treatment lies in our conception of the conditions and processes involved in its operation as such a capcity. First, we conceive of intelligence, though of course greatly affected by genetic components, to be predominantly acquired through socialization and learning processes. However, we conceive it not only possible to acquire intelligence but also to spend it through use in problem-solving activity.

Perhaps it will be helpful to explicate what we mean by the circulation of intelligence. If the human individual be taken as the primary point of reference — as seems appropriate for most purposes — we conceive that the level of intelligence of such an individual as an adult, let us say, is the outcome of combinatorial confluence of factors which have operated on him in the course of his life history. Among these factors clearly must be included the relevant apsect of the genetic constitution with which he was born. But the genetic factor does not stand alone. It is combined with cognitive learning experience and with a primarily noncognitive framework of socialization expectations.

Intelligence as cognitive capacity may then be conceived as capable of growth for long periods. Once available it can then be "used" in a wide variety of ways, notably in the solution of specific cognitive problems. The question then becomes whether and how such an actor of reference can recoup expenditure of intelligence on problem-solving activity. The answer seems to be that he "learns from experience" and the next time around can — on a certain average — do better than he could have without the experience.

Thus, rather than treating a person's intelligence as something he simply "has," we treat it as a fluid resource which can be acquired and enhanced in the course of action and effectively used by being "spent." [31]

There is a primary line of distinction between intelligence as medium and intelligence as trait. Our model here for intelligence as medium is that of other media, notably, money. We can speak of an individual as wealthy and in one linguistic usage his level of wealth is a trait of the individual; on the other hand, we know that his wealth was not part of his hereditary constitution, in the organic sense, and that the possession of wealth, that is, of economically valuable assets, places the individual in a network of interchange transactions where he can not only acquire such assets but also use those he has in the further interchange system.

We therefore posit that intelligence, considered as a medium, must meet the criteria of circulation. Its relative specificity seems scarcely to be in question, and the fact of the mode of its involvement in the cognitive complex, including the various levels of education, points to the primacy of the factor of institutionalization, which we also have stressed for media in general. I will not try to enter into an analysis of the non-zero-sum properties of intelligence conceived in this way, but will assert most emphatically that it fits the model of money as essentially a non-zero-sum pheonomenon, and not the more traditional one of power as bound by zero-sum limitations. Indeed, I think one of the most serious objections to the conventional psychological conceptions of intelligence lies in the tendency to subject it to the zero-sum condition.

The relation to social structure comes from the fact that we think of the entire cognitive complex as institutionalized at the social system level. Without this state of institutionalization there could be no such thing as the modern university. As institutional type, we think of the university as belonging to a distinctive category of social organization which, unfortunately, has not in our opinion been adequatley stressed in most recent sociological writing. The technical term we choose to refer to it by is a "collegial association." This should clearly be distinguished from a market system on the one hand, from a bureaucratic type of organization on another, and within the broader category of associated types, from purely democratic associations. It is distinguished from the last by a fiduciary component, in this case responsibility for the complex of cognitive interests and their involvement in certain respects in the larger action system, and a related pattern of stratification.

As concrete organization, the modern university has, of course, a bureaucratic component of considerable magnitude; and it is involved in the market nexus through its multifarious economic transactions. But the core, in our opinion, consists in the faculty—student collectivity which we define as predominantly a collegial association. [. . .]

The academic version of the collegial association belongs to a larger family of such associational structures in modern society. To us the most notable others are the kinship association, especially in the form in which it has developed in the more recent phases of modern society, the national or societal community, and the predominantly religious association. If space permitted, the similarities and differences among these four types could be considerably elaborated.

All of these major types of fiduciary association tend to have a collegial character and some concept of membership of which in a certain sense prototypical is that of citizenship, as that idea has been defined and developed by T. H. Marshall. [32] All are social structures within which certain functions can be performed with relative success and which are to important degrees insulated from the generally recognized "play of interests" which in a society like ours focuses at the economic and political levels. From the point of view of the more simplistic conception of the determination of social phenomena by interests in this sense, they are relatively useless from a utilitarian point of view. Perhaps a classical statement of this point of view is the one attributed to Stalin, I believe at the Yalta Conference, in which there was some reference to the Pope. Stalin's query in evaluating the importance of the Pope was alleged to be, "how many divisions does he have?" Quite clearly neither the military nor the economic significance of universities, of families, of religious bodies, and indeed, of communities in the sense of this discussion are the primary criteria of their importance. They are not primarily characterized by sheer control of means or coercive sanctions by political power or wealth.

This, however, is not a criterion of their lack of importance as components of the social structure. As I have several times said in print, [33] I concur with Daniel Bell [34] in the judgment that the university has become strategically the most important single category of structural collectivity in modern society, especially in what Bell refers to as its post-industrial phase. This is not because it has become the center either of wealth or of power, though it must participate in both of these interchange systems. It is rather because it is the center of the mobilization of a type of resource which has acquired a quite new level of significance in the more recent phases of social development which Bell characterizes, correctly I think, as focusing on the importance of "theoretical knowledge."

In order not to leave the concept of intelligence as a generalized medium functioning at the level of the general system of action entirely alone, perhaps it would be appropriate at this point to introduce a brief discussion of another medium which I have been calling *affect*. [35] Whereas I conceive intelligence to be anchored in what the Lidz brothers [36] call the behavioral system, I conceive of affect as anchored in the *social* subsystem of the general action system. It is, however, conceived to circulate not only within the social system but between it and the other primary functional subsystems of action, namely, the cultural, personality, and behavioural subsystems. Affect thus conceived is the generalized medium most definitely concerned with the mobilization and control of the factors of solidarity in Durkheim's sense. [37]

Solidarity as a primary property of social collectivities grounded in a value category is dependent on factors mobilized from all four of the primary subsystems of action. These factors include the cathectic commitments of individual persons to participation in solidary collectivities; the moral standards which underlie social order as this concept was employed by Durkheim, which is a contribution from cultural sources; and finally, rational grounds for the allocation of affect as between the societal and nonsocietal commitments and within the latter as between plural memberships in different social subcollectivities.

Back of this way of looking at affect as a generalized circulating medium lies a Durkheimian conception of the social system as playing a dual role in action. On the one hand, from the point of view of the acting individual, it is an environment which constitutes the focus of the individual's primary adaptive orientations. On the other hand, it is not part of the "natural" environment, which is analytically separate from the field of human action, but is itself part of the system of action and a creation of past processes of action. As such, its constitution consists of action components, of which a particularly important aspect is provided by the element of moral order which is a primary regulator of solidary relationships within the same social system. [38]

Affect we conceive to be the medium through which the stabilities essential to the moral order of a social system are adjusted to the ranges of variation that occur in the more concrete social environment in which the individual acts. We have stressed that the level of the general system of action must be intimately articulated with that of the internal imperatives of the social system. We would like, therefore, to draw a parallel between the functions of intelligence and the functions of affect as media which are involved in these processes of articulation. In fact, affective attachment of individuals to the collectivities which are constitutive of the structure of the social system and to the other individuals who share membership status with them are at the center of the mechanisms by which general action factors can achieve the status of institutionalization in defining the structure of social units. We have already illustrated this in the case of the modern university considered as a social system. These considerations can and should be generalized to a wide variety of other types of collective structure which play a part in social systems, particularly of the modern type characterized by an advanced division of labor. [39]

[...]

READING 14:
NOTES AND REFERENCES

[1] Cf. John Stuart Mill, *Principles of Political Economy,* edited with an Introduction by W. J. Ashley (London: Longmans, Green and Co., 1909). First published in 1848.

[2] Victor Lidz, "Blood and Language: Analogous Media of Homeostasis," Paper submitted to a *Daedalus* Conference on the Relations between Biological and Social Theory, Cambridge, Mass., 1974, and "The Analysis of Action of the Most Inclusive Level: An introduction to Essays on the General Action Systems," in J. Loubser, R. Baum, A. Effrat, and V. Lidz (eds.), *Explorations in General Theory in Social Science: Essays in Honor of Talcott Parsons* (New York: Free Press, 1976).

[3] Cf. Talcott Parsons, *Politics and Social Structure* (New York: Free Press, 1969), Chapters 14—16.

[4] Talcott Parsons, Robert F. Bales, and Edward A. Shils, *Working Papers in the Theory of Action* (New York: Free Press, 1953).

[5] Talcott Parsons and Neil J. Smelser, *Economy and Society* (New York: Free Press, 1956).

[6] Cf. Talcott Parsons, "On the Concept of Political Power," *Proceedings of the American Philosophical Society,* 107 (1963). Reprinted in Talcott Parsons, *Politics and Structure, op cit.,* pp. 352—404.

[7] Cf. Talcott Parsons, "On the Concept of Influence"; "Rejoinder to Bauer and Coleman," *The Public Opinion Quarterly,* Vol. 27 (1963), pp. 37—62 and 87—92. Reprinted in Parsons, *Politics and Social Structure, op cit.*

[8] Cf. James S. Coleman, "Comment on 'On the Concept of Influence,'" *The Public Opinion Quarterly,* Vol. 27 (1963), pp. 63—82.

[9] Max Weber, *The Theory of Social and Economic Organization,* ed. by T. Parsons, trans. by A. M. Henderson and T. Parsons, "Power, Authority and Imperative Control" (New York: Free Press, 1947), pp. 152—153.

[10] Cf. Thomas Hobbes, *The Leviathan: or the Matter, Form and Power of a Commonwealth, Ecclesiastical and Civil* (London: Crooke, 1651).

[11] See C. J. Friedrich, *Man and His Government: An Empirical Theory of Politics* (New York: McGraw-Hill, 1963); H. Lasswell and A. Kaplan, *Power and Society* (New Haven: Yale University Press, 1950); and C. Wright Mills, *The Power Elite* (New York: Oxford University Press, 1956).

[12] Cf. Talcott Parsons, "On the Concept of Political Power."

[13] Cf. Emile Durkheim, *The Division of Labor in Society,* trans. by George Simpson (New York: Free Press, 1964), Book 1, Chapter 7. Originally published in French 1893.

[14] Hobbes, *The Leviathan.*

[15] Max Weber, "Class, Status and Party," in H. H. Gerth and C. W. Mills (eds.), *From Max Weber: Essays in Sociology* (New York: Oxford University Press, 1946), p. 180.

[16] On the concept of bindingness, see Parsons, "On the Concept of Political Power," pp. 381–382.

[17] Chester I. Barnard, *The Functions of the Executive* (Cambridge, Mass.: Harvard University Press, 1938).

[18] Cf. Parsons, "On the Concept of Political Power."

[19] *Ibid.*

[20] Parsons, *Politics and Social Structure,* pp. 412, 413, 415 ff.

[21] Parsons, *Politics and Social Structure,* pp. 430–438,

[22] See Talcott Parsons and Gerald M. Platt, *The American University,* in collaboration with Neil J. Smelser (Cambridge, Mass.: Harvard University Press), 1973.

[23] Cf. Talcott Parsons, "Considerations on the American Academic System," *Minerva,* Vol. 6, No. 4 (Summer 1968), and Talcott Parsons and Gerald M. Platt, "The American Academic Profession: A Pilot Study" (Cambridge, Mass.: multilith, 1968).

[24] See Talcott Parsons, "On the Concept of Value-Commitments," *Sociological Inquiry,* Vol. 38 (1968). Reprinted in Parsons, *Politics and Social Structure.*

[25] Victor Lidz and Charles Lidz, "The Psychology of Intelligence of Jean Piaget and its Place in the Theory of Action," in J. Loubser, R. Baum, A. Effrat and V. Lidz (eds.), *Explorations in General Theory in Social Science: Essays in Honor of Talcott Parsons* (New York: Free Press, 1976).

[26] Talcott Parsons, *The Structure of Social Action,* (New York: McGraw-Hill, 1937). Reprinted by The Free Press, New York, 1949.

[27] Talcott Parsons and Edward A. Shils, *Toward a General Theory of Action* (Cambridge, Mass.: Harvard University Press, 1951).

[28] Cf. Parsons and Smelser, *Economy and Society.*

[29] Parsons and Platt, *The American University.*

[30] See Lidz and Lidz, "The Psychology of Intelligence of Jean Piaget and its Place in the Theory of Action." See also Parsons and Platt, *The American University,* pp. 33 –102.

[31] *Ibid.*

[32] T. H. Marshall, *Class, Citizenship and Social Development* (Garden City, Anchor Books, 1965).

[33] Cf. Parsons and Platt, *The American University*, pp. 1–7, and Talcott Parsons, "Social Stratification" in *Encyclopaedia Italiano*, Vencenzo Cappelletti (ed.) (Rome: Istituto della Enciclopedia Italiano, 1976).

[34] Daniel Bell, *The Coming of Post-Industrial Society* (New York: Basic Books, 1973).

[35] Cf. Parsons and Platt, *The American University*.

[36] Lidz and Lidz, "The Psychology of Intelligence of Jean Piaget and its Place in the Theory of Action."

[37] Among those concerned with media theory at the general action level there has been a disagreement with respect to the placement of affect. Notably, Mark Gould and Dean Gerstein have opted to use it as the medium anchored in the first instance in the personality system and to introduce an alternative concept for the social system medium. My own preference is definitely to use it in the social system context, but I do not feel dogmatic about it and hope that it will eventually prove possible to reach terminological consensus in this important area.

[38] Cf. Talcott Parsons, "Durkheim on Religion Revisited: Another Look at *The Elementary Forms of the Religious Life*," in Charles Y. Glock and Philip E. Hammond (eds.), *Beyond the Classics? Essays in the Scientific Study of Religion* (New York: Harper and Row, 1973).

[39] We consider the process of institutionalization, as previously referred to, to be the action-system equivalent of natural selection as that concept has come to be an integral part of biological theory, that is, the theory of the nature and functioning of organic systems. The general action system, and particularly its cultural component, we conceive to be analogous to the genetic constitution of species and the primary source of genetic variation. As such, the cultural system promulgates patterns of what at the value level may be characterized as desirable modes of action. By no means all of these, however, become institutionalized as operative characteristics of ongoing social systems. The intervening process is one of selection according to which some such patterns prove to be favorable in meeting the conditional exigencies of more concrete societal functioning, whereas others prove to be less successful. There develops, that is to say, a differential survival probability among those that are better and less well adapted to coping with such exigencies.

Reading 15
DEATH IN THE WESTERN WORLD

That the death of every known human individual has been one of the central facts of life so long as there has been any human awareness of the human condition does not mean that, being so well known, it is not problematical. On the contrary, like history, it has needed to be redefined and newly analyzed, virtually with every generation. However, as has also been the case with history, with the advancement of knowledge later reinterpretations may have some advantages over earlier.

I start from the proposition that if we are to speak of the death of individuals, we need some conceptualization, beyond common sense, of what a human individual, or "person," is. First, I do not propose to discuss the meaning of the deaths of members of other species, insects, elephants, or dogs, but only of human individuals. Second, I propose to confine discussion to individual persons and not to examine societies, civilizations, or races in this sense.

I

Within these limitations I should like to start with the statement that the human individual is a synthesized *combination* of a living organism

Reprinted with deletions, with permission, from T. Parsons *Action Theory and the Human Condition,* Macmillan, New York (1978), pp. 331–351.

and a "personality system," conceived and analyzed at the level of "action" in the sense in which I had and various others have used that term. [1] In older terminology, he is a combination of a "body" and a "mind." The concept of a personality as *analytically* distinguished from an organism is no more mystical than is that of a "culture" as distinguished from the human population (of organisms) who are its "bearers." The primary criterion of personality as distinguished from the organism, is an organization in terms of symbols and their meaningful relations to each other and to persons. In the process of evolution, personalities should be regarded as emergent from the organic level, as are cultural systems in a different, though related way.

Human individuals, seen in their organic aspect, come into being through bisexual reproduction — and birth — as do all the higher organisms. They then go through a more or less well defined life course and eventually die. The most important single difference among such individual organisms is the duration of their lives, but for each species there is a maximum span: for humans, it is somewhere between ninety and one hundred years. In this sense death is universal, the only question being "at what age?" Within these limits the circumstances of both life and death vary enormously.

It seems that these considerations have an immediate bearing on one of the current controversies about death, namely, the frequent allegation that American society — and some say others — attempts to "deny death." [2] Insofar as this is the case (and I am skeptical), the contention has to be in the face of a vast body of biological knowledge. If any biological proposition can be regarded as firmly established, it is that, for sexually reproducing species, the mortality of individual, "phenotypical" organisms is completely normal. Indeed, mortality could not have evolved if it did not have positive survival value *for the species,* unless evolutionary theory is completely wrong. This fact will be a baseline for our whole analysis.

The human individual is not only a living organism but also a special kind of organism who uses symbols, notably linguistic ones. He learns symbolic meanings, communicates with others and with himself through them as media, and regulates his behaviour, his thought, and his feelings in symbolic terms. I call the individual in this aspect an *actor.* Is an actor "born"? Clearly not in the sense in which an organism is. However, part of the development of the human child is a gradual and complicated process, which has sometimes been called *socialization,* whereby the personality becomes formed. The learning of patterns of relation to others, of language, and of structured ways of handling one's own action in relation to the environment is the center of this process.

Does a personality, then, also die? Because the symbiosis between organism and personality is so close, just as no personality in the human sense can be conceived to develop independently of a living child organism, so it is reasonable to believe that no human personality can be conceived as such to survive the death of the same organism, in the organic sense of death. With respect to causation, however, if the personality is an empirical reality, it certainly influences what happens to the organism, the person's "body," as well as vice versa. The extreme case is suicide, which surely can seldom be explained by purely somatic processes, without any "motives" being involved, as often can a death from cancer. But more generally there is every reason to believe that there are "psychic" factors in many deaths, all manner of illnesses, and various other organic events.

It is firmly established that the viability of the individual organism, human and nonhuman, is self-limiting. Thus, even in the absence of unfavorable environmental conditions, in the course of the "aging" process, there will occur gradual impairment of various organic capacities, until some combination of these impairments proves fatal. Organic death can be staved off by medical measures but cannot be totally prevented. There seems every reason to believe, but there is less clear-cut evidence on this point, that the same is in principle true of the action-personality component of the individual. This means that, with aging, various components of that complex entity lose the necessary capacities to maintain its balances, which eventually will lead to a breakdown. The cases in which there is virtual cessation of personality function without organic death are suggestive in this sense. More generally, if, as I strongly believe, the phenomena of mental illness are real and not merely epiphenomena of organic processes, then it stands to reason that some of them can be severe enough to eventuate in personality death, partly independent of organic death.

We have already noted that at the organic level the human individual does not stand alone but is part of an intergenerational chain of indefinite, though not infinite, durability, most notably the species. The individual organism dies, but if he/she reproduces, the "line" continues into future generations. This intergenerational continuity is as much a fact of life as are individual births and deaths.

There is a direct parallel on the action side: An individual personality is "generated" in symbiosis with a growing individual human organism and dies with that organism. But the individual personality is embedded in transindividual action systems, at two levels, social systems (most notably, whole societies) and cultural systems. There is a close analogy between these two and the relation between somatoplasm and germ plasm on the organic side, both of which are "carried" by the individual organism. Thus, the sociocultural "matrix" in which the individual personality is embedded is in an important sense the counterpart of the population-species matrix in which the individual organism is embedded.

At the organic level the individual organism dies, but the species continues, "life goes on." Also, the individual personality dies, but the society and cultural system, of which in life he was a part, also "goes on." I strongly suspect that this parallel is more than simple analogy.

What is organic death? It is of course a many-faceted thing, but as Freud and many others have said, it is in one principal aspect the "return to the inorganic" state. At this level the human body, as that of other organisms, is made up of inorganic materials but *organized* in quite special ways. When that organization breaks down, the constituent materials are no longer part of a living organism but come to be assimilated to the inorganic environment. In a certain sense this insight has been ancient religious lore; witness the Gospel, "Dust thou art, to dust thou shalt return."

Is the death of a personality to be simply assimilated to this organic paradigm? Most positivists and materialists would say, yes. This answer however, has not been accepted by the majority in most human societies and cultures. From such very primitive peoples as the Australian aborigines, especially as their religion was analyzed by Durkheim, [3] to the most sophisticated of the world religions, there have persisted beliefs in the existence of an individual soul, which can be conceived both to antedate and to survive the individual organism or body, though the ideas of pre-existence and of survival have not always co-existed in any given culture. The literature of cultural anthropology and of comparative religion can supply many instances. [4] The issue of the individuality of this nonorganic component of the human individual, outside its symbiosis with the living organism, is also a basis of variability.

II

Western civilization has had a historical background in which the dominant religious influence has been that of Christianity. Science has in recent times been the major focus of interpretation of the non-organic component. Let us then try to outline the main Christian patterns of orientation and indicate modifications of the old materialistic-religious dichotomy that seem to be dictated by the emergence of a complex of disciplines dealing with human problems at the level of action.

In collaboration with Renée Fox and Victor Lidz I have presented an analysis of the Christian orientation to death. [5] There is no doubt of the predominance of a duality of levels in the Christian paradigm of the human condition, the levels of the spiritual and the temporal, as one formula states it. There is a striking resemblance between this duality and that in the organic world between species and individual, as well as between the former and that in the action world between individual personality and sociocultural system. The Christian paradigm, however, seems to bracket the human condition within a still broader dichotomy. On the one hand, there is the material-temporal world, of which one religious symbol is "dust" as cited earlier. On the other, there is the spiritual world of "eternal life," which is the location of things divine, not human. The individual soul is conceived as in some sense an "emanation" from this second "world."

We attempted, [6] relying heavily on biblical documentation, to interpret this syndrome in terms of Marcel Mauss's paradigm of the gift and its reciprocation. [7] Seen in this way, the life of the individual is a gift from God, and like other gifts it creates expectations of reciprocation. Living "in the faith" is part of the reciprocation but, more important for us, dying in the faith completes the cycle. It is surely notable that our ordinary language is permeated with references to giving in this connection. Thus, a woman is said to *give* birth to a child and we often say that in dying a person *"gives* up the ghost."

The language of giving also permeates the transcendental level of symbolism in the Christian context. Thus, Mary, like any other woman, *gave* birth to Jesus. God also *gave* his "only begotten Son" for the redemption of humankind. Finally, Jesus, in the Crucifixion and thus the Eucharist *gave* his blood for the same purpose. By the doctrine of reciprocation mankind assumes, it may be said, three principal obligations, namely to "accept" the human condition as ordained by divine will, i.e., the gift of life, to live in the faith, and to die in the faith. If these conditions are fulfilled, salvation is the reward.

One further point should be stressed: the way in which the symbiosis of the organic and the action level of the human condition is symbolized in the Christian complex (that is, through the sacralization of the family, which is the primary social organization having to do with human reproduction, birth and death, health and illness, and their relations). The focus here is the Holy Family, and even the Trinity having certain family-like characteristics: witness God the Father and

God the Son. It may further be noted that the two most important Christian seasonal festivals "celebrate" the birth of Jesus — Christmas — and commemorate his death — namely, Easter, though with the doctrine of resurrection, commemoration also becomes celebration.

Christianity, in its Catholic form, has intitutionalized a special duality in the human societies and cultures in which it has existed; namely, in medieval terms, that between church and state. These institutional complexes have very closely corresponded to the duality, within the individual between soul and body, with the church having custody, as it were, of the soul. A major change, however, occurred with the Protestant Reformation. This particular version of Christian dualism was "collapsed" in that the sacraments no longer mediated (for Protestants) between God and man; no priesthood held the "power of the keys"; and withdrawal from the "world" into monasteries was abolished.

The primary consequence of this collapsing was not, as it has often been interpreted, so much the secularization of the religious component of society as it was the sacralization of secular society, making it the forum for the religious life, notably, though by no means exclusively, through work in a "calling" (as Weber held). [8]

Though Calvin, in his doctrine of predestination, attempted to remove salvation altogether from human control, this doctrine could not survive the cooling of the "effervescence" of the Reformation itself. Thus, later versions of Protestantism all accepted some version of the bearing of the individual's moral or attitudinal (faith) merit on salvation. Such control as there was, however, was no longer vested in the ecclesiastical organization but was left to the individual, thus immensely increasing this religious and moral responsibility.

The Reformation as such did not fundamentally alter the meaning of death in human societies. The collapse of the Catholic version of duality however, put great pressure on the received doctrine of salvation. Hence the promise of a *personal* afterlife in "heaven," especially if this were conceived to be "eternal," which must be taken to mean altogether outside the framework of time, became increasingly difficult to accept. The doctrine of eternal punishment in some kind of "hell" has proved even more difficult to uphold.

The conception of a "higher" level of reality, a "supernatural" world did not in any immediate sense give way; yet, it became increasingly hard to "visualize" it by simple extrapolation from this-worldly experience. Indeed, a fundamental challenge did emerge as part of the penumbra of the rise of modern science, which by the eighteenth century had produced a philosophy of scientific "materialism." The primary form of this was a "monism" of the physical world. There was, at that time, little "scientific" analysis of the world of action, or even of the organic world, and there was a tendency to regard the physical universe as unchanging and hence eternal. Death then was simple, namely, in Freud's formula, the "return to the inorganic" state, which implies a complete negation of the conception of "eternal life" since the physical, inorganic world is by definition the antithesis of life in any sense. [9]

The development of science has over time changed these matters. The sciences of organic life underwent their first great efflorescence in the nineteenth century and have gone much further in the present one. Moreover, a conception of evolutionary change came to be at the very center of biological thought, crystallizing in the work of Darwin, [10] This development laid the foundations for the view of the biological normality of death.

A second and more recent development was the maturing of what we have been calling the sciences of *action*. These of course have deep roots in humanistic tradition, but only in recent times can a cluster of generalizing sciences be said to have branched off from the humanistic "trunk." Indeed, these disciplines may well not yet have had their "Darwin," though I am inclined to think that the Durkheim–Weber–Freud combination comes close to filling such a role. It seems that a conception of evolutionary change, articulating with the organic theory, has also become an integral part of this scientific movement.

There is also a parallel in that not only has this development of the action disciplines produced a useful conception of the human personality as analytically distinguished from the organism but also it has created an intellectual framework within which the mortality of this personality can be understood to be normal. Moreover, this personality, as entity, can be seen to develop, live, and die within a matrix that is analogous to the physico-organic species matrix of the individual organism. Seen in terms of the nature of societies and cultures, the death of individual persons is presumably just as is that of individual organisms. Of course, again, this action matrix is conceived as evolving, in a sense parallel to organic evolution.

Not least important of the developments of science, finally, was the altered conception of the physical universe in recent times. First, there occurred the relativization of our knowledge of the physical world to the conditions of human observation of it, most saliently put in the ways in which Einstein's theory of relativity modified the previous assumptions of the absolute, empirical givenness of physical nature in Newtonian tradition. [11] Second, evolutionary ideas were extended to the physical cosmos. If one adds the physical to the organic and the action field one comes to the conclusion that for modern man the *whole* of empirical reality is in certain senses conceived to be relative to a human perspective and to be involved in evolutionary changes.

There is a parallel problem of relativization on the other side of the bracketing framework of the human condition. In the philosophical wake of Christian theology, as it were, there has been an energetic search for the conceptualization of the "metaphysical" *absolute*. In the context of the present analysis it seems that this can be likened to the search for the equally absolute, universal laws of physical nature. This quest, too, has been subjected to severe strain as a result of the altered conception of the human condition since the Reformation and has tended to break down in a comparable sense.

[...]

VII

So far as it is accessible to cognitive understanding at all, the meaning of death for individual human beings must be approached in the framework of the human condition as a whole. It must include both the relevant scientific and philosophical understanding and must attempt to synthesize them. Finally, it must, as clearly as possible, recognize and take account of the limits of our scientific as well as our philosophical understanding.

We have contended that the development of modern science has so changed the picture as to require revision of many of the received features of Christian tradition, both Catholic and Protestant. This development of science took place in three great stages marked by the synthesis of physical science and the seventeenth century, that of biological science in the nineteenth, and that of the action sciences in the nineteenth to twentieth.

The most important generalizations seem to be the following. First the human individual constitutes a unique symbiotic synthesis of two main components, a living organism and a living personality. Second, both components seem to be *inherently* limited in duration of life, and we have no knowledge which indicates that their symbiosis can be in any radical sense dissociated. Third, the individualized entity *both* is embedded in and derives in some sense from a transgenerational matrix which, seen in relation to individual mortality, has indefinite but not infinite durability.

From this point of view, death, or the limited temporal duration of the individual life course, must be regarded as one of the facts of life that is as inexorable as the need to eat and breathe in order to live. In this sense, death is completely normal, to the point that its "denial" must be regarded as pathological. Moreover, this normality includes the consideration that from an evolutionary point of view, which we have contended is basic to *all* modern science, death must be regarded as having high survival value organically at least to the species, actionwise to the future of the sociocultural system. These scientific considerations are not trivial, or conventional, or culture-bound but are *fundamental.*

There is a parallel set of considerations on the philosophical side. For purpose of elucidating this aspect of the problem complex I have used Kant's framework as presented in his three critiques. On the one hand, this orientation is critical in that it challenges the contention that absolute knowledge is demonstrable in *any* of the three aspects of the human condition. Thus, any conception like that of the ontological essence of nature, the idea of God, or the notion of the eternal life of the human soul are categorized as *Dinge an sich,* which in principle are not demonstrable by rational cognitive procedures.

At the same time, Kant insisted, and I follow him here, on the cognitive necessity of assuming a transcendental component, a set of categories in each of the three realms, that is not reducible to the status of humanly available inputs from either the empirical or the absolute telic references of the human condition. We have interpreted this to mean that human orientation must be relativized to the human condition not treated as dogmatically fixed in the nature of things.

The consequence of this revitalization that we have particularly emphasized is that it creates a new openness for orientations, which men are free to exploit by speculation and to commit themselves in faith but with reference to which they cannot claim what Kant called apodictic certainty. At the same time, we again insist with Kant that this openness must be qualified by the continuing subjection of human life to the constraints of the transcendental aspects of the human condition, which presumably cannot be altered by human action.

If this is a correct account of the situation, it is not surprising that there is a great deal of bafflement, anxiety, and indeed downright confusion in the contemporary attitudes and opinions in this area. I think that in its broad lines what I have presented is indeed an accurate diagnosis of the situation, but it would certainly be too much to claim that such an orientation is fully institutionalized.

It can be said to be most firmly established at philosophical levels and those of rather abstract scientific theory. Even there, however, there is still much controversy and anything like full consensus seems to be far off. Yet I still maintain that the development, say, from the medieval Catholic synthesis, is the *main line*. The grounds for this belief rest on the conviction that no equally basic alternative is available in the main cultural tradition and that this broad orientation is the most congenial to "reasonable men" in our situation. So far as fundamentals are concerned, I am afraid that, within the limitations of this essay, it will be necessary to leave it at that.

It may help, however, to mitigate the impression of extreme abstractness if in closing I very briefly discuss three empirical points. First, though scientific evidence has established the fact of the inevitability of death with increasing clarity, this does not mean that the *experience* of death by human populations may not change with changing circumstances. Thus, Victor Lidz and I have distinguished between inevitable death and "adventitious" death — that is "premature" relative to the full life span and in principle preventable by human action. [12] Within the last century and a half or so, this latter category of deaths has decreased enormously. The proportion of persons in modern populations over sixty-five has thus increased greatly, as has the expectancy of life at birth to seventy-two in 1975 in the United States. This clearly means that a greatly increased proportion of modern humans live out a full life course. Perhaps precisely because of this change, premature deaths from diseases, wars, accidents, or natural disasters like earthquakes have become more, rather than less disturbing events than they were previously.

Moreover, persons who live to a ripe old age will experience an inevitably larger number of deaths of persons important to them. These will be in decreasing number the deaths of persons younger than themselves notably their own children, but increasingly those of their parents and whole ranges of persons of an older generation such as teachers senior occupational associates, and public figures. (During this writing, for example, I learned of the death of Mao Tse-tung, certainly a figure of worldwide significance.) Quite clearly, these demographic changes have a strong effect on the balance of experience and expectation of the deaths of significant others and anticipation of one's own death.

Second, one of the centrally important aspects of a process of change in orientation of the sort described should be the appearance of signs of the differentiation of attitudes and conceptions in the relevant area. As Fox, Lidz, and I [13] have pointed out, there has indeed been such a process of differentiation, which seems not yet to be completed, with respect to both ends of the life cycle. With respect to the beginning, there is the controversy over abortion. However this controversy may eventually be resolved, it seems unlikely that public attitudes will go back to the traditional positions of either no abortions in any circumstances or only abortions that are strictly necessary to save the life of the mother. The interesting feature of this controversy is that it has entailed attempts to specify the point at which the life of a human *person,* as distinct from the human *organism* at conception, begins. Concomitant with this has been an attempt at redefinition of death. So far the most important approach has been to draw a line *within* the organic sector between what has been called "brain death," in which irreversible changes have taken place, destroying the functioning of the central nervous system, and what has been called "metabolic death," in which above all heartbeat and respiration have ceased. The problem has been highlighted by the capacity of "artificial" measures, say, mechanical respirations, to keep persons "alive" for long periods despite the fact that brain function has irreversibly ceased. The point of major interest here is the connection of brain function with the personality level of individuality. Hence, an organism that continues to "live" at *only* the metabolic level may be said to be dead as a person. We would expect still further elaborations of these themes in the future.

Third, we may make a few remarks about the significance for our problem of Freud's most mature theoretical statement. [14] It will be remembered that in his last major theoretical work, Freud rather drastically revised his views on the nature of anxiety, coming to focus on the expectation of the loss of an "object." By "object" Freud meant a human individual standing in an emotionally significant relation to the person of reference. To the child, of course, his parents become "lost objects" as he grows up in that their significance to him as growing child is inevitably "lost." The ultimate loss of a concrete human person as object (of cathexis, Freud said) is the death of that person. To have "grown away" from one's parents is one thing but to experience their actual deaths is another. Freud's own account of the impact on him of his father's death is a particularly relevant case in point. [15]

Equally clearly, an individual's own death, in anticipation, can be subsumed under the category of object loss, particularly in view of Freud's theory of narcissism, by which he meant the individual's cathexis of his own self as a love object. [16]

Anxiety, however, is neither the actual experience of object loss nor is it, according to Freud, the fear of it. It is an anticipatory orientation in which the actor's own emotional security is particularly involved. It is a field of rather free play of fantasy as to what might be the consequences of an anticipated or merely possible event.

Given the hypothesis, to which I subscribe, that in our scientifically oriented civilization there is widespread acceptance of death — meant as the antithesis of its denial — I see no reason why this should eliminate or even substantially reduce *anxiety* about death, both that of others and one's own. Indeed, in speaking earlier about the impact of demographic changes in the incidence of death, I suggested that in certain circumstances the level of anxiety may be expected to increase rather than the reverse.

It seems that the frequent assertions that our society is characterized by pervasive denial of death may often be interpreted as calling attention to widespread anxiety about death, which I submit is *not* the same thing. There can be no doubt that in most cases death is, in experience and in anticipation, a traumatic event. Fantasies, in such circumstances, are often marked by unrealism. But the prevalence of such phenomena does not constitute a distortion of the basic cultural framework within which we moderns orient ourselves to the meaning of death.

Indeed, in my opinion, this and the two preceding illustrations serve to enhance the importance of clarification at the theoretical and philosophical levels, to which the bulk of this essay has been devoted. Clarification is essential if we are to understand such problems as the shifts in attitudes toward various age groups in modern society, particularly older persons, the relatively sudden eruption of dissatisfaction with traditional modes of conceptualizing the beginning and the termination of human lives, and allegations about the pervasive denial of death, which is often interpreted as a kind of failure of "intestinal fortitude." However important recent movements for increasing expression of emotional interests and the like, ours remains a culture to which its cognitive framework is of paramount significance. It is a contribution to the understanding of this framework and its meaning, in an area that is emotionally highly sensitive, that I would like this essay to be evaluated.

READING 15:
NOTES AND REFERENCES

[1] Talcott Parsons, *Social Systems and the Evolution of Action Theory* (New York: Free Press, 1977).

[2] See Peter Berger and Richard Liban, "Kulturelle Wertstruktur und Bestattungspraktiken in den Vereinigten Staaten," *Kölner Zeitschrift fur Soziologie und Social Psychologie,* no. 2 (1960); and Robert Fulton in collaboration with Robert Bendiksen (eds.), *Death and Identity* (rev. ed.). (Bowie, Md: Charles Press, 1976),

especially the articles by Robert J. Lifton, "The Sense of Immortality: On Death and the Continuity of Life" (pp. 19–34), and by Erik Lindemann, "Symptomatology and Management of Acute Grief" (pp. 210.–221).

[3] Emile Durkheim, *The Elementary Forms of the Religious Life,* trans. J. W. Swain (New York: Free Press, 1965; first published in French in 1912).

[4] See Robert N. Bellah, "Religious Evolution," *American Sociological Review* (1961): 358–374, reprinted in idem, *Beyond Belief: Essays on Religion in a Post-Industrial World* (New York: Harper & Row, 1970), pp. 20–50.

[5] Talcott Parsons, Renée C. Fox, and Victor M. Lidz, "The Gift of Life and Its Reciprocation," *Social Research,* vol. 39, no. 3 (1972); 367–415.

[6] *Ibid.*

[7] Marcel Mauss, *The Gift: Forms and Functions of Exchange in Archaic Societies,* New York: Free Press, 1954; first published in French in 1925).

[8] Max Weber, *The Protestant Ethic and the Spirit of Capitalism,* trans. T. Parsons (New York; Scribner's, 1930; first published in German in 1904–1905).

[9] Sigmund Freud, *Beyond the Pleasure Principle,* in vol. 18 of *The Standard Edition of the Complete Psychological Works of Sigmund Freud* (London: Hogarth Press and the Institute of Psychoanalysis, 1955; first published in German in 1920), pp. 7–66.

[10] Charles Darwin, *On the Origin of Species by Means of Natural Selection, or The Preservation of Favored Races in the Struggle for Life* (London: Murray, 1859).

[11] See Alfred N. Whitehead, *Science and the Modern World* (New York: Macmillan, 1925).

[12] See Talcott Parsons and Victor M. Lidz, Death in American Society," In Edwin Schneidman (ed.), *Essays in Self-Destruction* (New York: Science House, 1967).

[13] Parsons, Fox, and Lidz, "The 'Gift of Life.' "

[14] Sigmund Freud, *Inhibitions, Symptoms, and Anxiety,* vol. 20 of *Standard Edition* (1959; first published in German in 1926), pp. 77–178.

[15] See Sigmund Freud, *The Origins of Psychoanalysis: Letter to Wilhelm Fliess, Drafts and Notes, 1887–1902* (New York: Basic Books, 1954).

[16] Freud, *Inhibitions, Symptoms, and Anxiety.*

Suggestions for Further Reading

A full bibliography of Talcott Parsons's published works is provided in the companion volume to this reader, Peter Hamilton (1983) *Talcott Parsons* (Ellis Horwood/Tavistock), as well as suggestions concerning useful commentaries and critiques of his theories.

In order to help the reader interested in finding the main publications of Talcott Parsons, I have listed below those which constitute his principal theoretical statements, or contain major essay collections.

1930 Max Weber *The Protestant Ethic and the Spirit of Capitalism* (translated by T. Parsons). London: Allen & Unwin; New York, Scribners.

1937 *The Structure of Social Action.* New York: McGraw-Hill. Reprint edition (1949). Glencoe, The Free Press.

1949 *Essays in Sociological Theory Pure and Applied.* New York: Free Press. Revised edition 1954.

1951 *The Social System.* New York: Free Press, London: Routledge & Kegan Paul.

Toward a General Theory of Action. Editor and contributor with Edward A. Shils *et al.* Cambridge, Mass.: Harvard University Press. Reprinted, Harper Torchbooks, 1962.

1953 *Working Papers in t' Theory of Action* (in collaboration with Robert F. Bales anc Edward A. Shils). New York: Free Press; Routledge and Kegan Paul. Reprint edition 1967.

1954 *Essays in Sociological Theory* (rev. ed.). New York: Free Press.

1955 *Family, Socialization, and Interaction Process* (co-authored with Robert F. Bales, James Olds, Morris Zelditch, and Philip E. Slater. New York: Free Press; London: Routledge & Kegan Paul.

1956 *Economy and Society* (co-authored with Neil J. Smelser). London: Routledge & Kegan Paul; New York: Free Press.

1960 *Structure and Process in Modern Society.* (A collection of essays.) New York: Free Press.

1961 *Theories of Society* (two vols.) (co-edited with Edward Shils, Kaspar D. Naegele, and Jesse R. Pitts). New York: Free Press.

1964 *Social Structure and Personality.* (A collection of essays.) New York: Free Press.

1966 *Societies: Evolutionary and Comparative Perspectives.* Englewood Cliffs: Prentice-Hall.

1967 *Sociological Theory and Modern Society.* New York: Free Press.

1968 *American Sociology* (A collection of essays edited by Talcott Parsons.) New York: Basic Books.

1969 *Politics and Social Structure.* New York: Free Press.

1971 *The System of Modern Societies.* Englewood Cliffs: Prentice-Hall. Companion volume to *Societies: Evolutionary and Comparative Perspectives* (1966).

1973 *The American University* (co-authored with Gerald M. Platt and in collaboration with Neil J. Smelser). Cambridge, Mass.: Harvard University Press.

1977 *The Evolution of Societies* (edited, with an introduction, by Jackson Toby). Englewood Cliffs: Prentice-Hall.
Social Systems and the Evolution of Action Theory. New York: Free Press.

1978 *Action Theory and the Human Condition.* New York: Free Press.

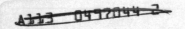